LEICESTERSHIRE AND RUTLAND
Unusual & Quirky

HALSGROVE

First published in Great Britain in 2016

British Library Cataloguing-in-Publication Data
A CIP record for this title is available from the British Library

ISBN 978 0 85704 274 3

HALSGROVE
Halsgrove House,
Ryelands Business Park,
Bagley Road, Wellington, Somerset TA21 9PZ
Tel: 01823 653777 Fax: 01823 216796
email: sales@halsgrove.com
website: www.halsgrove.com

Printed and bound in China by Everbest Investment Printing Ltd

Leicestershire and Rutland – Unusual and Quirky

Welcome to *Leicestershire and Rutland – Unusual and Quirky*. This is the third book in a new series that calls to mind that classic series of travel books called *The King's England*, written in the 1930s by Stapleford-born Arthur Mee, since each volume in Mee's series was suffixed with *"There have been many books on <insert county>, but never one like this…"* Well the very same tag line could be applied to this book, as some of its elements are certainly unique. Having said that, the book still has plenty to offer in terms of conventional reference, but it delivers this in a lateral and humorous format never seen before.

Essentially, then, the book is comprised of two main sections which are called *Conventional Leicestershire and Rutland* and *Quirky Leicestershire and Rutland*. The *Conventional* section kicks off with some county maps along with key facts and figures relating to the county – such as county town, population, highest point, key industries and famous sons and daughters. The facts are then followed by a history of the Leicestershire and Rutland *area* from the Stone Age to the 11th century – by which time both Leicestershire and Rutland, along with most of England's counties had been officially formed – after which the last one thousand years of county history is covered, bringing us up-to-date and into the 21st century. Nevertheless, in keeping with the title of the book, the *County History* also has forty small, but appropriately historical "Quirk Alerts" interspersed, too; like anecdotes covering Roman latrine management, how Robin-a-Tiptoe Hill became so-named, and the meaning of bizarre Leicestershire terms such as Gongoozlers and Yawny Box!

The *Conventional* section then hands over to the *Quirky* section … and it is here that we really begin to earn the *"… but never one like this …"* tag line. For although the *Quirky* section delivers some "seen it before" place-name origins and historic trivia, it does so via a quirky poem known as a Shire-Ode! Told in rhyming verse, the Shire-Ode portrays imaginary inhabitants of Leicestershire and Rutland but, as an extra twist, the poem contains dozens of place-names found within the two historic counties, each subtly woven into the tale – and it is these place-names upon which the *Quirky* section focuses. Firstly, the places have their location pin-pointed via a map of the two counties. A series of chapters then follow in (largely) alphabetical order for each place featured in the Shire-Ode – and it is here that the strangest and most interesting facts and features about each place are explored. As a result, you get a random almanac of places that would never ordinarily appear together – along with place-name status, population, earliest recording, name derivation, famous sons and daughters … and lots and lots of accompanying photographs.

So, feel free to commence your obscure Leicestershire and Rutland fact-digging; to read about some very famous people and their Leicestershire and Rutland exploits, to read about ancient battles and, quite frankly, some ridiculous legends, too … but to hopefully have a little chuckle along the way. For example, find out which mysterious stone kept all forms of Christianity at bay, and how doves dictated the build of the church at Breedon on the Hill! Alternatively, read about Hallaton's barking annual tradition involving bottle kicking, fighting and a huge hare pie – but not to be confused with Burley's "Dwarf in a Pie" tale. Or what about the huge Leicester gaoler who punched and floored a dancing bear after it attacked his dog, or the phenomena in a haunted house in Earl Shilton that caused hats and wigs to throw themselves off the heads of their wearers!

Parsons and rectors also feature heavily, including the blind Blaby rector who regularly participated in the local hunt, the Swinford parson who tied 58 bulldogs to 58 apple trees to prevent scrumping, and the Plungar clerk who used the parish registers to wrap up his lunch! And not forgetting the 14th century rector from Teigh involved in serious organised crime, or the parson who had five wives who died within thirteen years of each other!

Historically, Richard III's connections with Leicestershire are explored in depth, as is the county's pivotal connection with the English Civil War. But quirkiness always accompanies, including Richard's political machinations involving children, how the Siege of Leicester in 1645 was responsible for the conversion of John Bunyan, and why a Royalist rector was shot at whilst preaching in his pulpit – although all of these stories are surpassed by the mind-blowing historical revelation in Stoke Dry's church!

Alternatively, check out *The Signing of Magna-Parva*, the quirky Shire-Ode that drives the idiosyncratic *Quirky Leicestershire and Rutland* section and learn how two Glens become footballing superstars!

Anyway, that's the introduction completed. As you have probably gathered by now, this book is indeed "unusual and quirky"… so it's time to prime the quirk-ometer and pull up a pew at St Strangeways – oh, and did I mention the milking organist of Freeby, Kegworth's beer-swilling fox, the tiny Rutland village that is twinned with Paris …

Contents

Leicestershire Facts and Figures

County Status:	Ceremonial county and (smaller) non-metropolitan county (minus Leicester)
County Town:	Leicester
County Pop'n:	980,800
County Pop'n. Rank:	21st out of 48
Cities:	Leicester
Largest City:	Leicester
City Pop'n:	329,839
City Pop'n Rank:	9th English; 12th UK
City Status:	Unitary Authority
National Parks:	None
Other Areas:	Charnwood Forest, National Forest, Vale of Belvoir
County Area:	804 miles^2/2,156km^2
County Area Rank:	28th out of 48
Highest Point:	Bardon Hill (912ft/278m)
Longest River:	Soar (59 miles/95km)
Football Clubs:	Leicester City (Premier League), Coalville Town (Northern Premier League First Division South), Hinckley United (Midland Football League First Division)
Rugby Union:	Leicester Tigers (RFU Premiership)
Industries (Present):	Brewing, Cheese, Crisps, Engineering, Finance, Footwear, Livestock Farming, Metalfacture, Motorcycle Manufacture, Pet Food, Pharmaceuticals, Pork Pies, Retail, Services, Sports Cars
Industries (Past):	Bellfounding, Coal Mining, Engineering, Knitwear and Hosiery, Livestock Farming, Shoemaking

Born in Leics: Lemuel Francis Abbott, Tony Allcock, James Allen, Richard Armitage, Elizabeth Arnold, Henry Ernest Atkins, Robert Bakewell, Ian Baraclough, Julian Barnes, Dave Bartram, Henry Bates, Biddy Baxter, Frank Benbini, Andrew Betts, Lydia Rose Bewley, Manish Bhasin, Jeremy Bulloch, Robert Burton, Pat Butler, David Campton, Charles Henry Carter, Graham Chapman, Selina Chilton, Charlie Clapham, John Cleveland, Thomas Cooper, Nathaniel Corah, Mark Cox, Henry Curry, John Deacon, Louis Deacon, Betty Driver, Dion Dublin, Terri Dwyer, Julie Etchingham, Anne Fine, Glenn Flear, John Flower, George Fox, Stephen Frears, Martin Gillingham, Ernest Gimson, Martin Goodman, Lady Jane Grey, Emile Heskey, Augustus Hobart-Hampden, Clare Hollingworth, Thomas Hooker, Harold Hopkins, Kelvin Hopkins, Tom Hopper, Colin Hurley, David Icke, John Illsley, William Inman, John Arthur Jarvis, Anthony Jenkinson, John Johnson, Tony Kaye, Dominic Keating, Alison King, Chris Kirkland, Michael Kitchen, Daniel Lambert, Hugh Latimer, John Leeson, Barry Letts, William Lilly, Gary Lineker, Jon Lord, Ned Ludd, Joe Mattock, Tom Meighan, Joseph Merrick, Sir John Moore, Rendall Munroe, Parminder Nagra, David Neilson, Sir Henry Norman, Andy Nyman, Kate O'Mara, Joe Orton, Lynda Page, Samit Patel, Helen Pearson, John Barclay Pick, Jenny Pitman, Norman Plummer, Chris Pyatt, Bali Rai, Steve Redfern, Benjamin Ward Richardson, Michael Robinson, Mark Selby, Peter Shilton, Tony Sibson, Josette Simon, M.J.K. Smith, Ollie Smith, Molly Smitten-Downes, C.P. Snow, Una Stubbs, Willie Thorne, Sue Townsend, Luke Varney, George Villiers, Gok Wan, William Whiston, Roger Williamson, Colin Wilson, Mark Wingett, William Wyggeston

Rutland Facts and Figures

County Status:	Ceremonial county and Unitary District	**Football:**	Oakham United, Uppingham Town (both Peterborough & District Football League)
County Town:	Oakham	**Rugby U:**	Oakham RFC (Midlands 2 East[South])
County Pop'n:	37,600	**Industries (Present):**	Agriculture, Brewing, Cement Manufacture, Retail, Services, Stone, Tourism
County Pop'n Rank:	47th out of 48		
National Parks:	None		
County Area:	147 miles^2/382km^2		
County Area Rank:	45th out of 48	**(Past):**	Agriculture, Brewing, Iron Ore, Stone
Highest Point:	Cold Overton Park (646ft/197m)	**Born in Rutland:**	Robert Browne, Sir Jefferey Hudson, Simon de Langham, Titus Oates, Vincent Wing
Rivers:	Chater, Eye, Gwash, Welland		

Leicestershire and Rutland Maps

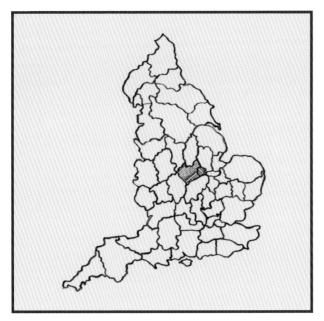

Administrative Counties of England – 1889-1965

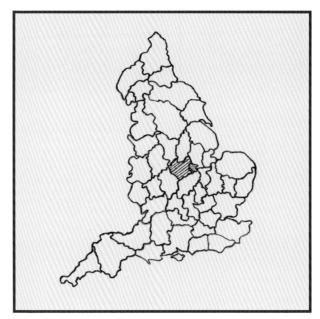

Administrative Counties of England – 1965-1974

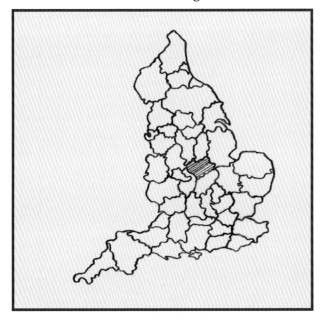

Ceremonial Counties of England – 1974-1997

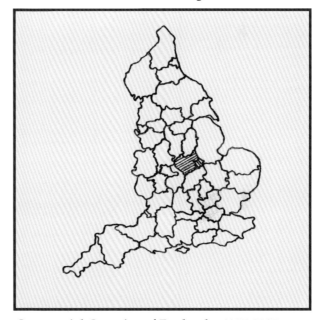

Ceremonial Counties of England – 1997-2015

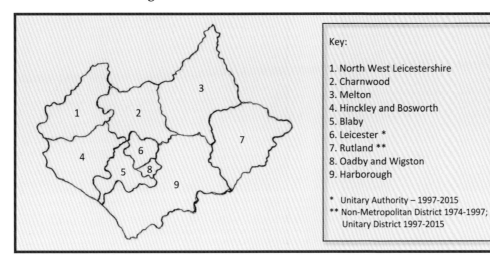

Key:

1. North West Leicestershire
2. Charnwood
3. Melton
4. Hinckley and Bosworth
5. Blaby
6. Leicester *
7. Rutland **
8. Oadby and Wigston
9. Harborough

* Unitary Authority – 1997-2015
** Non-Metropolitan District 1974-1997;
   Unitary District 1997-2015

Leicestershire & Rutland – Non-Metropolitan and Unitary Districts – 1974-2015

Conventional Leicestershire and Rutland

Prehistory

Like most other English historic counties, Leicestershire dates from the 11th century, and was formed towards the end of the two hundred year conflict on English soil between Anglo-Saxon and Viking. Rutland, however, is something of an exception to this rule. Although it existed as an entity at this time, and indeed is referred to as *Roteland* in the will of Edward the Confessor in around 1060, it is not thought to have been formalised as a county until 1159 (more on this later). The meaning of the name is also different to your standard shire, with "Rutland" commonly thought to mean "estate of a man called Rōta", thus deriving from the Old English personal name, *Rōta*, plus the Old English name *land*, meaning "tract of land, cultivated land, or estate". Having said that, another theory suggests that the name is somehow connected with the Ruthlanders that came from an area of Essex called the Ruth, while yet another theory suggests that it could be derived from the Old English words *hrythr* and *land*, where the former means "cattle" – and thus the meaning is "land of cattle". Leicestershire is more straightforward, meaning "shire or district of the town of Leicester", and is clearly derived from the place-name *Leicester*, plus the Old English word *scīr*, meaning "shire or district". Leicester, however, is much older than the shire it lends its name to – but we'll come to that shortly, for the history of the *area* of both Leicestershire and Rutland, goes back much further still.

The oldest part of the area in terms of landscape can be found around the Charnwood Forest vicinity. Here, numerous rocky outcrops are the result of volcanic activity over 700 million years ago during the Pre-

ANCIENT CHARNWOOD

The Old Man of Beacon Hill, one of many rocky outcrops in Charnwood Forest that were formed by nearby volcanic activity, 700 million years ago. Note the profile of the rock which resembles a side-on view of a human face.

Looking north-west from Pre-Cambrian Leicestershire towards Derbyshire.

Cambrian era, and which took place towards the north-western area of Charnwood Forest, with the lavas, ash and volcanic bombs spreading out in a south-easterly direction towards Leicester. In time, these rocky outcrops were buried beneath the accumulating sands of the Triassic period some 200 million years ago, while later sculpturing due to frost-shattering during the Ice Age finalised the current state of the many Charnwood crags. As a result, the area is one of Leicestershire most visited for walking and climbing, with a key focal point at Beacon Hill Country Park. Here, the summit of these fine-grained igneous rocks rise to 814ft above sea level (248m) and offers panoramic views as far afield as the Derbyshire Peak District to the north-west and Lincoln Cathedral to the north-east, while the whole area of Beacon Hill, Hangingstone and Outwoods is a designated Site of Special Scientific Interest (SSSI).

Leicestershire and Rutland are not particularly blessed with pre-Bronze Age evidence. That isn't to say that there weren't any stone circles, henges, long barrows or tumuli, though, as aerial reconnaissance has revealed potential shapes of ancient henge monuments that would date from the late Neolithic/early Bronze Age period, like a site at High Cross on Leicestershire's western border. Similarly, a pattern of field systems that pre-date the medieval ridge and furrow have been identified from the air in the valley between the River Chater and the Eye Brook in southern Rutland. Then in recent years, what are known as King Lud's Entrenchments – banks and ditches a mile north-east of Saltby – and which were previously assumed to be Anglo-Saxon, have been reassessed as prehistoric, while a series of Bronze Age round barrows have also been found nearby. However, the only tangible evidence of prehistoric man having lived in the two counties comes in the form of flint implements discovered in the gravel terraces of the Rivers Soar and Wreake. Here, Palaeolithic hand axes of over 70,000 years old have been found at Ratcliffe-on-the-Wreake, while flint flakes found at Wanlip date from the same era. Moving forward to the Mesolithic period (c.10,000-4,500 BC), and finds suggest evidence of hunter gatherer groups, with a number of microliths discovered at Leicester, Stoney Stanton and Burrough – microliths being the tiny flint blades used by Mesolithic hunters. Further Mesolithic flint implements were discovered at

Ratcliffe-on-the-Wreake in 1951, suggesting that this might actually have been a location where such implements were worked and fashioned into ancient tools. The majority of these finds are from the Soar Valley, suggesting that the people of these times either clustered about its banks or the tools were carried down from the headwaters of the Soar Basin. That said, the skeleton of a Stone Age man was also found at Great Casterton in Rutland, along with his tools and weapons.

For the Neolithic period (c.4,500-2,000 BC), evidence is similarly limited to stone axes and hammers (around 50 of them) along with flint arrow heads, blades and scrapers. However, what is fascinating about these axes and hammers is that many of them originated from much further afield, with petrographical analysis proving that a batch found in the Leicester vicinity originated from the Langdale Pikes area of the Lake District. Similarly, others found at Leicester and Glenfield originated from the Menai Straits in North Wales, while another at Sharnford was sourced from as far south as Mounts Bay near Penzance in Cornwall. That isn't to say that tools weren't fashioned locally, though, as evidence suggests one such centre existed on the narrow outcrop of pre-Cambrian rocks to the south of Nuneaton, on modern Leicestershire's western frontier, with axes and hammers turning up from this source inside the county boundaries at Barrow-on-Soar, Leicester and – again – at Ratcliffe-on-the-Wreake. Furthermore, similar axes have been turned up at Leicestershire locations that were clearly manufactured in Charnwood Forest, with examples including two axes found near Whitwick that were made from Blackbrook rock, another implement that was found in the east of the county at Goadby Marwood and which was hewn out of the pre-Cambrian rocks of Beacon Hill, and an axe that turned up on the lower slopes of High Sharpley that actually originated from half a mile away. Again, most of the Neolithic evidence was discovered in the Soar Valley, although there were discoveries elsewhere such as a Neolithic flint axehead showing up at Somerby in eastern Leicestershire. As for this presence of tools manufactured many miles away, this suggests some kind of widespread trade between the Neolithic farmers and the toolsmiths of the day.

In terms of pottery finds, these don't come to light in

Quirk Alert: *Oooh Arrgghhh!*

The largest collection of Leicestershire Bronze Age artefacts was discovered a couple of miles north of Melton Mowbray, and is known as the Welby Hoard. The artefacts date from between 1000 and 800 B.C. and they were discovered in 1875 by a farmer digging in the Welby parish … although the hoard wasn't passed on to Leicester Museum until 1919. Alas, by this stage, only a small proportion of the hoard remained intact, as the blissfully ignorant farmer had taken large parts of it away to be melted down at a local foundry! Luckily, a local resident witnessed this and rescued the remaining artefacts by purchasing them off the farmer. What survives today are a sword, three socketed axes (now known as Welby Axes), a small bowl, five circular mounts, cauldron mounts and a few other pieces. The original hoard was also thought to contain many objects that originated from central Europe, supplying further evidence that the Bronze Age inhabitants of the area that would eventually become known as Leicestershire and Rutland were engaged in long distance trade, too.

Leicestershire and Rutland until the end of the Neolithic period, when we start to see long-necked beakers being buried with their owners. Seven have been unearthed in Leicestershire, suggesting an incursion into this area up the Welland Valley by the Beaker people from across the North Sea. Moving into the Bronze Age (1650 BC to 500 BC), and there is evidence to suggest that a stronghold existed on Bardon Hill, while unearthed artefacts from this period include cremation urns and fragments of pottery as well as spearheads, axes, hammers and bronze daggers such as that found in the River Wreake near Syston – and where a tumulus known as Round Hill has been classed as a Bronze Age burial site, too. The most impressive discovery, though, is the Welby Hoard and which includes metalwork design that cannot be matched anywhere else in Britain.

For the final Bronze Age haul, we return to Beacon Hill, site of some of the country's oldest rocks, and of a definite Iron Age hillfort, too. However, as a Bronze Age haul was also found here, within the Iron Age earthwork, it is thought that the hillfort might also have been occupied during Bronze Age times, and perhaps even before then, too. The haul was discovered in 1858 and included two spearheads, a looped socketed axe and a socketed gouge, while a bronze axe-mould and a bronze bracelet were also found nearby; the axe-mould may also suggest an element of bronze production in the vicinity. Finally, an aerial reconnaissance in the 1950s did demonstrate evidence of a possible Bronze Age barrow which showed up as a ring in the soil at Lockington, close to the River Trent.

It is also Beacon Hill that provides some of the clearest evidence of Iron Age occupation in Leicestershire and Rutland, although it is actually bettered by classic former Iron Age hillforts at Breedon on the Hill at the north-western edge of Leicestershire, and at Burrough Hill on the opposite eastern edge of the county. Beacon Hill is probably the oldest of these hillforts, perhaps dating from the late Bronze Age as evidenced by the more lightweight defences when compared to classic

The trig point on Beacon Hill, which sits at 814ft (248m) above sea level, and marks the location of an Iron Age hillfort, and possibly a Bronze Age predecessor.

Iron Age hillforts like those at Breedon and Burrough. For example, the bank and ditch of the Beacon hillfort sits nearer to the top of the hill, and is easily traceable for around two thirds of the circumference, while the remaining third was made up of natural rocky outcrops.

As for the 400ft Breedon Hill, this was occupied during the Bronze Age and the early Iron Age, with excavations revealing hut circles of up to 47ft (14.3m) in diameter. However, evidence here suggests that the Iron Age hillfort was probably constructed around 300 BC, with saddle querns, hammer stones and numerous pottery finds suggesting continuous occupation from this point and right the way through the Roman occupation of Britain and possibly beyond. As was typical in those Iron Age times, the hillfort appears to have been constructed in order to turn the hill into a strategic, defensive settlement using a combination of ditches and ramparts, and which are today known as The Bulwarks. The hillfort covered around 23 acres, and the clear evidence of localised rampart work implies that the fort was kept in a good state of repair throughout its heyday. Alas, much of the ancient evidence has now been destroyed by 20th century quarrying on the south-

The limestone outcrop of Breedon Hill, crowned with the church of St Mary and St Hardulph which is visible for miles around. During the British Iron Age, this was the location of a significant hillfort.

Some of the surviving Iron Age ramparts along Breedon Hill's western flank, and which are known as The Bulwarks.

Looking north-eastwards from the trig point on Burrough Hill, one of the most important Iron Age hillforts in Leicestershire. The entire hilltop forms a vast arena-type feature, with stunning views all around.

Looking south-eastwards from the topograph on Burrough Hill, and demonstrating more of its defensive ramparts and natural amphitheatre.

ern and eastern sides of the escarpment, which has removed more than half of the original hill and hence more than half of its ancient defences. Hence, today, only a single bank and external ditch pass around the western side of St Mary and St Hardulph's churchyard. The Breedon site was excavated in 1946 and 1957, though, which is why we know that Breedon was a major producer of a distinctive pottery type known as Ancaster-Breedon Ware. Given types of this pottery were also found at Burrough Hill, this suggests an element of trade between the two Iron Age communities. Breedon was also home to cereal growing, as is evidenced by the number of corn grinders that were unearthed, while the community may have also engaged in some form of religion, given that another archaeological find was a rare, miniature bronze oval shield, an object that is often associated with Iron Age religious enclosures.

As for Burrough Hill, these impressive earthworks were built on an ironstone promontory that rises to a height of 690ft (210m) above sea level in eastern Leicestershire and commands panoramic views all around. The hillfort that was built here dates from the early Iron Age (c.500 BC), and is thought by many to be the ancient capital of the Celtic *Corieltauvi* tribe, thus making it the political, economic and social centre of the East Midlands; certainly the size of defences and other excavated evidence tends to support that viewpoint, as does proximity to known trackways of those times. The hillfort was surrounded by a single ditch along with a single stone and earth rampart (known as univallate) and which was accompanied by a counterscarp beyond the northern rampart. The fort was trapezoidal in shape and covered around 12 acres (4.8ha), while the main entrance was from the south-east via a typical inward turn of the ramparts and which formed a passage of around 150ft long; evidence of huge double gates and a guard chamber have also been found in this area as well as some of the original cobbled roadway which led through the gates. The site

may even pre-date the Iron Age, and certainly the area around Borough Hill was the location of older settlements although it cannot be stated whether or not they were contemporary with the hillfort. However, the hillfort itself saw the most intensive period of use occur much later between 100 BC and AD 50 and it continued to be used all the way up until the 4th century, with the focal point during these times of Roman occupation being towards the northern end of the fort.

Excavations carried out at Burrough Hill in 1935, 1960, 1967 and 1970-71 yielded the inevitable Iron Age and Roman artefacts, and included beehive querns or corn grinders, the usual pottery and bone fragments, and a La Tène brooch that dates from the late Iron Age. Despite these finds, though, it was also generally accepted that much of the purpose and history of the hillfort remained little understood. However, since 2010, the University of Leicester School of Archaeology and Ancient History, in conjunction with the University of Leicester Archaeological Services have been conducting a five-year excavation programme of Burrough Hill. They initially focussed on a number of large storage pits, finding a significant number of objects including around a hundred items of Iron Age metalwork. Further finds provided insight into Iron Age social life, with artefacts including a bone dice, gaming pieces, a polished bone flute and a beautifully decorated blue glass bead from a necklace. However, these artefacts were surpassed in 2014 when the fittings of an extremely rare Iron Age chariot were discovered, with the bronze fittings dating from 300 to 200 BC. It is thought that the chariot would have belonged to a local chieftain or a warrior – certainly someone of high status – but which was either dismantled or perhaps never built, but buried in a box and burnt as part of a religious ritual.

Today, Burrough Hill is a Scheduled Ancient Monument, as are The Bulwarks earthworks on Breedon Hill and the enclosure and linear boundary on Beacon Hill. Of course, it is almost certain that other

Quirk Alert: *Another Tall Story*
One possible site of an Iron Age hillfort is the intriguingly named Robin-a-Tiptoe Hill. It actually used to be called Howback Hill or Hawback Hill many centuries ago, but was re-named in the 16ᵗʰ century following the hanging here of a sheep-stealer known only as Robin (which presumably, he had been!) Anyway, legend has it that Robin was so tall that he managed to cheat death by periodically touching the ground with the tips of his toes, and thus lessening the effects of the asphyxiation. Then, when the authorities exited the scene assuming him to be dead, his friends rushed in to cut him down before the noose could claim his life.

Robin-a-Tiptoe Hill, a Scheduled Ancient Monument and former ancient settlement of undetermined origin, but which acquired its name more recently (explained left).

Iron Age settlements existed in Leicestershire and Rutland, but some – like Buddon Hill and Croft Hill – have been destroyed by quarrying, while most of those others suspected are as yet unproven. Examples include Bury Camp near Ratby, Life Hill near Billesdon in south-eastern Leicestershire, and also a couple of miles north of there at Robin-a-Tiptoe Hill – and which is also only 3 miles south-west of Burrough Hill. Robin-a-Tiptoe is yet another Scheduled Ancient Monument, but although it was clearly once a defended enclosure of around 11 acres (4.5ha), archaeologists aren't sure of their dates; it may well be contemporary with Roman Britain, or even later – perhaps Anglo-Saxon or even Danish – but certainly, its embanked fortifications survive to this day. The site, however, is on private land and therefore remains unexcavated – a similar situation to each of the nearby quartet of Whatborough Hill, Sconsborough Hill, Ranksborough Hill and the previously mentioned Life Hill. As for Rutland and the Iron Age, the most likely place for a hillfort was at Market Overton, where the medieval church was later erected within a rectangular-shaped earthen rampart close to a limestone escarpment that looks out over the Vale of Catmose; the earthworks are thought to most likely date to Roman times, but they could be older.

Romans, Anglo-Saxons and Vikings

By the time the Romans invaded Britain in AD 43, the territory of the Celtic *Corieltauvi* tribe stretched from Lincolnshire down to all but the south-western slice of Warwickshire. In the middle of this province was the *Corieltauvi's* capital city, which the Romans named as *Ratae Corieltauvorum*, and which was the ancient predecessor settlement to Leicester. The Roman name meant "fortified city of the Corieltauvi", with the word *Ratae* a latinate form of the Brythonic word for "ramparts".

This choice of name therefore suggests that the settlement was an Iron Age oppidum – a large and defended Celtic Iron Age settlement of the type that first emerged in Europe between 200 and 100 BC.

It is thought that just before the Romans invaded, the *Corieltauvi* were heavily under the influence of their south-eastern neighbours, the *Catuvellauni*, whose main base was at *Verulamium* (St Albans in modern-day Hertfordshire), although the *Corieltauvi* certainly issued their own coinage, as coin moulds have been discovered at both Leicester and Old Sleaford in Lincolnshire. By AD 45, the Romans had defeated the *Corieltauvi* although they didn't actually settle in the area until after AD 60. They had, however, built the Fosse Way by AD 47 and which stretched from *Isca Dumnoniorum* (Exeter) in the South West to *Lindum Colonia* (Lincoln) in the East Midlands, thus taking it right through the middle of what would eventually become Leicestershire on a south-west to north-easterly bearing. The Fosse Way was also thought to mark the temporary frontier of the embryonic province of *Britannia*; temporary because, having quickly established control over the south-eastern section of Britain, the Romans didn't advance north and west for another two decades. Whether or not there was a garrison at *Ratae Corieltauvorum* is not known for certain. Despite its ideal position on the River Soar and its proximity to the Fosse Way, the only evidence to indicate a Roman fort here is one military-style V-shaped ditch with one side steeper than the other and a drainage slot at the bottom. However, further evidence to support an early garrison at *Ratae Corieltauvorum* is supplied by a little-known Roman road called Gartree Lane, which ran south-eastwards from modern-day Leicester to Medbourne (on today's county border with Northamptonshire). Opinion is divided as to the road's importance. There was certainly an outlying estate and villa at Medbourne, so one view is that Gartree Lane simply linked the two settlements. The other view, though, suggests that the road continued across the Welland Valley and swept all the way down to the early Roman base at *Camulodunum* (Colchester), with the route used as a military conduit into the Midlands and, in particular, to an early Roman fort at *Ratae Corieltauvorum*. Certainly after AD 70, though, there wouldn't have been a need for a garrison here, as by this stage, the legions had swept through to the north and west, and Leicestershire and Rutland ceased to be of any military importance.

This latter move into northern and western Britain also explains the other major Roman roads that passed through Leicestershire and Rutland. As well as the Fosse Way, Watling Street (the modern A5) marked what is today's south-western boundary between Leicestershire and Warwickshire before heading off to the key Roman settlements of *Viroconium Cornoviorum* (Wroxeter) and *Deva Victrix* (Chester), while Ermine Street passes through eastern Rutland on its march towards *Lindum Colonia* (Lincoln) and *Eboracum* (York). On Watling Street, there were three Roman settlements that skimmed the modern-day Leicestershire border. The most southerly was known as *Tripontium*, and is today located in the Warwickshire parish of Newton

and Biggin, around 3 miles south of Lutterworth, while the most northerly was known as *Maduessedum*, and is today pinpointed by the Warwickshire village of Mancetter. In between the two, and where Watling Street crossed the Fosse Way, was *Venonae*, and which later became known as High Cross. Given its position at one of the most important junctions of Roman Britain, one might expect *Venonae* to have been a major Romano-British settlement, but archaeological evidence suggests not. Excavations carried out in the 1950s do confirm that the site was continuously occupied from the 1st through to the 4th century, but no evidence of stone structures or of a military base or of large-scale industrial usage has been revealed. This may well be because the major Celtic settlement of *Ratae Corieltauvorum* had already been developed and Romanised, a few miles to the north-east.

Throughout Roman Britain, a recurring arrangement was that of the villa-estate, but Leicestershire and Rutland don't appear to have been the location of particularly grand villas, with the exception of perhaps one on the western bank of the River Soar at Leicester. We are able to pinpoint smaller Roman villa sites, though, courtesy of archaeological finds such as fragments of building material, pottery, coinage, tiles,

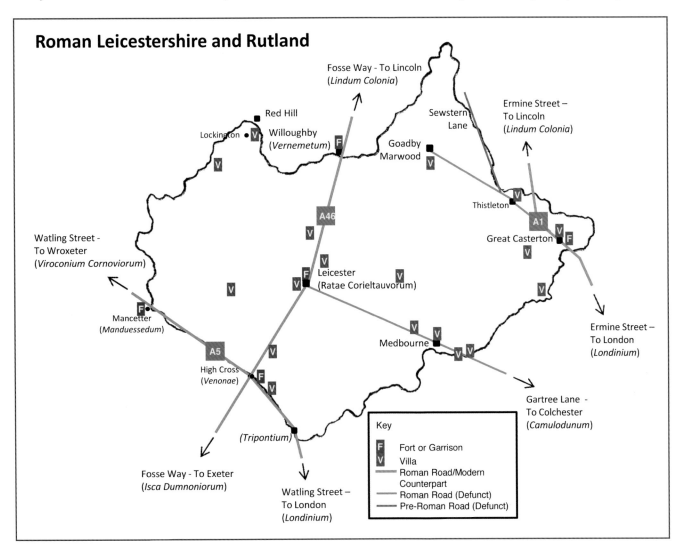

plaster and mosaic flooring. Of these more modest villas, three of the best examples were at Great Casterton in modern-day Rutland, at Medbourne in the Welland Valley, and at Sapcote just east of modern-day Hinckley. Another was discovered in the 1950s close to Goadby Marwood in modern-day north-east Leicestershire. Named the "Wycomb Villa" it was also subject to a resistivity survey in 2002 which showed the position of the villa walls, while further excavations in 2003 and 2004 turned up pottery fragments, part of a mortarium, a number of wall foundations, and building debris. One room was also found to have a hypocaust (underfloor heating system), and a small area of complete mosaic was uncovered, too. Collectively, the excavations indicate that the site was occupied from the late 1st century to the 4th century.

Returning to *Ratae Corieltauvorum*, the town didn't initially appear to be overly wealthy, with few amenities, none of the usual public buildings and a simple open marketplace at the centre instead of a forum. Nevertheless, by the early 2nd century, larger and better-quality stone houses had been built along with central courtyards. Those excavated in more recent times reveal tessellated and mosaic floors, and decorative plaster walls, with one also boasting an elaborate frieze

around its courtyard depicting theatrical masks, doves, pheasants, cupids, and flowers. Eventually, in the 2nd century, the forum and basilica were built. Public baths soon followed in around AD 145, and which were fed by an aqueduct, while they also had a large exercise room alongside. A second marketplace was eventually laid out in the early 3rd century and a new market hall constructed, while by the end of the 3rd century, *Ratae Corieltauvorum* had been surrounded by stone defences with four gateways. Cemeteries were placed outside each gateway and a suburb was built to the north of the town, while inside the town walls, there may have been two temples. As for industries in the Roman town, these included pottery production as well as metal and glass working.

Remarkably, the foundations of the Roman baths survive to this day in Leicester, along with an impressive section of the eastern wall known as the Jewry Wall and which is made of local granite, limestone and sandstone. Layers of red tiles also run along the Jewry Wall, this being a typical Roman building technique used for levelling and bonding, and thus making the wall more robust. This is one reason why the wall has survived so long, but this particular wall has also survived longer than its counterparts as it was also built into the wall of

ROMAN RATAE

The Jewry Wall and some of the remains of the Roman baths of Ratae Corieltauvorum, *the Celtic and then Roman forerunner to Leicester.*

Another view on the Roman bath foundations with the Jewry Wall Museum behind.

A further view on the Roman bath foundations seen through the Jewry Wall and with somewhat less elegant 20th and 21st century architecture behind!

a church that was at least one incarnation younger than the current medieval church of St Nicholas. As for the origin of the name "Jewry", this isn't known for sure, but it is neither Roman, nor is it linked to the medieval Jewish community of Leicester. The most likely derivation is from the "jurats", the senior members of the Corporation of Leicester who may have met in the churchyard just behind the wall between the 13th and 15th centuries. Arthur Mee offers a similar, but slightly earlier alternative, suggesting that the Norman system of 24 jurors used to meet by the wall to settle disputes, deliberately holding court by this ancient place of justice – a nod to the fact that in Roman times, the baths were situated next to the forum. As for that forum, we will never know its original layout, as centuries of stone robbing, followed by modern redevelopment have put paid to that. Thankfully, though, we do have the beautifully preserved foundations of the Roman baths, thanks to the excavation carried out under the direction of Dr Kathleen Kenyon in the late 1930s.

Throughout the Roman occupation, the native Britons of Leicestershire and Rutland lived in relative harmony with their Roman masters. Recent aerial photography shows evidence of a large number of Iron Age settlements along the banks of the Trent at the northern end of Leicestershire and the Welland at the southern end of the county, plus others right through the centre of the county along the valleys of the Soar and the Wreake. It is thought that these settlements retained their characteristics throughout the Roman occupation, suggesting that the fabric of Celtic society survived the Roman occupation intact. One of the best examples is at Lockington, and close to the confluence of the Rivers Trent and Soar. Here, the markings of a score of circular huts are revealed from the air, most within ditched enclosures, and located on either side of a long droveway, with surface finds indicating the settlement was occupied as late as the 2nd century. Less than half a mile to the east is the site of a small villa, leading to the inevitable conclusion that the huts marked the location of a village of serfs who worked on the villa estate.

One of the other constants of Roman occupation was industry, and the slate in Charnwood Forest was quarried throughout Roman times, while the famous stone from the Ketton area in southern Rutland turned up in

LEICESTER'S ROMAN PAVEMENTS AND WALL PAINTINGS

Part of the remarkable Blackfriars Pavement which dates to the late 1st century. It was first discovered in the basement of a house in Leicester in 1832 which was later demolished to make way for the Great Central Railway's "Leicester Central" Station in the late 1890s. However, a special chamber was built around the mosaic beneath the station to protect it, before it was moved to the Jewry Wall Museum in the late 1970s.

This mosaic is known as the Peacock Pavement (the peacock is in the centre of the octagon shown top left). It was found in 1898 and was moved to the Jewry Wall Museum in 1966.

Mosaic of Cyparissus and his stag. This was discovered in the 1670s at High Cross Street.

This is what is known as the Norfolk Street Wall Painting. The original had actually fallen onto its front in the cellar of a house in Norfolk Street, thus preserving much of the pattern.

Quirk Alert: *Bath Recursion*

In the late 1930s, the Leicester Corporation put together plans for building new municipal baths alongside St Nicholas' church. However, before doing this, the area around the Jewry Wall was excavated between 1936 and 1939. This was also the first large-scale excavation of the former Roman town, and indeed, 6ft of topsoil had to be removed to get down to the Roman level. Anyway, the archaeologists were hoping to find the Roman forum, but instead they soon realised that what they had actually discovered was a 2000 year-old predecessor to the very edifice their own council were looking to erect; they had uncovered the Roman public baths!

buildings at key Roman strongholds such as *Verulamium* (modern day St Albans). Then at Great Casterton in eastern Rutland, there is evidence of Roman iron smelting, as there is at Market Overton, too, while in between those two places, at Pickworth, a group of three shaft furnaces have been found that date from the early 2nd century.

As for Great Casterton, the very name (*Castretone*, 1086) means "the larger farmstead near the Roman encampment", with the "Caster" part of the name deriving from the Old English word *cæster*, meaning "Roman station or walled town". The Roman encampment in question was a very early fort established on the north bank of the River Gwash in AD 44 during the early Claudian campaigns of Aulus Plautius. The fort was large enough to house a mixed unit of cavalry and infantry, although military occupation is thought to have ceased around AD 80, with forces presumably redeployed further north. However, the Romano-British settlement or *vicus* that had developed in the protective lee of the fort, continued to expand along the line of Ermine Street and it continued to be occupied into the 4th century. The walled town defences, evidence of which still remain, were constructed around the turn of the 3rd century, and resembled an elongated polygon of seven or eight sides and which enclosed an area of 18 acres (7.3ha). They consisted of an 8ft wide stone wall, backed by a 30ft wide earthen rampart, fronted originally by a 7ft wide berm and three ditches, but later replaced in the early 4th century by a single ditch measuring an average 62ft wide and 11ft deep. As for the aforementioned ore-smelting evidence, this was discovered within the defences and dates to the late 1st century. Excavations have also revealed a possible late 1st century bath house, while a pottery kiln dating from AD 150 to AD 180 was found along with two other as-

yet undated kilns. The Roman cemetery lay to the south of the settlement along Ermine Street, and continued in use during Saxon times. Interestingly, Great Casterton is the only place in Leicestershire and Rutland where you can still see Roman defensive walls.

Other Roman remains or finds in Rutland include tiles built into the walls of Caldecott church, a tessellated pavement found at Ketton, a small bronze statue found at Langham, thousands of Roman coins found at Market Overton covering 350 years of their occupation, and a Roman brooch found at Seaton.

The Romans eventually left Britain in around AD 410, and their departure had a severe effect on Britain's economy which didn't really return to similar levels again until the late Anglo-Scandinavian period. But what of the Leicestershire and Rutland area after the Romans departed? This is a difficult question to answer, for once the literate Romans had departed, the largely illiterate Britons were unable to record their own progress. It is likely that some form of life persisted on the villa sites for an undefined length of time, whilst those who lived in Romano-British settlements and farmsteads must have continued their lives much as before. What we do know, though, is that the country gradually became settled by the Angles and Saxons of northern Europe, with Leicestershire and Rutland playing host to the Angles who came from the Schleswig-Holstein peninsula between modern-day Germany and Denmark. The traditional view of Anglo-Saxon colonisation of England is that these particular Angles had originally settled in Lincolnshire before pushing their way up the Trent Valley into Nottinghamshire and then into Derbyshire and Leicestershire, as is evidenced by mid-6th century heathen burial sites found from Newark to Burton-on-Trent. Much of Leicestershire and Rutland was thought to have been unreclaimed forest wilderness during these times, and the Angles were credited with founding villages and hamlets in self-created clearings. However, more recent research suggests that the Angles reached Leicestershire and the limestone country of eastern Rutland much earlier, in the first half of the 5th century, and potentially even earlier, before the Romans had even departed. This viewpoint is based on the evidence of pagan burial grounds close to Roman roads and Romano-British settlements, with sites discovered close to the walls of Roman Leicester, as well as close to Roman roads at Glen Parva, Oadby, Rowley Fields and Thurmaston. The cemetery at Thurmaston alone revealed 96 cremation urns that date from either the late 4th century or the early 5th, clearly evidencing an

Quirk Alert: *Bath Diversion*

For the Romans, bathing was a highly social thing and was open to all; young or old, male or female, rich or poor, most people visited the baths and many on a daily basis. People played games, conducted business or just socialised. There were warm rooms (Tepidariums), hot rooms (Caldariums), cold rooms (Frigidariums)…and then there were the latrines! And in those latrines … they used a communal sponge on a stick! So when you're next about to complain about your job, spare a thought for the official with the responsibility for assessing and effecting replenishment...

Saxon stonework built into the inside west wall of a Norman part of St Mary de Castro church in Leicester. Its previous usage is unknown.

Anglo-Saxon cremation urns on display at the Jewry Wall Museum.

early Anglo-Saxon presence of sorts in the Soar Valley – although it is thought that these early Teutonic migrants may well have been soldier mercenaries known then as the *foederati*. A similar pattern of pagan cemeteries close to Roman settlements is also revealed in Rutland too, with cemeteries excavated at Cottesmore, Market Overton and North Luffenham. Significantly, the latter dates from the early 5th century to the late 6th century, and has yielded metal buckles and harness equipment – typical soldier mercenary gear of the late Roman occupation!

One very interesting theory is put forward to support this viewpoint, by Roy Millward in *A History of Leicestershire and Rutland*. He mentions the fact that the Anglo-Saxon –*ham* place-name suffix dates from AD 400 to AD 650, and that three such places in the ironstone belt of east Leicestershire (Waltham, Wymondham and Wycomb) probably date from that time. He then links this to the fact that Wycomb is close to the sites of two Anglo-Saxon cemeteries, and therefore asks the question as to whether or not the –*ham* at Wycomb (*Wicham*, 1207) may have commenced as a community of Teutonic mercenaries guarding or perhaps providing labour for Roman iron-ore mines before the end of the 4th century (the *Oxford Dictionary of British Place Names* also states that the name means "Homestead associated with a *vicus*", and derives from the Old English word *wīc-hām* – and, of course, a *vicus* is another name for a Romano-British settlement). Millward then goes on to point out that other place-names ending in –*ham* are also found close to Roman Roads, such as Clipsham in the east (close to Ermine Street), and Goatham, Higham and Measham in the west (close to Watling Street). But later, towards the end of the pagan Anglo-Saxon period, place-names started to be suffixed with –*ing* and –*ingham*, and these Leicestershire and Rutland places generally *aren't* situated close to former Roman roads or settlements. Rutland examples in this category, and founded in then-heavily forested territory include Uppingham and Whissendine, while Leicestershire sees one batch of places in the upland areas between the trib-

utaries of the Welland and the Soar – for example, Horninghold, Loddington and Skeffington – and another batch to the south of the county, such as Saddington and Theddingworth.

By the end of the 6th century, the majority of the Leicestershire and Rutland area had become part of the Anglo-Saxon kingdom of Mercia. The kingdom was centred on the Trent Valley and its territories covered much of modern South Derbyshire, Leicestershire, Rutland, Nottinghamshire, Staffordshire and northern Warwickshire, with its capital sited at Tamworth. The most authentic source of information at this time was from the early 8th century Northumbrian monk and scholar known as the Venerable Bede, and who describes Mercia as being divided in two by the River Trent. Slightly earlier, in 679, the Mercian church underwent a reorganisation, and the large see of Lichfield was subdivided. Leicester became the bishopric of the Middle Angles and its territory spread across the southeast Midlands as far as the valley of the upper Thames. Alas, when the Vikings invaded in the late 9th century, many of Mercia's monastic records were destroyed, although thankfully, a list of the Bishops of Leicester did survive, revealing that the final incumbent was

> **Quirk Alert:** *Speaking in Tongs*
> The Venerable Bede refers to a priest at Breedon in 741, called Tatwin. Later to become Archbishop of Canterbury, Tatwin's talents also included poetic riddles, such as this one:
>
> Marvellous is my fate, which I now relate to you,
> For my strength lies in two arms.
> I have great confidence that I can grasp with gaping
> jaws
> Unalarmed by anything hard, rough or hot:
> With jaws gaping fearlessly I try to seize all things.
>
> He was, of course, referring to a pair of tongs!

The church of St Thomas a Becket at Tugby. The top two sections of the tower are Norman, but the bottom two sections (inset) are Anglo-Saxon.

Ceolred in 872. Also destroyed by the Vikings was Leicester's first cathedral, and which is thought to have been on the site of St Nicholas' church; indeed, it is rumoured that some of the former cathedral's stones survive in the present incarnation of the church.

In terms of surviving relics from the Anglo-Saxon centuries, these include a bronze Saxon spearhead found on Bardon Hill, a Saxon sword found at Round Hill near Syston, further spears and shields found at Hungarton, two Saxon coffin lids now in Hallaton church and a stone decorated with knotwork at Harston church. A further site at Saxby revealed the Saxon remains of men, horses, bridle bits and brooches, while another at Wigston Magna revealed Saxon horse trappings. Saxon remains in Rutland are confined to pre-Norman carvings at Greetham church, a tympanum in a Norman doorway at Stretton thought to be made from a Saxon coffin lid, and a Saxon hoard found at North Luffenham including spearheads, arrowheads, fragments of shields, urns, buckets, bronze ornaments, glass beads and fine brooches. However, the finest treasures were discovered at Market Overton, including a foot high Saxon urn, a magnificent brooch, and a Saxon clock which Arthur Mee describes as a "national antiquity", while Market Overton's church also contains the only Saxon arch in Rutland. As for that

Saxon clock, it is bronze, saucer-shaped, pierced by a single hole and was designed to measure one hour. It worked by placement in water so that it gradually filled up and sank, and when tested, it was found to take 62 minutes to sink.

Of course, churches also abounded during Anglo-Saxon times, but very little remains of these today – with a handful of exceptions, such as the lower two stages of the church at Tugby and the arch in the church tower at Market Overton. Otherwise, we have to be content with "successor to successor" churches standing in virtually the same place, or those surviving Norman churches that either retained the lower stonework of their Anglo-Saxon predecessor, or incorporated Anglo-Saxon stone into their walls. However, Leicestershire does have one outstanding example of Anglo-Saxon stonework in the medieval church of St Mary and St Hardulph at Breedon on the Hill, and which Arthur Mee describes as having no equal in Western Europe, never mind in England. It is known that an Anglo-Saxon monastery was founded here around 675, and certainly Bede writes of a priest in the monastery here in 731, called Tatwin, and who was later made Archbishop of Canterbury. The monastery was built right inside the defences of the former Iron Age hillfort, with the old defences topped by a wall or timber palisade, and it went on to play an important role in Mercian politics during the next century as Mercia flourished and expanded. It was also the burial place for various saints and other notable people of the day, which probably made Breedon a place of pilgrimage. One of those buried here – St Aerdulfus rex – owns a name that suggests a king made into a saint and he might even be a variation of St Hardulph, after whom the current church is co-named. Also buried here was St Fretheric, who may also be the Friduricus who was granted the lands of Breedon in 675 for the construction of the monastery.

Alas, it is highly likely that Breedon monastery was sacked by the invading Danes in the winter of 874-875, along with many other religious Mercian institutions, as that is when their army established their quarters at nearby Repton. The monks of Breedon almost certainly fled south, but for some reason, it is thought that the Danes didn't destroy Breedon monastery and this is presumably why around 30 of its Anglo-Saxon sculptured stones survived.

These carvings fall into four groups. The first two groups were friezes with widths of seven inches and nine inches respectively, with the first depicting continuous interlacing vine scroll patterns and the second much more complex designs, some depicting geometrical interlace patterns and others what are known as "inhabited vine scrolls". These latter carvings include birds, foliage, strange beasts and human figures, including charging mounted huntsmen with spears and one depicting a crouching warrior in short-sleeved tunic and knee-length kilt defending himself with a spear. One carving on the inside east wall of the chancel, of a vine decoration alongside a charging mounted warrior armed with a spear, is astonishingly intricate and of stunning quality given its age. Then on the south wall, there is a carving of a lion-like creature with an owl-like face, the largest animal carving in the collection, and which is known as the Anglian Beast. It is thought that many of these works of art were perhaps carved by Frankish sculptors, as their character resembles similar carvings in north-western France. Initially, the two friezes were around 63ft in length, and would have run in parallel bands around both the inside and outside of the Saxon church. When the church was rebuilt in the 13th century, these two groups of carvings were then built into scattered lengths around the interior of the new church.

The third group of carvings are a series of figure panels set in arches mainly depicting saints, plus the spectacular Breedon Angel, and collectively, they amount to the largest collection of Anglo-Saxon human figure sculptures in Britain. They are set in decorative frames with the largest of them behind the altar in the south aisle. The aforementioned Breedon Angel now resides in the bell-ringing chamber of the church tower and is not accessible to the general public; we have to make do with a copy that is on display in the south aisle of the church. Thought to represent the Angel Gabriel, the Breedon Angel is one of the finest surviving examples of Anglo-Saxon figure sculpture and perhaps the earliest known carved angel in Britain. The body is covered in robes and the angel's wings are clearly seen draping down his back. He also holds a cross-headed staff in one hand while the other is raised to give the Byzantine-style blessing; the latter gesture, and which is also portrayed in one of the other carvings, helps to date the sculptures to the 8th or 9th centuries.

BREEDON'S ANGLO-SAXON STONEWORK: WITHOUT EQUAL IN WESTERN EUROPE

Here are some of the most remarkable carvings in Britain. They are Anglo-Saxon and some of them date from way back in the 8th century, making them some of the oldest carvings in Western Europe. They once belonged in a 7th century monastery that was founded at Breedon on the Hill, but when the church was rebuilt in the 13th century, the builders of the day worked these gems into the ancient walls. The carvings can be subdivided into four groups: a seven inch frieze of vine scroll patterns, a nine inch frieze of birds, human figures and strange creatures, a series of figure panels depicting mainly saints, and a small selection of free-standing decorated Viking cross fragments.

From Group 1, here is a stretch of the vine scroll frieze as it runs behind the altar, and which was probably built into the wall in medieval times.

From Group 2, here is part of the nine inch frieze in the south aisle, depicting a series of strange beasts.

From Group 3, here are three of the figure panels. Those shown left and right can be found in the Lady Chapel, with the one on the left depicting a person holding a book in the left hand and giving a Byzantine blessing with the other, thus dating the sculpture to the 8th or 9th century. Also delivering a Byzantine blessing is the Breedon Angel (centre). Located in the south aisle, this is a copy of the original, which is in the bell tower and not accessible to the public. It is one of the very finest surviving examples of Anglo-Saxon figure sculpture anywhere in the world, and is also perhaps the earliest known carved angel in Britain.

Also from Group 3, on the left we have another figure panel from the Lady Chapel this one of two sets depicting three saints. Note that their haloed heads also have the same drilled eyes that the figure on the top row (left) has. They also each carry books that may once have had their names inscribed upon them. On the right, and also in the Lady Chapel, is the carving that is known as the Anglian Beast, and which appears to have a lion-like body with an owl-like face.

The final group of carvings are a small collection of free-standing decorated Viking cross fragments, now located at the west end of the north aisle. The tallest has a vine scroll design and was initially re-used as a staircase step before being released and restored in the 20th century, while many of the other crosses show various dragon-like beasts. The most spectacular cross piece, though, depicts the Garden of Eden, with Adam and Eve picking the forbidden fruit from the Tree of Knowledge and the evil serpent wrapped around it. Interestingly, this collection of 9th and 10th century crosses are post-Danish Christianisation, thereby suggesting that the church, if not the monastery, was active again relatively soon after its late 9th century sacking.

The other famous surviving remnant from the Dark Ages in Leicestershire and Rutland is the remarkable, yet brooding "Celtic goddess", an ancient stone figure that stands outside All Saints' church at Braunston-in-Rutland. Also known as the Braunston Goddess, she sits at the base of the west tower. Amazingly, she was actually used for many years, face-down, as a doorstep to the church, but was rediscovered in around 1920 when the doorstep needed to be replaced; the carving was revealed on the underside when the stone was lifted from its former position. Perhaps someone from a more discrete age felt she would preserve her modesty better in such a position! As to the carving's origins, some historians believe her to be a Saxon fertility goddess, while others feel sure she is older and hence

This magnificent Anglo-Saxon cross can be found in the churchyard of St Mary and St John's church at Rothley.

The Braunston Goddess sits outside All Saints' church at Braunston-in-Rutland. Some call it the Celtic Goddess and believe it might be some form of Sheela na Gig, *originally intended to ward off evil. Others think it could be an Anglo-Saxon fertility goddess.*

The Sproxton cross, thought to date from either the 10th or 11th century.

the alternative Celtic moniker – with some suggesting an approximation to a *Sheela na Gig* carving (the church website also refers to her as Shelagh). Some have argued that it might be a more recent church gargoyle, while others have suggested some type of apotropaic purpose – i.e. to ward off evil – which again, fits in with the *Sheela na Gig* theory. What doesn't fit with the *Sheela na Gig* theory, though, is the clear absence of any genitalia. The figure therefore remains something of a mystery, but it is certainly very strange with its two noses, large rubbery styled mouth and the deep, concertina-like striations in the neck area. The *Creature from the Black Lagoon*, perhaps?

We've already mentioned the marauding Danes who sacked Breedon monastery in around 874, and certainly, Mercian power was already on the wane at that time, making the east of the kingdom easier pickings for the invaders from across the North Sea. The late 860s had seen the Vikings[1] harrying much of north and eastern England, and the Danish army under Halfdan established a base at Nottingham where he was joined by a second army led by Guthrum. By 874, they had set up another base at Repton, while the Bishop of Leicester had fled south to Dorchester, thus bringing an end to Leicester's 200 year-old bishopric and which wouldn't be restored again until the 20th century. The Danes then expelled King Burgred of Mercia and replaced him with their puppet, Ceolwulf.

By 877, the Danes had begun to partition Mercia and it was at this stage that Leicestershire began to take shape, along with Derbyshire, Lincolnshire and Nottinghamshire, with four of the five new "shires" named after their respective military strongholds (Rutland had to wait a few more years to be formed as a shire, but its area probably aligned to the stronghold at Stamford). The entire area became known as the Five Boroughs, the name deriving from the Old English word *burh* meaning "fortified place or stronghold", and the strongholds in question being at Derby, Nottingham, Lincoln, Leicester and Stamford. Then in the following year (878), King Alfred of Wessex and the Danish King Guthrum agreed to carve up England between them following the Treaty of Wedmore and a temporary peace was established. The Five Boroughs became occupied by separate divisions of the Danish army, and the Danes who settled the area introduced their native law and customs known as the Danelaw. Each of the Five Boroughs was ruled as a Danish Jarldom, controlling lands around the fortified *burh*, which served as the centre of political power.

Interestingly, the Five Boroughs were divided from West Mercia on its south-western frontier by Watling Street, which by this stage was a Roman relic of around eight hundred years of age – and therefore Roman was now defining the boundary between Saxon and Dane! Also throughout this time, it is thought that Breedon

[1] The term "Viking" is a general one applied to Scandinavian pirates, raiders, marauders, rapers, pillagers, etc., who had been plaguing the east coast of Britain for decades. Once they settled in Britain and established the Danelaw, these settled Vikings, most of them originating from Jutland/Denmark, became known as Danes.

monastery became active again, as evidenced by fragments of carved Viking crosses of the late 9th and early 10th centuries – this after the Danes had also become Christian. It is also thought that the monastery recovered much of its importance in the late 10th century.

Meanwhile, the early 10th century saw the Anglo-Saxon half of Mercia forging strong links with its old enemy Wessex. Æthelflæd, 'Lady of the Mercians' then set about fortifying Mercia's eastern borders, before taking the Danish fortress at Derby in July 917 and annexing the whole region back into English Mercia again. When Æthelflæd died in 918, the Mercians accepted Edward the Elder of Wessex as their king and he proceeded to take back Nottingham and Leicester in 920. However, the Five Boroughs continued to oscillate between Anglo-Saxon and Viking for another hundred years or so, until 1035, when what was by then known as the *Earldom* of Mercia was in Anglo-Saxon hands, under Leofric, Earl of Mercia. Throughout these times, and particularly during the first forty-or-so years of the Danelaw, the Scandinavians left their permanent mark on Leicestershire and Rutland, particularly in terms of place-names. For starters, there are around 60 places in Leicestershire that end in -*by*, each deriving from the Old Scandinavian word *bý*, meaning "farmstead or settlement". Around half of these are also preceded by a Danish personal name, such as Kettleby, Rotherby and Saxelby (farmsteads belonging to men called Ketil, Hreitharr and Saksulfr, respectively), while a number of Saxon –*tūn* endings are also prefixed by Scandinavian personal names, such as Thurmaston (farmstead or village of a man called Thormóthr), thus suggesting a Scandinavian takeover of a Saxon estate.

Intriguingly, where the Anglo-Saxons had already established their communities – such as along the Soar Valley – we don't see quite so many Scandinavian place-names. However, we do see lots of Scandinavian places along the Wreake Valley, thereby suggesting that they actually established new communities here. Of further interest, though, is that the number of such places falls away again beyond Melton and towards the river's source. And indeed, the river ceases to become the Wreake further upstream, and takes on the Anglo-Saxon name of the River Eye, which derives from the Anglo-Saxon word *ēa*, meaning "river"; unsurprisingly, *Wreake* is of Scandinavian origin, meaning "twisted or winding".

Historians are divided on the nature of settlement in the Wreake Valley, though. Some think that the area was quickly settled by members of the Danish army very early – in around 877 – and that this perhaps represents the last-surviving evidence of a Danish army unit that was deliberately settled on new land where they could fairly rapidly swing into action – in this case, for the defence of Leicester should the Anglo-Saxons threaten to re-take it. However, other historians think that the Wreake Valley was settled by Scandinavian farmers over a much longer period of time – although they still agree that these were Danish colonists largely occupying virgin sites as opposed to taking over existing Anglo-Saxon settlements.

As for Danish settlement in Rutland, we have a very different story. There are no place-names ending in –*by* for a start – these being *primary* settlements, while there are only six place-names that derive in part from a Scandinavian personal name. There are, however, eleven places ending in –*thorpe*, this indicating a *secondary* Scandinavian settlement – and therefore suggesting at only a token settlement of the county area. And yet there is no evidence that *Roteland* maintained its Anglo-Saxon identity through military resistance. One possible answer to the lack of a Scandinavian imprint in today's Rutland, is that in the late 9th century, *Roteland* might have stretched further east, and included Stamford and other parts of Lincolnshire's Kesteven district. And here, the Danes most definitely did stamp their presence. So perhaps the land to the west of Stamford just didn't hold any strategic importance, and settlements tended to be funnelled up and down Ermine Street.

As well as place-names, the Scandinavians also left a profound impression in terms of language, vocabulary, grammatical construction … even down to tone and inflexion. And yet despite this, there is limited tangible evidence of Danish influence. One area where their mark was left, though, was in Leicester, where the town was converted from a Mercian cathedral city into a Danish garrison town. The Old Scandinavian word *gata*, meaning road or street, was also imprinted on the town from its period of Danish occupation all the way up to today; witness street-names of Belgrave Gate, Church Gate, Gallowtree Gate, Humberstone Gate and Sanvey Gate, all of which lie to the north and the east of the former Roman and Anglo-Saxon settlement. This meant that 10th century Leicester must have had two distinct towns: the Anglo-Saxon one and the Danish one. Interestingly, a Christian church was also established by the Danes at the top of Sanvey Gate in the Danish quarter, probably as early as the 9th century, thus confirming the Danish conversion to Christianity within a generation of their occupation. Today, the site is occupied by the 15th century St Margaret's church – and which, significantly, was aligned to the diocese of Lincoln (ex-Danelaw), while the parishes of the older Anglo-Saxon town were aligned to the diocese of Lichfield (ex-Mercian).

Finally, as already stated, it was in the middle of the Anglo-Saxon/Viking struggle that Leicestershire was first created, and with very similar borders to today. Internally, the shires of the Danelaw were divided into wapentakes, the equivalent of the Anglo-Saxon hundreds. There were four wapentakes in Leicestershire, Goscote covering the north-west and north of the county, Framland covering the north-east, Guthlaxton the south-western quadrant and Gartree the south-east. The wapentakes later became hundreds, with the division of Goscote into West Goscote and East Goscote, plus the addition of Sparkenhoe hundred.

During the 10th century, though, we also see evidence in various charters where distinct areas within Leicestershire are allocated to Mercian thegns (Anglo-Saxon noblemen), and which closely resemble our modern-day parishes.

The Domesday Book of 1086 then became the first concise recording of towns, villages and estates in Leicestershire and Rutland, recording most of the current settlements of each county, bar those that emerged during the Industrial Revolution. Leicestershire itself is first formally referenced as a shire in 1087, when it was recorded as *Laegrecastrescir*, but it had clearly been recognised as a distinct *area* long before that, particularly throughout its Five Boroughs lifetime. Of course, the *town* of Leicester dates back to pre-Roman times, but the modern version of the name only started to appear at the beginning of the 10th century when it was recorded as *Ligera ceastre*, and again as *Ledecestre* in Domesday Book (1086). Both names mean "Roman town of the Ligore people", where Ligore is a tribal name, derived from the ancient River Legro (now the River Soar). The rest of the name is derived from the Old English word *ceaster*, meaning "Roman station or walled town". But what is also clear, is that the name was now Anglo-Saxon, and the Celtic version of the name which had been based on the ancient *Corieltauvi* tribe, had long-since disappeared.

From the Normans to the Dissolution

Following the Norman Conquest, William I attacked Leicester, and took the city by storm in 1068. In the assault a large portion of the city was destroyed, along with St Mary's church. William then promptly handed the manor of Leicester over to one of his Norman nobles, Hugh de Grandmesnil, who had fought alongside him at Hastings, and who came from a family famous for the breeding and training of great war horses. William also gave de Grandmesnil one hundred manors for his services, sixty five of which were in Leicestershire and appointed him Sheriff of the county of Leicester and Governor of Hampshire; later on, his family would also acquire the title of Earl of Leicester and later still, the principal title of Earl of Lancaster, while in the 14th century they became *Dukes* of Lancaster. A similar ruthless class system overhaul was then imposed on the majority of Leicestershire and Rutland, as out went the previous Anglo-Scandinavian incumbents, to be replaced by Norman gentry.

It was largely these new incumbents, or their immediate successors who were recorded in the Domesday Book survey of 1086. The same survey also revealed that Leicestershire was comprised of 296 settlements, while the area that would shortly become Rutland consisted of 39. The majority of settlement centres were therefore already laid out and very similar to today. The only differences are those deserted or shrunken medieval villages that were mainly lost to the plague between the 14th and 17th centuries, such as Baggrave,

Facets of Norman Leicester. In the foreground is part of Leicester Castle's defences while in the background is St Mary de Castro church, built in the mid-12th century by Robert de Beaumont.

Great Stretton and Quenby, a small handful of fields cleared from woodland in the 13th century such as Bondman Hays, rare new medieval settlements such as Newton Linford and, of course, those new villages and towns that sprung up during the Industrial Revolution, such as Coalville. One interesting insight afforded by Domesday Book, is that four particular manors in Leicestershire, had very complex ownership structures, with scattered holdings in several neighbouring and sometimes distant settlements. The manors in question were Barrow-on-Soar, Great Bowden, Melton Mowbray and Rothley, with Barrow-on-Soar alone owning land in 13 other villages.

Rutland, meanwhile, appears as *Roteland* in Domesday Book, and is referred to as "the King's soc of Roteland". Not yet a shire, it was actually a detached part of Nottinghamshire that covered just the north-western part of today's county. At the same time, the opposing south-eastern area of today's county was recorded as the wapentake of Wicelsea in Northamptonshire. As for the "King's soc of Roteland", the *soc* or *soke* in question was a term used around the time of the Norman Conquest to denote an area that held a special kind of jurisdiction. Its primary meaning seems to have involved "seeking", thus *soka faldae* was the duty of seeking the lord's court. The Soke of Rutland is also still referred to as late as the 14th century, although Rutland is generally deemed to have been a separate county, with an area very similar to its modern counterpart from around 1159 onwards, with the office of High Sheriff of Rutland having been introduced 30 years earlier in 1129. The *Roteland* area was also assigned as a dowry to Queen Isabella after her marriage to King John in 1200.

Back to Domesday Book, though, and the other thing that can loosely be derived from it is population, although the survey was never intended as a census; the information collected was gathered mainly for the purpose of taxation. However, as it records important heads of families, it is thought that by multiplying this number by a factor of five, you will get an approximation to the late 11th century population value. Therefore, given the recorded "population" in Domesday Book for Leicestershire and Rutland locations is 6406 and 1479, respectively, it is a fair bet that the actual population of the two counties was around 30,000 and 7000, respectively. As for Leicester, Domesday Book records 322 houses, so we can assume that the town's population was perhaps between 1500 and 2000. The fact that 65 burgesses are mentioned confirms that Leicester was designated a borough at that time, while it also boasted its own mint, too; Domesday Book also records *Ledecestre* as a *civitas* – in other words, a city. However, it lost its city status in the 11th century and didn't regain it until 1919. Nevertheless, under the Normans, Leicester continued to be comprised of its two distinct parts, Anglo-Saxon and Danish, with the former still largely within the ancient Roman wall and the latter a suburb to the north-east.

Shortly after the Norman Conquest, Leicestershire and Rutland also underwent the other standard Norman process: that of fortification. In total, Leicestershire and Rutland are home to around 20 castle sites that date from the Norman Conquest to the end of the mid-12th century period known as The Anarchy when Stephen and Matilda fought over the throne. The most significant castle was built in Leicester in the late 1060s, and somewhat inevitably by Hugh de Grandmesnil. Designed to help quell any local uprisings, the castle was strategically placed in the south-west angle of the Roman town defences, which dominated the town and also overlooked the River Soar. Indeed, rather than reinvent the wheel, the Norman castle actually *used* some of the Roman defences in places! Unsurprisingly, de Grandmesnil built a typically early Norman castle, including motte and bailey along with an oval defensive rampart and ditch with a timber palisade on top. Inside the ramparts, there would have been a series of timber buildings including a Great Hall, a church, an armoury, stables, and a kitchen. As for the motte, this large mound would have been surmounted by a timber tower, or a keep – the castle's last line of defence. Today, there is no trace of the timber keep, but the mound that was the motte still survives, standing at around 30ft (9m) high and 95ft (30.5m) wide.

It was Robert de Beaumont, the second Earl of Leicester, who began replacing the timber castle with a stone one, probably in the mid-12th century. The stone church that was built at this time was named St Mary de Castro (St Mary of the Castle), a name selected to differentiate it from St Mary de Pratis (St Mary in the Meadow) and which would later become known as Leicester Abbey. Robert de Beaumont's church was located within the castle bailey and was founded as a college served by a Dean and twelve Canons. Also rebuilt in stone at this time was the Great Hall, some of which also survives to this day, and which has been described as "the oldest surviving aisled and bay-divided hall in Europe". The castle eventually passed to the de Montforts (much more on them later), while the castle also played host to Edward I in 1300 and Edward

LEICESTER CASTLE

Part of the remaining walls of Leicester Castle, known as the Turret Gateway. The castle was originally built in the late 1060s by Hugh de Grandmesnil.

This mound, that was located in the south-west angle of the Roman city wall, is what remains of the motte of the former Leicester Castle.

II in 1310 and 1311. Many of the castle's owners rebuilt and enhanced the structure, initially improving defences, but eventually merely improving the comfort of the residence as the threat of local uprisings gradually receded.

Rutland's county town, Oakham, also had a medieval castle. Oakham Castle was built between 1180 and 1190 for Walkelin de Ferrers. However, it wasn't built along traditional Norman castle lines and was more of a fortified manor house, although it did have a curtain wall, a gatehouse and a drawbridge. Remarkably, the Great Hall remains today, completely intact, and comprises a nave and two arcaded aisles, each with three large stone columns. It is the earliest complete hall of its kind anywhere in England.

Another fine example of earthwork remains of a Norman motte and bailey castle can be found at Hallaton in the south-east of Leicestershire. Contrary to the norm, though, the castle was built low-down, almost on the valley floor, so it was unlikely to have been built for defensive or strategic purposes. It was owned by Geoffrey Alselin, another of William I's right-hand men and was around 118ft (36m) high and 630ft (190m) in circumference. Excavations carried out in the late 19th century turned up pottery, leather shoes and wooden bowls along with evidence of iron-making.

A similar excavation at the 12th century motte at Groby revealed that it may well have been built on the site of a much older building. There is also dispute as to which Norman built Groby Castle. Some think that it was built by Hugh de Grandmesnil who owned the manor in the years after the Conquest, while others think it was built later by one of the first two Robert de Beaumonts, first and second Earls of Leicester, with the latter theory more favoured as the motte appears to have supported a stone and not a wooden tower. Whoever built it, historians are fairly certain that it was destroyed by Henry II during the Revolt of 1173-74, a rebellion against the King by three of his sons, his wife Eleanor of Aquitaine, and their rebel supporters, one of whom was the Earl of Leicester – and hence the slighting of Leicester Castle, too.

One other "castle" that was built in the 12th century was Ashby-de-la-Zouch Castle, although it was originally built as a fortified manor house; it wasn't raised to the status of a castle until the 15th century. It was gradually extended between the 12th and 15th centuries by the Zouch family, but reverted to the Crown in 1461 before Edward IV bestowed it upon William, Lord

ST MARY DE CASTRO

Today's Grade I listed St Mary de Castro church, was built in the mid-12th century as a collegiate church by Robert de Beaumont, second Earl of Leicester.

The sedilia in the chancel extension of the church, which Pevsner describes as "the finest piece of Norman decoration in the county".

When St Mary de Castro was extended in the 13th century, what is now the south aisle became the parish church, making the entire building two churches in one, separated by screens. What had been the outer south wall of the older collegiate church now became the inner north wall of the parish church – and external features of the older church survive such as part of a Norman arch shown here above the main arch. Services were regularly conducted simultaneously at the two altars.

Hastings along with a "license to crenellate" in 1474. Hastings became Edward's Lord Chamberlain, and soon built what was known as the Hastings Tower which was 90ft (27m) high, as well as a chapel in the north-east corner of the castle. Alas, in 1483, Hastings fell victim to Richard, Duke of Gloucester, a charge of treason and the executioners axe – this despite supporting the future Richard III's installation as Lord Protector; revenge must have been sweet for Hastings' son, Edward, two years later at Bosworth Field! Centuries later, the castle was a Royalist stronghold during the English Civil War, which proved to be its undoing, for following a prolonged siege between September 1645 and March 1646, the Royalists eventually surrendered the castle which was then partially destroyed by the Parliamentarians. As a brief aside, it was also the first Baron Hastings who owned the castle at Castle Donington that had been built by Henry de Lacy during the late 13th century. Alas, by the time it was owned by Sir George Hastings in 1595, the castle was a ruin and was eventually replaced by a house. No trace of the castle remains today.

MEDIEVAL LEICESTERSHIRE AND RUTLAND CASTLES

The timber-framed gatehouse of Leicester Castle, built in the 1450s.

Ashby-de-la-Zouch Castle. Originally a fortified Norman manor house, it became a castle in the 15th century, was partially destroyed during the English Civil War, and then became a tourist hotspot after its inclusion in Walter Scott's Ivanhoe (1819) as the scene of a tourney.

View towards the remains of the motte of Hallaton Castle, built for Geoffrey Alselin in south-east Leicestershire in the late 11th century.

This mound at Groby marks the position of the motte of Groby Castle, which was slighted following the Revolt of 1173-74.

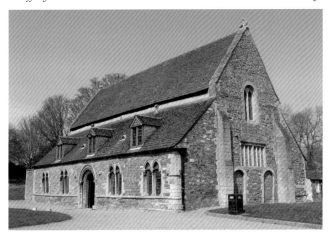

The Great Hall, sole surviving remnant of Oakham Castle which was built between 1180 and 1190 for Walkelin de Ferrers.

Internally, Oakham Castle is blessed with many late Norman features. The horseshoes are explained in a later Quirk Alert!

As mentioned earlier, Leicester was also home to the Abbey of Saint Mary de Pratis, more commonly known as Leicester Abbey. The abbey was founded in around 1139 for the Augustinian order, again by Robert de Beaumont, 2nd Earl of Leicester. It soon grew to become the wealthiest religious establishment in Leicestershire, through the patronage of scores of churches, donations, the acquisition of a considerable amount of land and several manorial lordships, while the institution was also exempt from paying certain tithes, too. The abbey also acquired granges in the Peak District along with their valuable stock-piles of wool – and which found a ready outlet with Leicester's many merchants. Nevertheless, the abbey began to suffer financially towards the end of the 14th century, and was forced to lease out its estates. Then, from the 15th century onwards the abbey became hamstrung by a series of corrupt and extravagant abbots, and by the time of the Dissolution of the Monasteries in the late 1530s, the abbey's considerable income was exceeded by even more considerable debts! It was therefore never going

to survive Henry VIII's wrath, and it was duly dissolved in 1538, rapidly demolished and the building materials re-used by new buildings across Leicestershire, including a new mansion built on the site of the abbey. The other notable milestone for the abbey was in 1530, when Cardinal Thomas Wolsey died there whilst travelling south to face trial for treason.

In the two centuries after the Norman Conquest, a number of other monasteries were founded, including an early 12th century Augustinian priory on top of Breedon Hill. We've already talked about the Saxon monastery there which was badly sacked by the Danes. But sometime between 1109 and 1122, Robert de Ferrers gave the parish church (which was probably the ruins of the Saxon monastery), to the Augustinian Priory of St Oswald at Nostell in Yorkshire. By 1122, a prior and five canons were established at Breedon, and they went on to either rebuild the eastern part of the ancient minster or they built it from scratch. Cloisters and domestic quarters were added, but the priory always remained small and dependent upon Nostell. By the

LEICESTERSHIRE'S "SURVIVING" MEDIEVAL RELIGIOUS HOUSES

The layout of Leicester Abbey, as plotted by archaeologists following excavations during the 1920s and 1930s. The abbey was originally built in 1143. However, it was dissolved in 1538, rapidly demolished and a mansion, Cavendish House, built in its place. The above outline has now been designated a scheduled ancient monument as well as receiving Grade I listing.

Part of the ruins of Ulverscroft Priory, originally founded in 1134 by Robert de Beaumont, who also founded Leicester Abbey.

Following the Dissolution of the Monasteries, Launde Priory was acquired by Thomas Cromwell in 1539. He was executed the following year, but his son, George, built a new manor house in its place, retaining most of the 12th century priory chancel (shown above) which became a private chapel.

This chapel at Rothley Court Hotel also survives. It was once part of Rothley Temple, founded in 1231 for the Knights Templar.

15th century, the priory was in debt and its buildings dilapidated, while a century later, it was surrendered to the Crown in 1539 as part of the Dissolution of the Monasteries. However, the chancel of the priory church survived and makes up a significant portion of today's parish church.

Another Augustinian priory was founded at Ulverscroft in the heart of Charnwood Forest in 1134, again, by Robert de Beaumont, 2nd Earl of Leicester. The original priory was probably built of wood, but the 13th and 14th century buildings that followed were built of Charnwood Stone. A small priory, it still only had three canons in 1220, although by 1438 the number had risen to eight, and by 1532 the priory was home to nine canons and the prior. It accumulated modest donations over the four centuries of its existence, gaining 70 acres of "waste" at Groby in 1323, and the advowson of Syston Church. Thomas de Ferrers then donated the advowson of the splendid Bunny church, in Nottinghamshire, in 1345, while in around 1465 the smaller Charley Priory, nearby, was merged with Ulverscroft. As for the Dissolution, Ulverscroft Priory survived the first cull in 1535, but was finally dissolved in September 1539. Happily, the last Prior, Geoffrey Whalley, was granted an annual pension of £20 and fared much better than many of his peers. As was common elsewhere, post-Dissolution, the priory building was granted to someone with a title, in this case, Thomas Manners, 1st Earl of Rutland. All that remains today are some extensive ruins, medieval walls, ditches and fishponds, while the prior's lodging and refectory is incorporated into a farmhouse. And talking of fishponds, these are also traceable at the site of another monastic house over in the east of Leicestershire where Owston Abbey once stood. The abbey was founded in the mid-12th century by Robert Grimbald, Chief Justice of England, and was endowed with the church and manor of Owston; by 1166 it had also acquired the advowsons of the Leicestershire churches of Burrough, King's Norton and Slawston along with Tickencote in Rutland and North Witham in Lincolnshire. Further additions followed in the 14th century, including the manors of Muston and Normanton. Despite these endowments, though, Owston Abbey remained one of the smaller and poorer Augustinian houses, and although there were 17 canons at the abbey in 1377, by 1534 the number had fallen to 11 and by 1536 only 6 remained – this also being the year that the abbey was dissolved. By 1556 the abbey was a ruin, although parts of it – including the chancel – were incorporated into St Andrew's church at Owston. Some of the original stonework also exists, albeit below ground, and therefore the site is a scheduled monument.

Of course, this section has only represented a handful of Leicestershire and Rutland's medieval religious establishments, but there were many more. Most of these are captured in a table that can be found under the *Author, Book Supplements, Leicestershire and Rutland: Unusual and Quirky* menu options on the following website: www.andybeardmore.com.

St Nicholas' church, Leicester is famous for its surviving Saxon stonework (c.900), and the Roman tiles built around a Saxon arch in the north wall of the nave. It also boasts a Norman tower. **Inset:** *Looking down the nave towards the chancel at St Michael and All Angels, Hallaton. The arches in the north aisle date to the late Norman period.*

STORMING NORMAN FEATURES IN LEICESTERSHIRE AND RUTLAND

St Mary de Castro, Leicester.

St Mary the Virgin, Ketton.

St Michael and All Angels, Hallaton.

St Peter's, Tickencote.

Norman tympanum at St Edmund's church, Egleton.

Horninghold St Peter, 12th century south doorway.

Norman carvings on the tower arch at St Luke's church, Tixover.

The magnificent chancel arch at Tickencote St Peter's church. There surely can't be a more stunning internal feature in any other small UK parish church.

Even the chancel roof is spectacular!

Similarly, there are many churches in Leicestershire and Rutland that still retain Norman features. Most of these are captured in a table that can be found in the same section of the same website.

Throughout the late 11th and 12th centuries, the town of Leicester remained largely confined within the medieval walls that had been raised above the foundation of the Roman defences. In the centre, close to St Nicholas' churchyard, two important thoroughfares crossed; Welford Road running from London to the North Midlands, and the Fosse Way still running between Exeter and Lincoln. Each road entered and exited via a walled gate, thus dividing the centre up into quadrants, and within those walls, there were actually *seven* parish churches – although All Saints, St Clement's, St Michael's and St Peter's had all disappeared by the end of the 16th century; St Margaret's still lay outside the core of Leicester to the north-east and thus came under the control of nearby Leicester Abbey.

It is almost certain that the northern part of the medieval walled town was the busiest and most densely populated area. It was also where the main industries of the day were concentrated, and which initially included bell-founding, cloth manufacture, leather-working and the wool trade. In 1196, the oldest surviving Guild Merchant Roll lists fifty different occupations amongst its members, while at around the same time, a medieval court known as the Portmanmoot existed for the settlement of minor disputes. These two factions – merchants and justices – came together at this time to manage the affairs of Leicester, and therefore both Guild and Moot became the forerunner to the Town Council, and which became known as the Corporation by the end of the 15th century. In the interim period, Leicester Guildhall was built in 1390, close to St Martin's church, and became the meeting place of the Corpus Christi Guild, while a century further on it was used for meetings by the governing body of the town. Amazingly, the Guildhall survives to this day, and is a Grade I listed building, its survival undoubtedly due to the fact that it remained in use as a town hall until 1876, when the "new" town hall was built.

Industry-wise, the 13th century saw the Leicester clothiers clothing royalty. Again, their premises were situated in the northern part of the town – which is also where five footwear manufacturers were located at the beginning of the 14th century, a number which had risen to 13 by 1376. However, it is known that the northern quarter fell into decline not long after that, probably caused by changing economics at the end of the 14th century with cloth no longer as important, and very much superseded by wool production and export to northern Europe.

The 13th century also saw Leicester play a significant role in English history when, in 1265, Simon de Montfort, 6th Earl of Leicester, forced King Henry III to hold the first Parliament of England at the by now-ruined Leicester Castle. This followed on from the Second Barons War 1263-64, which de Montfort had led against the King due to the King's hostility towards reform. He scored a spectacular victory over the King at the Battle of Lewes, on the 14th May 1264, after which he set up a national government. Henry was allowed to retain the title and authority of King, but all decisions and approval now rested with his council, led by de Montfort and subject to consultation with parliament. What became known as De Montfort's Parliament (of 1265) was comprised of two representatives from each English county and a select list of boroughs, plus for the first time, elected ordinary citizens from the boroughs. It is therefore from this period that parliamentary representation derives, while the right to vote in Parliamentary elections for county constituencies was uniform throughout the country to all those who owned the freehold of land to an annual rent of 40 shillings.

The turning point for de Montfort came in May 1265, when Henry's son, Prince Edward, gained the support of the Welsh Marcher Lords. This was followed by the defection of de Montfort's former ally at Lewes, Gilbert de Clare, the Earl of Gloucester, and the most powerful of the barons … and who had grown resentful of de

Leicester Guildhall, built in 1390, and originally used by the Corpus Christi Guild, but which remained in use as a Town Hall all the way up to 1876.

Statue of Simon de Montfort, 6th Earl of Leicester. He was briefly de facto ruler of England in 1265 before his death at the Battle of Evesham (1265).The statue is one of four Leicester giants to adorn the Haymarket Memorial Clock Tower in Leicester City Centre.

Montfort's growing power. Prince Edward then attacked de Montfort's forces at Kenilworth, capturing many of his allies, before the two met at the Battle of Evesham on 4th August 1265. In a distinctly uneven battle, Simon de Montfort was stabbed in the neck by a lance and died. His body was then horribly mutilated by the royalists, with his head severed from his body, his hands and feet cut off, and his testicles removed and hung on either side of his nose. Such remains that could be found were buried under the altar of Evesham Abbey by the canons. Nevertheless, despite this grisly demise, for a short time, de Montfort had actually been de facto ruler of England and during his rule he had called the first directly elected parliament in medieval Europe. He is thus regarded today as one of the fathers of modern parliamentary democracy. He was also held in such high regard, that his grave was frequently visited by pilgrims. Meanwhile, today, a number of buildings in Leicester are named in his honour, such as De Montfort University and the concert venue, De Montfort Hall, whilst a statue of Simon de Montfort can be found in the City Centre on Haymarket Memorial Clock Tower.

> **Quirk Alert:** *Mangled by a Mangonel*
> *The father of Simon de Montfort, 6th Earl of Leicester, was Simon de Montfort, 5th Earl of Leicester. Alas, he was killed at the Siege of Toulouse in 1218 by a stone hurled from a mangonel – the latter being a type of catapult or siege engine used to throw projectiles at castle walls, albeit with less accuracy than a trebuchet, throwing at a lower trajectory, but higher velocity.*

From the end of the 13th century, the hall of Leicester Castle was used as an assize court. However, in 1426, what became known as the Parliament of Bats was held at Leicester Castle during the infancy of King Henry VI. Despite its title, this was the genuine Parliament of England, but it was so-named because members were not allowed to be armed with swords, and thus took in clubs and bats instead. The reason behind the tension was due to the ongoing dispute between Cardinal Beaufort (also the Bishop of Winchester and Lord Chancellor), and the Duke of Gloucester, the King's uncle and regent. The Parliament saw Beaufort removed permanently as Lord Chancellor and replaced with John Kemp. Throughout the Parliament of Bats, meetings took place in the Great Hall, whilst one session saw the young King knighted across the road in St Mary de Castro church.

One of the changes brought about by the downgrading of Leicester Castle's fortifications during the 13th and 14th centuries was the development of the area to the south of the castle that became known as the Newarke (basically the New Work). This process began with the foundation of the Trinity Hospital just to the south of the castle in 1331. It was founded by Henry, 3rd Earl of Lancaster and Leicester, and comprised a church at the east end with adjoining accommodation to the west. By this stage, the Earls of Lancaster were one of the three wealthiest and most powerful families in the country, so it was no surprise when in 1352, Henry, the 4th Earl, was elevated to Duke of Lancaster. He then set about transforming the castle, adding an outer bailey to the north of the castle and major redevelopment to the south, including the doubling of the size of Trinity Hospital. He also established a religious precinct to the south of the castle, including a large new church, the Collegiate Church of the Annunciation of St Mary, complete with its own college of clergy who supported one hundred poor persons; the clergy lived in dwellings located around the church while the poor lived in cubicles in the hospital. A wall was then built around the precinct and included two large gatehouses, one towards the middle of the south side and one in the north-east corner, the Magazine Gateway, and which still stands today.

MEDIEVAL MELTON MOWBRAY AND MARKET HARBOROUGH

 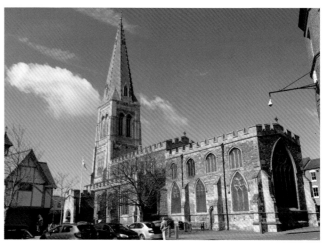

Here we have not only two of the most acclaimed churches in Leicestershire, but in England, too. St Mary Magdalene church in Melton Mowbray (left) was begun in the 13th century and includes a magnificent clerestory of 48 windows (largely obscured by the trees). Meanwhile, Market Harborough's St Dionysius church (right) was initially only a chapel that is first mentioned in 1220 and which was dependent upon the parish church of St Mary in Arden. However, when the latter fell into disuse, St Dionysius took over, having been significantly developed throughout the 14th and 15th centuries.

Quirk Alert: *Doveine Intervention*
The village of Breedon on the Hill actually sits at the foot of the striking hill after which it is named, with the medieval church of St Mary and St Hardulph perched alone at the hill's summit. For centuries, therefore, worshippers have had to ascend a steep and winding path to attend services. One may wonder, therefore, at the rationale for the church's placement, which must have defeated many of the local aged and infirm over the centuries. Of course, we know today that it is history that dictated the placement, with an Iron Age hillfort succeeded by Roman settlement, which was succeeded by a Saxon monastery, which was succeeded by a Norman priory, which was succeeded by the current church. However, that didn't stop an interesting legend from surfacing several centuries ago, stating that the villagers were actually consulted regarding the location for the church and they originally selected a spot at the base of the hill. However, the story goes that the foundations were dug, but after the first day of building, all of the stones were carried away in the night by doves, and skilfully reconstructed in exactly the same manner on top of the hill. Awestruck by this intervention, the builders agreed to continue with the structure begun by the doves!

The Magazine Gateway in central Leicester dates back to the 14th century, when Henry, 1st Duke of Lancaster built a religious precinct to the south of Leicester Castle. The area was known as the Newarke, and that name is continued today in the area by a number of streets, houses, gardens and a museum. As for the Magazine Gateway, that was so-named because the gatehouse was used as a magazine for storing arms during the English Civil War, three centuries later.

The work was eventually completed by Henry's son-in-law, John of Gaunt, who inherited the Dukedom in 1361 as Henry died without a male heir. John of Gaunt also happened to be the father of Henry Bolingbroke who, in 1399 became Henry IV of England. The title Duke of Lancaster thus became an honorary title of the monarch, and Henry and his successors had their principal residence in London and were buried in Westminster Abbey. However, Leicester Castle continued to be regarded as the traditional seat of the Dukes and to be used for ceremonial occasions, such as the knighting of the future Henry V. The ceremonies continued there until the outbreak of the Wars of the Roses in the mid-15th century, mainly due to the fact that between 1461 and 1485, the throne was in the possession of the House of York, the sworn enemy of the Dukes of Lancaster. The Yorkists neither occupied nor maintained the castle or the Newarke, so by the time Richard III stayed in Leicester prior to the Battle of Bosworth, in 1485, the place was no longer habitable and Richard stayed at a local inn instead.

Despite Leicester Castle's neglect during the Wars of the Roses, it still contained one of the town's principal parish churches, St Mary de Castro, and the Great Hall was also still used as a court. Here, major cases were brought before judges who travelled around the country conducting trials in the name of the Crown. Parts of the Great Hall were demolished in the 16th century, while the main entrance dates from the late 17th century. Further alterations in the 18th and 19th centuries saw the Great Hall divided into two courtrooms which remained in use until the 1980s.

As for the Collegiate Church, its college continued to prosper for over two hundred years, and even survived the dissolution of religious houses in the late 1530s – perhaps due to its close connection with Henry VIII's ancestors. However, the college was surrendered to the Crown in 1545, and when Edward VI succeeded his father, he held no such affinity for the building; the college was therefore dissolved in 1548, the property seized and the clergy dismissed. Shortly afterwards the Collegiate Church was demolished. Some of the church ruins survived until the early 20th century, but even they disappeared when an Art and Technical School was built on the site, and which eventually became De Montfort University. Meanwhile, and despite taking a battering during the English Civil War in the 1640s, the walls of the Newarke survived for around 500 years before eventually being demolished in the early 19th century, leaving only two upstanding structures. One of these was a building known as Prince Rupert's Tower which was eventually demolished in 1935. The other, the previously mentioned Magazine Gateway, still survives to this day, although it had a close shave in the 1960s when the inner ring road was being built. Thankfully a public outcry saved what was by then a scheduled monument, and there it remains as the only major survivor of the great 14th century Collegiate Church and the precinct that enclosed it.

One of the main pastimes of Norman and medieval gentry was hunting. It is likely that during the Middle Ages, the western part of Leicestershire was still heavily wooded. Reaching to the North Gate of Leicester was an area known as *Hereswode*, a name which means "wood of the army", and which was probably associated with the Danish army during the early 10th century. Stretching from Leicester down to Earl Shilton, this particular woodland tract was owned by the Earls of Leicester until the 13th century; thereafter it belonged to the Duchy of Lancaster. However, the wood eventually became known as Leicester Forest – although it was never officially a royal forest. Meanwhile, despite its name, there is no evidence to suggest that the area today known as Charnwood Forest was a royal forest, either, although some historians believe that it could have been prior to the Norman Conquest. That leaves just the Royal Forest of Leicestershire and Rutland as the only known royal hunting ground. In the 13th century, this royal forest covered the area of south-east Leicestershire where it borders Rutland, plus around half of the Rutland county area, although by the 15th century, the area had become known as Leighfield Forest.

Throughout the Middle Ages, many of Leicestershire and Rutland's towns and villages were awarded market charters or fairs – 44 of them, in fact, by 1350. All but two of these were issued after 1200, the exceptions being Melton Mowbray and Belvoir, although it is pretty clear that some towns had market places that date to before 1200, Leicester being the prime example even though it didn't receive its charter until 1229. Conversely, many of those places that were explicitly granted a market charter, certainly don't run markets today, and haven't done so for several centuries; examples include Gaddesby (charter granted in 1306), Kibworth Beauchamp (1223), Lubenham (1327) and Wymondham (1303).

We've already covered the medieval cloth, leather and bell-founding industries in Leicester, but in terms of county-wide industries, coal mining had already become a significant industry in North West Leicester-

LEICESTERSHIRE AND RUTLAND'S MEDIEVAL MARKET CROSSES

The market cross and stocks at Bottesford date from the 14th century.

The market cross at Oakham is also known as the Butter Cross, as this is where dairy products were sold. It is shown on Speed's map of 1611.

The medieval village cross at Hathern is a scheduled ancient monument.

The medieval village cross at Muston.

The 15th century market cross at Billesdon.

shire – albeit open seam, near-surface coal-mining. The Leicestershire coalfield is effectively split into two by what is known as the Ashby Anticline, a crest running through Ashby in a north-west to south-easterly direction. To the east, the coalfields run between the Ashby Anticline and the western edge of Charnwood Forest, while to the west, the coalfield includes the region from South Derbyshire down to Measham – with both coalfields supporting around 20 workable seams. The first official record of coal mining is via a charter dating from 1204, while in 1270, Garendon Abbey was formally granted "the whole wood at Worthington" and which also included "coalmines". A further 13th century record in 1293 tells of an annual rent of four cart-loads of coal arising from the land at Donington-le-Heath. All of these 13th century references refer to the eastern portion of the Leicestershire coalfield; the first official reference to the western part dates from 1477 when a record from Leicester Abbey talks of the possession of a coal mine at Oakthorpe. Other contemporary documents state that at Worthington and Staunton Harold, coal exploitation was controlled by the lord of the manor, while at Swannington, any freeman could dig coal on the common land of the township. By 1498, coal mining is clearly recognised as a profession, with two locals of Coleorton recognised as *collyers*.

As already mentioned, the early medieval cloth industry was superseded by the wool industry, and one of Leicester's most famous sons made his fortune from it, exporting wool to the Flemish weavers through the port of Calais. In fact, wool merchant William

Statue of William Wyggeston on the Haymarket Clock Tower in Leicester City Centre.

Quirk Alert: *Horseshoeing Around*

Oakham is home to a centuries-old tradition where members of royalty and peers of the realm who visit or pass through the town for the first time, have to pay a forfeit in the form of a horseshoe. There are now around 230 of these commemorative shoes on display on the walls of the Great Hall of Oakham Castle, with the earliest datable horseshoe commemorating a visit by King Edward IV in about 1470. It is thought that this tradition is linked to the de Ferrers family name, as ferrier *was the Norman French word for "farrier" and the horseshoe has been a symbol of the de Ferrers family since Henry de Ferrers arrived in England with William I in 1066. Today, the donation of a horseshoe only happens on Royal visits, when a specially made ceremonial horseshoe is presented and hung in the Great Hall. Recent horseshoes commemorate visits by HRH The Princess Royal (1999), HRH The Prince of Wales (2003), HRH Princess Alexandra (2005) and HRH the Duchess of Cornwall (2014). Interestingly, the horseshoes actually hang upside-down – a tradition generally held to be unlucky, based on the theory that this way, your luck runs out, whereas the other way around, the "cup" holds your good luck. However, in Rutland, having the shoe point upwards was akin to inviting the Devil to build his nest in the hollow, not to mention being a representation of the devil's horns! As for the upside-down horseshoe motif, this also appears on the county emblem as well as appearing on the local Ruddles beer labels, too. And as* Rutland Times *editor, Eddie Hudson ranted back in 1997, on hearing of a plan to celebrate Rutland's reinstatement as a county by turning the county emblem around: "How dare they! Rutland has got it right. It's everyone else that's wrong!"*

Some of the horseshoes paid as a forfeit by royalty, including the first donated by King Edward IV in around 1470, Queen Elizabeth in 1967, right up to the Duchess of Cornwall in 2014.

WYGGESTON AND LATIMER

Today's Newarke Houses Museum (white building) incorporates Wyggeston House (nearside), a former chantry chapel founded by William Wyggeston in 1512.

Latimer House, Thurcaston, probably built in two stages during the 15th and 16th centuries. It was the birthplace of Hugh Latimer (1487-1555), who became Bishop of Worcester in 1535. However, he resigned his bishopric in 1539 following the passing of the Act of the Six Articles, and was eventually burnt at the stake as a Protestant martyr in 1555, one of Catholic Mary Tudor's 300 victims. He was also known as one of the three Oxford Martyrs of Anglicanism, to one of whom, Nicholas Ridley, he stated on sentencing: "We shall this day light such a candle, by God's grace, in England, as I trust shall never be put out".

Wyggeston (1467-1536), also known as William of Wigston, became so wealthy, that in 1522 he paid 22 per cent of all tax levied on Leicester. Other accounts state that in 1523-24, Wyggeston personally paid £600 of a special tax raised by Henry VIII – over a quarter of the tax – while another survey of 1524 showed that he owned over 20 per cent of Leicester's taxable property.

During his lifetime, Wyggeston was four times Mayor of the Staple of Calais, Mayor of Leicester in 1499 and 1510, and MP for Leicester in 1504. However, he also devoted much of his wealth to charitable works, including the founding of Wyggeston's Hospital in Leicester in 1513, which was initially sited close to St Martin's church, but later moved to Hinckley Road in

MEDIEVAL BRIDGES

This packhorse bridge over the Rothley Brook at Anstey is thought to date from around 1500, and was part of a medieval track from Leicester through Charnwood Forest.

Most of this packhorse bridge over the Medbourne Brook at Medbourne, bar the wooden handrails and brick paving, is thought to date from the 13th century.

1869. The initial hospital housed 12 poor men and 12 poor women who were to be *"blind, lame, decrepit, paralytic or maimed of their limbs, or idiots wanting their natural senses, so that they may be peaceable, not disturbing the hospital"*, as well as being *"unmarried and without friends or relations to support them"*. Wyggeston also founded a chantry chapel in 1512, which was connected with the Collegiate Church in the Newarke. The college was dissolved in 1547, but the chantry house has survived to this day and has been incorporated as part of the Newarke Houses Museum. After his death, William Wyggeston's brother, Thomas, used part of the endowment from his brother's estate to establish a grammar school in Leicester in 1577 and, although this school eventually became defunct, it lent its name to the later Wyggeston Grammar School for Boys, founded in 1877 on the site of the original Wyggeston Hospital. Wyggeston Girls School was also established in 1878, initially in Humberstone Gate before moving to Regent Road in Leicester.

Finally for this chapter, we come to one of Leicestershire's most famous historic events: the Battle of Bosworth Field, 1485, and the events that led up to it during the Wars of the Roses which were fought between 1455 and 1487. But before we cover Leicestershire's role in the Wars of the Roses, we'll start with the year 1470 – for this was the year that saw Rutland's most important contribution to the conflict when it provided the location for a pivotal battle between the Yorkists and the Lancastrians, the site being roughly half way between Empingham and Pickworth. The battle was triggered when the Lancastrians persuaded Sir Robert Welles of Lincolnshire to rally to their cause and rebel against Edward IV. However, the King's response was to take Welles's father hostage, and then ordering Welles Junior to disperse his men. Welles Junior refused, so Edward killed Welles Senior in full view of the rebel army, and then ordered his men to attack. The rebels were soon overwhelmed, and as many of them fled, they discarded their distinguishing livery to escape capture. This act thus provided the Battle of Empingham with its alternative name, the Battle of Losecoat Field. The battle site, which is alongside the Great North Road, is also still known as Bloody Oaks – a name that adds weight to the theory that the Battle of Losecoat Field led to the depopulation of nearby Pickworth; certainly in the 13th century it was quite a substantial village, but by the end of the 15th century it was almost non-existent. The only surviving remnant of the church today is one arch on private land, hinting that the Yorkists destroyed the church and the remaining villagers didn't have the heart or the resource to restore it.

As for the Battle of Bosworth Field, this was the last significant battle of the Wars of the Roses, and certainly the *most* significant. Richard III had ascended the throne in 1483 when his nephew, the 12 year-old Edward V, and for whom he was acting as Lord Protector, was declared illegitimate and therefore ineligible for the throne. Edward and his younger brother, Richard – the famous Princes in the Tower – then disappeared in mysterious circumstances, and to this day, it is strongly rumoured that Richard had something to do with their disappearance and probably their murder. Hearing such rumours across the English Channel in Brittany was Henry Tudor, a Lancastrian, who decided that the time was right to stake his claim for the throne.

On the 7th August 1485, therefore, Henry landed unopposed on the south-west coast of Wales and began his long and convoluted march towards London, gathering support as he went. News of Henry's landing reached Richard on 11th August, but it took three or four days for his messengers to notify his lords of their mobilisation. Richard's two main commanders were

A sculpture at Bosworth Battlefield Heritage Centre and which is encircled by chairs and posts depicting all of the major players at the Battle of Bosworth Field in 1485.

King Richard's Well is also located close to the Heritage Centre. It is thought that Richard III took his last drink from this well, shortly before meeting his end in the battle.

Left: *The flags of the Lancastrians (nearside) and the Yorkists (farside) at Bosworth Battlefield Heritage Centre.*

the Duke of Norfolk and the Earl of Northumberland. Norfolk set off for Leicester on the 16th August, as did Northumberland, although his northern army had much further to travel; a further 80 men were also sent from York to join the King. Richard himself reached Leicester on 20th August, and was joined by Norfolk; Northumberland arrived the following day.

In the meantime, Henry had not marched directly on London as expected. Instead, he had headed north-eastwards for Shrewsbury where he acquired the services of Gilbert Talbot and other allies, including deserters from Richard's forces. Despite the swelling of his ranks, though, Henry's army was still no match for Richard's in terms of numbers, perhaps totalling around 5000 to Richard's 8000. He thus slowed his pace through Staffordshire in order to acquire more troops, including those belonging to the Stanleys, and who had mobilised their forces on hearing of Henry's landing. From here, Henry's forces marched eastwards towards Leicestershire. On the 21st August, the Stanleys made camp on the slopes of a hill north of Dadlington, while on the same day, the royal army struck out westwards from Leicester to intercept Henry's forces. Having passed Sutton Cheney, Richard then moved his army towards Ambion Hill, thinking it would offer a tactical advantage, and it was here that he made camp on the night of 21st August.

On the day of the battle, Thomas, Lord Stanley, and Sir William Stanley also brought their forces to the battlefield, but initially held back from entering the fray. Meanwhile, Richard had divided his larger army into three groups led by himself, Norfolk and Northumberland, while Henry kept most of his force together and placed it under the command of the experienced Earl of Oxford. Richard's vanguard, commanded by Norfolk, attacked but made little impact against Oxford's men, Norfolk himself was killed, and some of Norfolk's troops actually fled the field. Northumberland took no action when signalled to assist his King, so Richard gambled everything on a charge across the battlefield to kill Henry and end the fight. Seeing the King's knights separated from his army, the Stanleys then finally intervened, and Sir William led his men to Henry's aid. It is said that Richard fought bravely and ably during this phase of the battle and actually came within a sword's length of Henry Tudor, before he was surrounded by Stanleys men and killed – thus becoming the last English king to be killed in battle. It is thought that the killer blow came from a Welsh soldier wielding a halberd while Richard's horse was stuck in marshy ground, and that the blow was so hard that the King's helmet was driven into his skull, while a contemporary account also talks of a Welshman having "killed the boar and shaved his head".

After the battle, Henry was crowned King below an oak tree in nearby Stoke Golding, and thus began the Tudor dynasty in England, while the death of Richard marked the end of the Plantagenet dynasty; that day

Quirk Alert: *Dark Dealings*
In 1478, Anne Mowbray of Cold Overton Hall was married at Westminster to Richard, Duke of York – the younger son of Edward IV. Of course, poor Richard went on to become one of the two tragic Princes in the Tower, who mysteriously disappeared in 1483, while Anne had died tragically young two years earlier. On Anne's death, an Act of Parliament conveniently passed the Mowbray estates to Richard, Duke of York and, on his disappearance, the estates even more conveniently passed to his scheming uncle – along with the somewhat more significant crown of England! As for the 1478 wedding of Richard and Anne, it is remarkable simply because he was four years of age and she was five!

on 22nd August in Leicestershire was a hugely defining moment in English and Welsh history. There has subsequently been some dispute as to the exact site of the battle, due to inconclusive evidence. Nevertheless, the Bosworth Battlefield Heritage Centre was built in 1974 around 2 miles to the south-west of Market Bosworth, at Ambion Hill, although various other sites have since been suggested within the triangle of the Leicestershire villages of Shenton, Sutton Cheney and Dadlington.

As to what happened to the body of Richard III, that has also been subject to myth and rumour over the centuries. It was widely accepted that Richard's naked body was taken from the battlefield and transported to Leicester draped over a horse. It was then exposed for a while in Leicester before being buried at the church of a friary in the centre of the town known as Greyfriars. Myth then surfaces again during the Dissolution of the Monasteries, for it was rumoured that during the destruction of Greyfriars, Richard's body was cast into the River Soar. But then you have the early 17th century story that a memorial stone existed in a garden built on the site of Greyfriars. Of course, if you want to know the truth, then you'll need to flip forward to the end of this history section, and to the extraordinary revelations, proven by science, between 2012 and 2014!

Quirk Alert: *Seeriously*
A local legend suggests that Richard III had consulted a seer in Leicester before the Battle of Bosworth Field, who foretold that "where your spur should strike on the ride into battle, your head shall be broken on the return". On the ride into battle, his spur is said to have struck the bridge stone of Bow Bridge in Leicester (shown as it is today, right). The legend goes on to state that as his corpse was carried from the battle, draped over the back of a horse, his head struck the same stone and was broken open!

Throughout the period from the Norman Conquest to the Dissolution of the Monasteries, Leicestershire and Rutland's populations moved in step with most other counties. The first two significant population markers are the Domesday Book of 1086 and the Poll Tax Returns of 1377. For Leicestershire, it is reasonable to derive a population of between 25,000-30,000 from Domesday Book, and the Poll Tax Returns records 31,730 people who fall into the category of "adults over the age of fourteen upon whom a tax of fourpence per head was levied". Given that figure and criteria, J.C. Russell in his *British Medieval Population* estimates that

Kirby Muxloe Castle, built for William Lord Hastings in the 1480s. This was the same Lord Hastings that had raised the Ashby-de-la-Zouch fortified manor house to the status of a castle a little earlier, and who was also Edward IV's Lord Chamberlain. Unsurprisingly, Hastings opposed Richard III's seizure of the throne in 1483. Alas, this resulted in his execution and the immediate cessation of castle build. The Hastings family did occupy the completed buildings, but even these were abandoned in the 16th century and the castle gradually became ruinous.

The Anne of Cleves public house in Melton Mowbray is one of Leicestershire's most historic buildings. It was originally built for chantry priests of the Cluniac order who served the parish church, St Mary's, from the 12th to the 16th century. Following the Dissolution of the Monasteries, the house was then owned by Henry VIII's Lord Chancellor, Thomas Cromwell, from 1538 until his execution in 1540. It was then included in 1540 by Henry VIII as part of the settlement to Anne of Cleves.

the total population of Leicestershire in 1377 would have been 47,595. However, given the four major outbreaks of plague in the Midlands between 1348 (when it first visited these shores to devastating effect) and 1377, it is likely that the population had doubled between 1086 and 1348 to around 60,000. For many, Russell's estimate of 47,595 may be over-pitching somewhat, and therefore under-selling the effect of the plague, which many deem to have claimed at least a third of the population, and maybe even half. Certainly, its effect on England was acute. For example, after the middle of the 14th century there is no evidence of the founding of new villages and hamlets, and indeed, conversely, the plague was largely responsible for the disappearance of 65 medieval villages in Leicestershire alone. In other words, the mid-to-late medieval period saw 15 per cent of Leicestershire's rural communities disappear – although a number of these communities also fell victim to the growth of the wool trade as arable fields were converted to pasture, and indeed, those rural communities that were part of the wool-flourishing estates of priories and abbeys were particularly prone to desertion. As for the effect of the plague on Rutland, the outbreak of 1348-49 alone claimed one quarter of Rutland's clergy. In terms of population impact upon Leicester, the town's population grew steadily from a 1086 Domesday Book-suggested total of around 2000, to a 1377 Poll Tax Return-suggested total of around 3000 (derived from 2000 taxpayers). It is not thought that the population grew by much between then and the 1530s; indeed, at the accession of James I in 1603, Leicester still only totalled around 3000 inhabitants. It is thought that the regular outbreaks of plague throughout the preceding three centuries meant that the number of births and the number of deaths tended to cancel each other out. However, the 17th century saw the population begin to increase again, rising to around 5000 inhabitants by 1670.

From the Elizabethan Era to the Onset of Industrial Change

One of the most lasting legacies of the late 16th to the 18th centuries in Leicestershire and Rutland, is the number of stately homes that were built, usually by a resident member of the aristocracy. Probably the most splendid of these homes, and certainly the largest, is Belvoir Castle, initially built in the 11th century by Robert de Todeni. That building no longer stands, and neither does its successor, built by Earl Manners in 1528, as it was largely destroyed during the English Civil War. Even the next mansion, built by the eighth earl between 1654 and 1668 no longer exists, because it was replaced by the current building in the 19th century, and which was erected by the fifth *Duke* of Rutland (see *Quirky Leicestershire and Rutland [Belvoir]* for more).

The second largest house in the two counties is Staunton Harold Hall, which was designed and built by the 5th Earl Ferrers between 1760 and 1778, replacing an earlier 17th century building that had been built for the 1st Earl Ferrers. Built in grand Georgian style in limestone and red brick, the building forms a square enclosing a quadrangle. The grounds also contain the now Grade I listed Holy Trinity church, built in 1653 by Sir Robert Shirley, and a rarity in that it is a church built during the Commonwealth period. The hall, however, started to slip out of the grasp of the Shirleys during the 10th Earl Ferrers' tenure who having inherited it in 1859, proceeded to sell off most of the land. The 12th Earl Ferrers (1894-1954) then gifted Holy Trinity church to the National Trust and put the estate up for auction. In 1955 it was acquired by Leonard Cheshire for use as a Cheshire Home (for the disabled), but was then sold again in 1980 to be used as a Sue Ryder care home. The house moved back into private hands again in 2003.

Bradgate House was built a little earlier in the early 16th century by Thomas Grey, who was the grandson of Sir John Grey of Groby and Elizabeth Woodville (after Sir John's death, Elizabeth married King Edward IV). Bradgate House was therefore one of the earliest *unfortified* mansions to be built in England and one of the first houses of its scale to be built in brick. The two-storey house was around 200 feet in length, with two wings joined by a Great Hall and parlour. It was also in the 16th century that Bradgate House was home to one of the most famous Leicesterians of all time. Lady Jane Grey was born at Bradgate Park in 1537 to Henry VIII's sister and, of course, she was fated to reign as uncrowned Queen Regent of England for just nine days. Thus it was that although only third in line to the throne on the death of Edward VI in 1553, Lady Jane Grey became the victim of both family and religious power struggles. Favoured by Edward VI in his will, thanks to her Protestant background, it was Jane's father, the Duke of Suffolk who proclaimed her as Queen in July 1553. It was a move for which Jane was to ultimately pay with her head, after Mary I recruited sufficient support to ride into London and claim the throne as her own. Lady Jane Grey was charged with high treason and may have survived were it not for a later Protestant rebellion in January 1554, after which she was executed, aged only seventeen. As for Bradgate House, it was unoccupied by 1719, and by 1790 it was in ruins. Today plenty of the ruins remain, including Lady Jane Grey's Tower, but the only building that remains intact is the chapel – and which contains a fine alabaster memorial to Sir Henry Grey, cousin of Lady Jane.

Continuing with the great houses of this period, Stapleford Park is another Leicestershire Grade I listed country house, and is located a few miles east of Melton Mowbray. Today's version was built in the 1620s by Sir William Sherard, along with the park, while his son, Benet Sherard, greatly enlarged the house around 1670. Stapleford Park was the seat of the Sherard family for 484 years, and who were later created the Earls of Harborough. However, the house was bought in 1894 by John Gretton – later created Baron Gretton in 1944 – a successful brewer who owned Bass, Ratcliffe and

Gretton, and who was also Conservative MP at various times for Derbyshire South, Rutland and Burton. However, the house was sold in 1988 to American fast-food merchant Bob Payton, who converted the property into a hotel. The grounds of Stapleford Park also contain a church, St Mary Magdalene, built in 1783 by George Richardson for the 4th Earl of Harborough.

Sticking with stately homes, Rutland is best represented by the spectacular and palatial Burley House (see *Quirky Leicestershire and Rutland [Burley]* for more).

Stapleford Park, built in the early 17th century by Sir William Sherard.

The ruins of Bradgate House, completed in around 1520 by Thomas Grey.

Bosworth Hall at Market Bosworth, home to the colourful Dixie family from its initial build in the late 17th century until 1885 when it had to be sold due to the gambling of Sir Alexander Beaumont Churchill Dixie, 11th Baronet of Bosworth.

It is also represented by Hambleton Old Hall, which was built in the early 17th century (the new hall, Hambleton Hall, was built in 1881), as well as by the other 17th century builds of Lyndon Hall and South Luffenham Hall. Hambleton Old Hall was built by Christopher Loveday in the early 17th century, but by 1611, he had sold it to Roger Quarles of Lincolnshire. Quarles died in 1616 and so the house passed onto his two nephews who sold the property to Abel Barker in 1634, with Abel Barker Junior taking over three years later after his father's death. This Abel Barker owned the property for more than forty years, during which time he was elected Sheriff of the county (in 1646), and was created a baronet by Charles II. Abel and his brother Thomas then purchased nearby Lyndon Hall in 1662 for £9300, and both properties remained in the Barker family until 1845. More recently, Hambleton Old Hall just about survived the creation of Rutland Water, as it sits at the end of the extensive promontory that thrusts out from the west bank, looking across the water to the less fortunate St Matthew's church at Normanton. As for Lyndon Hall, that has been owned by the Conant family since the 19th century.

> ## Quirk Alert: *Rough Justice*
> *In 1616, nine women were executed as witches in Husbands Bosworth, following a young boy's development of epileptic fits. Of course, the boy's seizures continued after the executions and so another six women of the village were condemned to death. Thankfully, common sense prevailed, and the six women earned a reprieve.*

Another member of the Leicestershire gentry who was created a baronet by Charles II was Sir Wolstan Dixie (1602-1682), this thanks to his loyalty to Charles I during the English Civil War. It was his eldest son, Sir Beaumont Dixie, 2nd Baronet of Bosworth, who built Market Bosworth Hall in the late 17th century, and on parkland acquired in 1589 by an earlier Sir Wolstan Dixie (1524-1594), a former Lord Mayor of London. The

> ## Quirk Alert: *Quaker Notes*
> *George Fox (1624-1691) is one of Leicestershire's most famous sons, since he was one of the earliest English Dissenters, and the founder of the Religious Society of Friends. The latter organisation was also more commonly known as the Quakers – so-named following a tirade by Fox against Derby magistrate Justice Bennett, whom he claimed should "tremble at the word of the Lord".*

hall stayed in the Dixie family for another 200 years, until both house and estate had to be sold in 1885 to pay off the gambling debts of Sir Alexander Beaumont Churchill Dixie, 11th Baronet (1851-1924). Described as "a spendthrift, a hopeless gambler and a heavy drinker", his family paid a heavy price for his failure to face up to his responsibilities.

As mentioned in the previous chapter, a large number of medieval villages were deserted courtesy of either aristocracy or religious institutions effectively ousting the villagers. One of those villages in the former category is Nevill Holt, initially built by Thomas Palmer in 1448, but much enhanced by the Nevill's towards the end of the 17th century. Other country houses actually profited from the Dissolution of the Monasteries, with hundreds of the aristocracy acquiring great religious houses and converting them into palatial country homes. One example was Grace Dieu Priory, where John Beaumont was the beneficiary in 1539, although by the end of the 17th century Sir Ambrose Phillips had demolished most of the original priory buildings (see *Quirky Leicestershire and Rutland [Belton]* for more). Then of course, there are those once magnificent stately homes that have been demolished, such as Gopsall and Garendon. The former was built by Charles Jennens (who had made his fortune in the iron industry), but was completely demolished in 1952, while the latter was converted from the dissolved Cistercian Abbey to a country house by Thomas Manners, 1st Earl of Rutland. This house also came into the possession of Sir Ambrose Phillips in 1684, and he redesigned, extended

On the left is a standard medieval pair of four-holed stocks on the green of Market Overton, but why there are five holes in the stocks underneath the Butter Cross at Oakham (right) is not known!

and rebuilt parts of Garendon House in the Palladian style, such that it became known as Garendon Hall. By the 19th century, Phillips' successor, Ambrose Charles Lisle March Phillips De Lisle (seriously) adapted the hall, adding elements of Gothic to the existing Palladian. However, following his death, the family moved out of Garendon Hall to Grace Dieu Manor, but returned in 1907...only to be forced out again during World War II, when it was used, and badly damaged, by the army. The house never recovered and was demolished in 1964.

Rutland is also represented in the "ruinous house" category by Old Hall in Exton Park, which was built by the Noels (Viscounts Campden and Earls of Gainsborough), but which sadly was burnt down in 1810. The ruin still stands today, indicating at its former glory with grand gables and beautiful Elizabethan chimneys. Rutland is further represented by Martinsthorpe where the Earl of Denbigh built a house in the 17th century, but which was demolished in 1775 by the Duke of Devonshire after his family had acquired it in the 1750s, and by Normanton Hall which was built by Sir John Heathcote between 1735 and 1740 to the design of Henry Joynes, but which was also demolished in the 1920s.

Two of Rutland's most famous sons originated from Oakham in the 17th century, and also ended up indirectly crossing paths, too. Jeffrey Hudson (1619 – c.1682) was an English dwarf at the court of Queen Henrietta Maria. He was famous as the "Queen's dwarf" and "Lord Minimus", and was considered one of the "wonders of the age" because of his extreme but well-proportioned smallness, with most reports stating that he was 18 or 19 inches tall. His life was utterly extraordinary and is covered in detail in the *Quirky Leicestershire and Rutland [Burley]* section of this book. Towards the end of his life, though, he found himself seriously inconvenienced by anti-Catholic activity, and that's where the second Rutlander comes in. For Titus Oates (1649-1705) was an Anglican priest born in Oakham, and ultimately a perjurer who fabricated what became known as the "Popish Plot" along with his friend, Israel Tonge, which was a supposed Catholic conspiracy to kill King Charles II. With the help of the Earl of Danby their list of alleged conspirators grew to 81, and Oates was given a squad of soldiers; a squad which he used for rounding up Jesuits, including those who had helped him in the past during a time when he had pretended to become a Catholic to "learn about the secrets of the Jesuits". But after nearly three years and the executions of at least 15 men who are now thought to have been innocent, opinion began to turn against Oates. When told to leave his apartments in Whitehall, he responded by denouncing the King and so was arrested for sedition, sentenced to a fine of £100,000 and thrown into prison. Later, James II had Oates retried and sentenced for perjury to annual pillory, loss of clerical dress, and imprisonment for life. Oates was thus annually taken out of his cell and put into the pillory at

Bede House at Lyddington was originally the wing of a medieval palace belonging to the Bishops of Lincoln. However, in 1600, Thomas Cecil converted it into an almshouse for "12 bedesmen over 30 years old and two women (over 45), all free of lunacy, leprosy or the French pox".

the gate of Westminster Hall where passers-by pelted him with eggs. The next day he was pilloried in London and a third day was stripped, tied to a cart, and whipped from Aldgate to Newgate. He was eventually released in 1688 following the accession of William of Orange and Mary.

As it had during the Wars of the Roses, Leicestershire was to play a significant role in the English Civil War of the mid-17th century. At the beginning of the war, in 1642, Leicester, along with most of the southern half of Leicestershire had declared for Parliament, and was held by John Grey of Groby. However, the northern half of the county was held for the King by Henry Hastings of Ashby-de-la-Zouch Castle. As happened elsewhere around England, and particularly in the Midlands, the ordinary folk of Leicestershire and Rutland villages were treated badly by both Parliamentarian and Royalist, who tended to commandeer houses and resources wherever they went. In terms of garrisons, though, there were five in Leicestershire and one in Rutland, the latter being at Burley House (see *Quirky Leicestershire and Rutland [Burley]* for more). Of the Leicestershire garrisons, Ashby Castle was held by Henry Hastings for three whole years, and therefore when Royalist defeat became inevitable in 1645, he was actually allowed to surrender honourably and marched out with full military honours.

The most significant garrison, at Leicester, remained staunchly Parliamentarian throughout the conflict, but in 1645, the town was about to endure two sieges and much barbarity. By May 1645, the war was going badly for the Royalists, and Charles resolved to regain control of the north. The King and Prince Rupert therefore headed north from Oxford with a huge army on 7th May 1645. However, they were soon greeted by the news that Oxford was besieged by the Parliamentarian's New Model Army, led by Sir Thomas Fairfax. This forced Charles into abandoning the march north, and instead, they decided to attack the Parliamentary stronghold of Leicester in the hope of luring Fairfax and his army away from Oxford. They also chose Leicester because they had information from Lord Loughborough, a staunch Royalist, that Leicester's defences were weak. Furthermore, taking Leicester would strengthen links to the Royalist towns of Newark and Ashby, thus creating a strong Royalist axis in what was largely a Parliamentarian region.

Moving the plan into action, Charles summoned his armies that were fighting in the West Country and in South Wales, along with Lord Loughborough's 1200 cavalry from Newark, for a rendezvous on 27th May at Ashby-de-la-Zouch. With 10,000 men under his command, the King then marched on Leicester the following day – a town that had by now lost its medieval walls and was only protected by earthen banks, ditches and timber fences around its three-mile perimeter. Leicester Castle fared slightly better, as its medieval walls had survived and had even been re-fortified, and the Newarke was also still enclosed by a medieval wall and gates. However, the Parliament-arians were also extremely low on artillery.

Knowing they were in grave danger, the Committee of the town appealed to the adjacent counties for support, as well as to the New Model Army, but the only response came from the Scottish Army who sent several hundred cavalry to Leicester. That left Leicester looking to its own for recruitment, and around 900 townsfolk and 150 from the county were enlisted to assist the 480-strong Leicester garrison plus Major Innes and his 200 horse from the Newport Pagnell garrison, who had arrived in Leicester just before the Royalists. In summary, it was around 2000 defenders vs. the 10,000-strong army of the King.

The Royalists arrived on 30th May and pitched their tents to the south of Leicester, with Charles making his headquarters at Aylestone vicarage. Despite bombard-ment from the town's defenders, the Royalists set up their battery on the remains of the Roman aqueduct known as Raw Dykes (see *Quirky Leicestershire [Aylestone]* for more). Under a flag of truce, Prince Rupert then met the Town Committee at the Mayor's Parlour of the Guildhall, where he requested their surrender. However, an agreement was not reached, and thus at 3 o'clock on May 30th, the Siege of Leicester commenced. By six o'clock that evening, the Newarke wall had suffered a significant breach, and by midnight, the town was attacked in seven different places at once, with the main bulk of the Royalist army storming the Newarke breach to the south of the town, and the remaining soldiers using scaling ladders to attack from the north and east. Many of the main attacking bulk to the south were cut down by the town's best cannon, but eventually, sheer numbers told and Sir Thomas Appleyard became the first Royalist to enter the town from the south, while Royalists to the north and east also successfully scaled the defences and gained entry into Leicester. Once inside, they tore down the town gates and began filling in the defensive ditches, thus

opening up the town to Prince Rupert's cavalry. Still the brave townsfolk refused to surrender, and fought hand-to-hand, street by street, until eventually, they were forced back into the market square. Here, faced with certain death from a charge of mounted cavalry, they finally laid down their weapons.

Alas, surrender didn't save them, with the Royalists taking brutal exception to isolated skirmishes, post-surrender. Perhaps using this as a weak excuse, they proceeded to use excessive violence against the towns-folk of Leicester, killing without distinction and inflict-ing barbarous acts of rape, murder and robbery, as well as indulging in mindless destruction. Some of the Town Committee were also hanged while others were simply cut to pieces. Small surprise, therefore, that when Charles I was put on trial, Leicester was highlighted as an example of his cruelty. Interestingly, Charles also saw the sacking of Leicester as a turning point for himself. In a letter to his wife, he writes: "I may without being too sanguine, affirm, that since this rebellion, my affairs were never in so hopeful a way."

The ruins of Cavendish House, once a splendid house built by the Earl of Huntingdon from the remains of Leicester Abbey, but destroyed on the whim of the King.

Having said that, Charles had initially got his own way, for not only had he secured his strategic axis of Newark, Leicester and Ashby, thus delivering a hammer-blow to the Parliamentarians, his actions also lured Sir Thomas Fairfax from Oxford who proceeded to march on Leicester. Meanwhile, the triumphant Royalists looted every house and shop in Leicester, and drank the inns dry in celebration amid a scene of utter carnage and devastation. As for King Charles, he briefly stayed at Cavendish House alongside the ruins of Leicester Abbey, but had little intention of staying and attempting to defend a town in such a ruinous state, so on 4th June, he left Leicester, leaving Lord Loughborough and a 1200 garrison the unenviable task of re-fortifying and defending! However, adding insult to injury, he sent a demand to Leicester's mayor for a further £2000 before his departure, and also gave the order to burn down Cavendish House, lest it be used in any future siege! So Prince Rupert led the Royalist army over the border and to a resounding defeat at the Battle of Naseby on 14th June, 1645. On realisation of their imminent defeat, the Royalists fled back towards Leicester, although many Royalist coaches and wagons overturned in the mud, prompting men to scrabble in the dirt to retrieve their loot of a few days before. Alas, a lot of the stragglers were caught by the Parliamentary troops, and they weren't about to take the moral high ground and treat the soldiers and their wives in a better way than the Royalists did in Leicester. Around a hundred of the wives were murdered in cold-blood, and many more were marked as "whores" by having their noses slit to the bone and their faces cut. A further 400 soldiers were caught up between Market Harborough and Leicester, and were killed, too, while 5000 infantry were captured and taken prisoner in Market Harborough, this adding to the 9000 weapons captured along with all of Charles' artillery.

Meanwhile, King Charles and Prince Rupert fled to Ashby-de-la-Zouch, where they set up quarters and slept for the night before heading off westwards the following day. As for the Parliamentarians, they stayed overnight at Great Glen on the 15th June, before surrounding Leicester the following day. They first offered up an opportunity to surrender, but the new Royalist garrison refused, and thus commenced the second Siege of Leicester inside a month. Somewhat ironically, the Parliamentarians also set up their battery on Raw Dykes, as the Royalists had done a couple of weeks earlier, and similarly commenced a battering of the south wall of the Newarke. Inevitably, a breach soon appeared, but this time, the defenders under Lord Loughborough surrendered. Unlike eighteen days earlier, the defenders – the Royalists – were guaranteed safe passage to Lichfield and Ashby, and were even allowed to take their horses and private arms with them. Leicester – scene of the bloodiest battle of the English Civil War – was back in the hands of the Parliamentarians.

In the aftermath, £1500 was granted to the town for repairs, with the money taken from the estates confiscated from Royalists. The money was spent on the demolition of the bulwarks, and on repairing the streets. However, that didn't help the homeless, with around 120 homes alone having been torn down by the Royalists as part of their last desperate defence. If Leicester had been poor before the siege – and it had been – it was now quite destitute and remained economically weak for decades after. In the end, the

town had suffered terribly for supporting the Parliamentary cause. Rutland, thankfully, enjoyed a quieter Civil War than its western neighbour, although the original hall at North Luffenham was the scene of a siege where 200 Royalists bravely held out against 1300 Parliamentarians – until the cannons were brought in, at which point the house was largely destroyed and its surviving occupants captured.

Leaving the English Civil War behind, we will cover one more partially destructive element of 17th and 18th

> **Quirk Alert:**
> *There but for the Grace of God ...*
> It would appear that the Siege of Leicester, in 1645, was responsible for the conversion of John Bunyan. Prior to the Civil War, he had not been noted for his piety. However, one night, while performing the duty of sentinel on top of the town walls, he handed over the duty to a friend of his, only for the friend to be shot dead by a Royalist sniper a few minutes later.

> **Quirk Alert:** *The Price of Loyalty*
> John Cave was the rector of Pickworth during the English Civil War. He was also a staunch Royalist in largely Parliamentarian territory, and his loyalty led to him being shot at whilst preaching in his pulpit! However, as happened elsewhere, Royalist family loyalty was rewarded when Charles II was restored to the throne in 1660, and John Cave's son was awarded the office of chaplain to the King.

> **Quirk Alert:** *Mortality and Adversity*
> A 17th century monument to William Jervis and his wife in All Saints' church, Peatling Magna, is accompanied by the following striking lines: "As you are so were we; as we are so will you be". Meanwhile, the only church in Leicestershire built during the Commonwealth period, was Holy Trinity at Staunton Harold. Built in 1653 by Sir Robert Shirley, an inscription over its doorway includes the words: "the best of things in the worst of times".

Old John Tower sits at the highest point of Bradgate Park (690ft). It was built in 1784 by the Earl of Stamford, and was used by his guests for the view, and to watch horse racing and fox hunting. It was allegedly named after an old retainer who was accidentally killed by a fire in 1786. Apparently, Old John also liked a drink – which is why the arch was added to resemble a giant tankard!

Quirk Alert: *Wrestling Dixie*

Sir Wolstan Dixie (1700-1767), 4th Baronet of Bosworth, was a colourful character with a reputation of being "a pugnacious bully with a penchant for using his fists" (Young Samuel Johnson, J.L. Clifford, 1955). He had employed the great Samuel Johnson as an usher at the local school, during Johnson's four months at Bosworth Hall in 1732, a period that Johnson always recollected with "the strongest aversion and even a degree of horror" (Samuel Johnson, Walter Jackson Bate, 1975). Anyway, as Dixie was also "legendary for his ignorance" (Samuel Johnson, A Life, David Nokes, 2009), this accounts for a rather amusing, yet seemingly typical tale about the man. For according to J.L. Clifford in Young Samuel Johnson, *the story takes place after Dixie had been involved in one of his many fights, this one with a neighbouring squire who objected to Dixie barring access to a footpath across his land. Shortly afterwards, Dixie was presented to King George II who, obviously keen to impart his local historical knowledge stated: "Bosworth, Bosworth! Big battle at Bosworth, wasn't it?" To which the self-important Dixie was said to have replied: "Yes, Sire. But I thrashed him!"*

century life, before moving onto more positive developments. For in the former category is the issue of land enclosure, and although the first official Enclosure Act in Leicestershire was passed in 1730 (for the parish of Horninghold), most of the open fields in that parish had already vanished in the first quarter of the 17th century, while it is estimated that 25 per cent of the whole *county* was enclosed before 1640, thus threatening village peasantry with ruin. But it was the 18th century where ownership of land became official, with twelve Acts passed in Leicestershire during the 1750s and 11 further Acts passed in 1760 alone; a further 41 were passed throughout the 1760s, and all this time, a move towards pasture was at the expense of arable farming and the common fields. Daniel Defoe, famous commentator of the early 18th century says of Leicestershire that "the whole county seems to be taken up in country business, particularly in breeding and feeding cattle". He also adds that Leicestershire is "a vast magazine of wool for the rest of the nation … in some places the graziers are so rich, that they grow gentlemen!" And of course, it was throughout these years that the enclosed and patchwork landscape of the England of today was formed, at the same time that gentlemen farmers and a wealthy rural middle class were emerging. There was the odd act of opposition in terms of ripping up hedges and filling in ditches, while clergy posted public objections such as John Moore, minister of Knaptoft, who published a pamphlet called "The Crying Sin of England of not caring for the Poor", in which he talks of the peasantry being cast into poverty by the extinction of the common lands. Of course, as it happened, many of the rural poor were on the cusp of gravitation towards the towns, with the Industrial Revolution just around the corner. That said, the 18th century did see great improvements in agriculture, with Dishley's Robert Bakewell leading the way with his pioneering selective breeding of livestock. The visionary Bakewell had seen that the newly concentrated town populations required supplies of meat and milk greatly in excess of that which could be delivered by existing, under-nourished livestock. He therefore set up a farm, irrigated by a mile-long canal, thus enabling him to mow the grass four times a year, to carry food to his stock and also to collect his crops by boat. This

Quirk Alert: *Attention!*

At the west end of the nave of St Helen's church in Ashby-de-la-Zouch, there is an extremely rare, early 18th century finger pillory. It was used to punish misbehaviour in church, which included not paying attention during a sermon!

Quirk Alert: *Blind Faith*

Edward Stokes was minister at Blaby All Saints' church for 50 years during the 18th century. He also liked to hunt – which is all the more remarkable considering he was blind! However, he was accompanied on each hunt by a companion who would ring a bell on approaching each fence. One would assume that the Reverend Stokes chose his companions wisely!

Quirk Alert: *Clerk Tales*

All of the pre-1754 parish registers at St Helen's church in Plungar are missing, and local legend suggests that they vanished when the parish clerk, who was also the village grocer, used them to wrap up his lunch! One wonders if he went to the same school as the Rearsby clerk, who round about the same time unearthed the lead coffin of Andrew Sacheverell (d.1658) and sold it for 28 shillings so that he could buy himself a new coat!

enabled him to develop new breeds of powerful horse, cattle with less bone and more flesh, and sheep providing sizeable and tender joints; his cattle increased from 370 pounds to 800, calves from 50 pounds to 150, sheep from 28 pounds to 80 and lambs from 18 pounds to 50. He has quite rightly been recognised as the greatest worldwide agricultural pioneer of his day, turning England into the stud farm of the world.

Before we launch into the Industrial Revolution, though, there are two critical developments that need to be discussed; namely turnpike roads and canals. Turnpike trusts were bodies set up by Acts of Parliament with powers to collect tolls in order to maintain principal highways. The first turnpike road in Leicestershire was opened in 1726, this being the portion of "the principal road from London" that passed through the county from Market Harborough to Loughborough via Leicester, and which was part of an Act of Parliament designed to repair the road. This was, of course, the modern-day A6, and the turnpike trust was charged with making a gravel track 14ft wide. By the 1760s, the turnpike system applied to most roads out of Leicester while county-wide, many new bridges were built and existing ones were either repaired or replaced. For example, the Hinckley Turnpike Trust of 1754 built a number of bridges to replace fords south of Earl Shilton – and thus putting the ferrymen out of business! Meanwhile, the existing bridge at the southern entrance to Lutterworth was re-built with a stronger version in 1778 in order to cope with the increased stage coach traffic. Road improvement continued to, well, *improve* in the first quarter or more of the 19th century, before the railways came along and triggered a whole new travel revolution. By the 1870s, all of Leicestershire and Rutland's turnpike trusts had become defunct, perhaps giving the spirits of the 18th century ferrymen a private moment of satisfaction!

Of course, the other 18th century transportation breakthrough involved canals, with James Brindley constructing Britain's first major canal, the Bridgewater Canal, between 1759 and 1761. In Leicestershire, a move to make the River Soar navigable from Leicester down to its confluence with the Trent had first been attempted in 1634, when Thomas Skipwith had obtained a grant to do so. However, the project ran into financial difficulty and was abandoned after only five miles had been completed. Remarkably, it was another 144 years before the county's first profitable canal was constructed, this being a one and a half mile stretch constructed in 1778 to link the River Soar to Loughborough, and which made the town a significant "inland port".

What was already known as the Soar Navigation had been funded by the Derbyshire coal magnates and Loughborough businessmen, the very same people who had funded the Erewash Canal coming down to the Trent from the north, and which therefore mirrored the Soar Navigation coming up to the Trent from the south. As a result of this small waterway, Loughborough's fortunes in the 1780s were transformed; a barge-building industry began in the town and new houses and warehouses appeared alongside the town's wharves.

Another two years on, and moves were afoot to improve the Soar Navigation down to Leicester, although it wasn't until 1791 that the Bill for Leicester Navigation was passed – the delay being due to a number of owners of estates and mills who were concerned that the improved waterway would impact their existing monopoly on the thoroughfare, while the coal magnates of north-west Leicestershire were positively aggressive in their opposition, primarily because their significant road traffic income was now under threat. In the same year (1791), Melton Mowbray was also opened up to river traffic by the Wreake and Eye Navigation and which would later open up Rutland, too, via the Oakham Canal. Three years later in 1794, the Charnwood Forest Canal linked north-west Leicestershire to the Soar Navigation at Loughborough, with the coal-masters of Coleorton and the surrounding area by now having warmed to the idea of water transport. There was a slight caveat in that the canal actually terminated at Nanpantan due to what would have been an expensive requirement for locks to traverse the average 1 in 78 descent between the village and Loughborough, and so a horse-drawn wagonway engineered by William Jessop took care of the last couple of miles. This "warming" of the north-west Leicestershire coal-masters was taken even further when the Ashby Canal was opened in 1804. This 31-mile stretch of canal now linked the collieries of Moira with the Coventry Canal at Bedworth in Warwickshire, with a number of tramways constructed at the northern end to service multiple collieries; indeed, one of these tramways stretched for 8½ miles from the canal

The 21st century terminus of Leicestershire's first canal, the 1.5 mile waterway built in 1778 that linked the wharf at Loughborough with the River Soar.

Part of the Oakham Canal that was opened in 1802 and ran from Melton Mowbray to Oakham.

terminus to the limestone quarries at Ticknall in South Derbyshire (see *Quirky Leicestershire and Rutland [Moira]* for more on the Ashby Canal).

Returning to the Soar Navigation, it finally became navigable down to Leicester in 1794, and its completion immediately triggered growth to the north-east of the town. This led to Belgrave becoming Leicester's first built-up suburb of the Industrial Revolution. It was also at this time that attention began to switch to not just linking the southern half of Leicestershire to what was now being termed the Leicester Navigation, but to linking this relatively new Leicestershire water navigation system to the *national* network, ultimately linking the Thames with the Trent, and thus internally linking London, Liverpool and Hull. However, further landowner opposition combined with the onset of war with France to limit progress. So although by 1797 the system had been extended down to around 3 miles to the north-west of Market Harborough, it wasn't until 1809 that the extension to the town, known as the Debdale Wharf, was completed. The vision of linking London, Liverpool and Hull also had to be deferred until around this time, and eventually came to fruition following the founding of the Grand Union Canal Company in 1814 – although this linking of the Leicester Navigation and the Grand Junction Canal, which was then-termed the Grand Union Canal, is now known as the "Old Grand Union Canal" so as not to be confused with the later and more famous 20th century version! Also part of this south Leicestershire section of the Old Grand Union Canal is a tunnel of 1166 yards (1066m) just north of Husbands Bosworth, and around 6 miles to the north-east of that are the Grade II listed Foxton Locks, the largest flight of staircase locks on the English canal system and which take around an hour to traverse. Constructed between 1810 and 1814, these ten canal locks consist of two "staircase" sets of five canal locks each.

As mentioned earlier, Rutland also got in on the water transportation revolution when the Oakham Canal was constructed between Oakham and Melton Mowbray. The Act of Parliament for its construction was passed as early as 1793, but the canal didn't actually open until June 1802. The detailed design was carried out by Christopher Staveley Junior, who then became the chief engineer for the project. However, he resigned in 1797 following a critical report on his work, and was replaced by William Dunn of Sheffield who saw the project through to completion. The 15.5-mile watercourse included 19 locks, rose by 126 feet between Melton and Oakham, and included wharves at Saxby, Stapleford, Market Overton, Cottesmore and the Oakham terminus. Unfortunately, though, the canal was never a success, primarily because deeply rural Rutland didn't have the industrial muscle that neighbouring Leicestershire had, although agricultural produce did proceed down the line to Melton with coal going in the opposite direction. The canal was also beset by a lack of natural water supplies, which combined with a series of summer droughts to hinder its optimisation.

The Oakham Canal was closed in 1847, shortly after the railways effectively put it out of business. The Charnwood Forest Canal was officially abandoned a year earlier in 1846, although it had actually been out of use since 1808, having never really recovered from the disaster of 1799 when a rapid spring thaw caused the embankment of its feeder reservoir to burst and which

Quirk Alert:
Bamboozled by Gongoozlers
The Foxton Locks, being the largest set of staircase locks in England, are a magnet for gongoozlers – a term used to describe people who enjoy watching canal-based activity but tend to not actively participate – so in other words, they're the canal-based equivalent of trainspotters! The term may have derived from canal workers' slang when describing towpath observers, although another theory is that it derives from the Lincolnshire phrase to gawn and to gooze, both meaning to stare or gape. One would expect the phrase to have originated from the late 18th or early 19th century, but in actual fact, the word isn't formally recorded until the turn of the 20th century; it was later given wider use by Chester-born writer L. T. C. Rolt, who used it in his book Narrow Boat*, published in 1944. It would also appear that some hardcore gongoozlers actually heckle, harass and ultimately bamboozle struggling boat crews, whilst other more empathetic gongoozlers actually visit locations such as Foxton Locks armed with a lock windlass, so keen are they to help boat crews with their passage, by opening the paddles or helping push open the heavy balance beams on the gates – although surely participation means they are no longer official gongoozlers!*

Quirk Alert: *Share and Share Alike*
The Leicestershire and Rutland canals of the late 18th century and early 19th century had contrasting fortunes which were particularly highlighted by shareholder returns. Top of the tree was the 1.5-mile Loughborough Navigation, a fairly small project supplying a commercially hungry town, and which was constructed long before the rising costs of the Revolutionary Wars hit the country. As a result, by 1804 its shares were earning a 96 per cent dividend, and by 1824, the original £100 shares stood at £4,600. Alas, bottom of the pile was the Ashby Canal, commenced in 1794 at the onset of the Revolutionary Wars, opened in 1804 during the Napoleonic Wars, and which remained unable to pay a dividend until 1828, when its original £100 shares were worth a measly £10. Somewhat cruelly, the Leicester and Swannington Railway then opened four years later, scotching any chance of shareholders turning in a profit.

THE AMAZING FOXTON LOCKS

Foxton Locks are probably the most famous feature of the original Grand Union Canal. Built between 1810 and 1814, they form two flights of five locks and are the largest flight of staircase locks on the English canal system. They take around an hour to traverse.

Here we see a narrow boat approaching the top-most lock...

...here we now look back up the first flight of five locks as a narrow boat comes through into the central pool between the two flights...

...and now for lock number two...

...and finally, here we see the lower set of five locks.

put the canal out of action for two years. The Melton Mowbray Navigation lasted a little longer but was eventually closed in 1877, but the other more high-profile Leicestershire waterways managed to keep going alongside the railways until well into the 20th century.

The seeds of the Industrial Revolution in Leicestershire were planted at Hinckley in around 1640, when William Iliffe became the county's first hosiery manufacturer, utilising the stocking frames that had been invented by William Lee in 1589. Within another 100 years, the industry had spread to a reported 118 of the county's villages and towns, and by the first census of 1801, it was thought that around half of the county population's livings depended upon the hosiery industry – namely the manufacture of clothing such as stockings, socks, shirts, gloves and cravats. This extraordinary fact is represented by the growing number of stocking frames deployed in the county: around 50 in 1660, around 1000 by the mid-18th century, and an astonishing 11,000 during the latter part of the

The statue known as The Leicestershire Seamstress, outside the City Rooms on Hotel Street, Leicester. It was unveiled in 1990 to reflect the female contribution to the local hosiery industry in the 18th century.

Napoleonic Wars. Certainly, the period of the Revolutionary Wars in the 1790s and the Napoleonic Wars between 1803 and 1815, saw a huge demand for clothing and hence the booming hosiery industry. However, although the number of stocking frames would eventually grow to around 20,000 by the mid-19th century, the years immediately after Waterloo (1815) saw fortunes change dramatically. Demand for clothing fell away, and thousands of soldiers returned, thus flooding the market with surplus labour.

The inevitable laws of supply and demand saw wages tumble, with an 1845-sourced Parliamentary Commission on framework knitting recording that wages dropped from 14s per week to 7s between 1815 and 1819 – and that was for 15-hour working days, too! This situation led to more famous disturbances in neighbouring Derbyshire (the Pentrich Revolution) and Nottinghamshire (the Luddite riots) – although the Luddites

Quirk Alert: *The Tragic Chippy*

One night in 1782, after a bell ringing session at St Leonard's church in Thorpe Langton, one of the bell-ringers stayed behind, thinking it would be a nice little joke to leave the tenor bell delicately balanced upside-down, so that it would turn over in the middle of the night and wake up all of the villagers. Alas, it didn't turn over in the night, but did so the next day, killing the village carpenter outright!

were actually named after Ned Ludd of Anstey who broke two stocking frames in his own village as early as 1779, allegedly in "a fit of passion". This was also coincidentally the year that Edmund Cartwright became rector of Goadby Marwood, and it was here that he designed his first power loom and patented it in 1785. By 1790, 500 of Cartwright's power looms were due to be installed at Knott Mill in Manchester, but with only 30 in place, the factory was burned down, probably as an act of arson on behalf of hand loom weavers. Similarly, John Heathcoat had opened a lace-making factory in Loughborough several years later, but after a wave of Luddite-based machine smashing in 1816, he moved the entire business to calmer Tiverton in Devon. The framework knitting bubble had pretty much burst, though, and despite there being around 20,000 frames in Leicestershire by the 1840s, it is estimated that around a third of those were not in use. The final nail in the coffin came when the first steam-powered hosiery factory opened in Loughborough in 1839. Rural framework knitting managed to hang on until the 1860s, but by the 1870s even that had been wiped out by 74 steam-powered factories in Leicestershire alone.

The hosiery industry, however, had left an indelible mark on Leicestershire's population, with the county's increases throughout the 18th century seeing the greatest impact in areas where the industry had begun to flourish. In the pre-census years of the 18th century, the best source of information on population came from the parish registers in terms of births, deaths and marriages. Based on these registers, it is thought that Leicestershire's population was around 80,000 in 1700, and had grown to about 98,000 by 1750. Another fifty-one years further on, though, and the 1801 census reveals a county population of 130,000 – thus confirming the population acceleration in the second half of the

18th century. Another measure of population increase in the 18th century is supplied by returns made to the bishop of Lincoln in terms of units of family. This reveals that Loughborough had 530 families in 1705, but which had risen to around 1000 families by 1900. Similarly, Hinckley's number of families increased from 300 to around 1000 during the same period, but Melton Mowbray, over in the east of the county where the impact of the hosiery industry was not as strong, only increased from 300 to 358 families. Similarly, Market Harborough only increased from 420 families to 538, but clearly didn't compare to the twofold and threefold increases of Loughborough and Hinckley where the hosiery industry had become firmly entrenched. By contrast, Market Harborough's growth during the 18th century was probably down to its position half way between Leicester and Northampton; in fact by 1755, it actually sat at the centre of *four* turnpiked roads, and by the 1760s, its inns provided six daily coach services to London, as well as services in the opposite direction to Derby and Nottingham. The town's popularity was also marked in the second half of the 18th century by the granting of additional fairs; one in April to add to the medieval-granted October fair, two more added in 1772 for January and July, and three more by the end of the century. Today, much of Georgian Market Harborough survives, including the three-storey town hall that was built in red brick in 1788 by the Earl of Harborough. As for Lutterworth, much of the western side of the town

The interesting baroque monument in the foreground is in St James' churchyard at Burton Lazars, and was built in 1721 with money left by local weaver, William Squire. He had instructed that the remaining money be spent on the education of poor children. Alas, the sculpture required the full amount!

Quirk Alert: *Leicestershire Parsons: Unusual & Quirky*

During the late 18th century, Melton Mowbray had two eccentric parsons. The first, also known as Orator Henley, left his post to preach in London, where he famously made good on his promise to demonstrate a rapid way of making shoes; he simply cut off the tops of boots! Meanwhile, Dr Ford became vicar in 1773, and he was able to precisely measure the distance from Melton to Leicester by reciting Handel's Messiah *during the journey, such that he always completed the Alleluia Chorus as he passed the cross in Belgrave Gate. However, their quirkiness paled into insignificance when compared to that of William Staresmore, parson of Swinford, who locked up his servants every night, kept 58 dogs and tied a bulldog to each of his apple trees each night to prevent scrumping. Alas, one morning in 1747, the pack of dogs greeted him so boisterously that he fell into the village pond and drowned!*

GEORGIAN TOWN HALL'S

Market Harborough Town Hall, built in 1788 by the Earl of Harborough.

Lutterworth Town Hall, built in 1830.

> **Quirk Alert:** *As easy as ABC*
> *The youngest of 14 children, Robert Hall (1764-1831) of Arnesby became a prominent Baptist minister, having written hymns aged eight, and preached sermons aged eleven ... prior to which he had actually learned his alphabet by reading gravestones!*

RUTLAND'S GREAT PUBLIC SCHOOLS

retains its late Georgian identity, including the town hall which was built in 1830, while the buildings at the lower end of Market Street in Ashby-de-la-Zouch date from the same period, including Leicestershire's most successful spa, the Royal Hotel and the Ivanhoe Baths.

Returning to industry, though, and of course, the hosiery capital of Leicestershire was its county town, and Leicester itself saw its population rise from around 6000 in 1700 to 16,953 in 1801. Moreover, for the first time since pre-Roman times, the focus of the town core shifted from the western quarter and the area inside the wall that had defined Roman, Saxon and medieval Leicester, and out to the east. In 1711, Peacock Street was laid out alongside St Martin's church, with Friars Lane running adjacent and both roads joined by New Street. By 1785, Georgian Leicester also saw the development of New Walk, a tree-lined promenade laid out along the boundary of the South Field, although many of the buildings didn't follow until the early 19th century – which is also when further roads were added such as Bishop Street and Belvoir Street. At around the same time, a new middle-class suburb evolved around Kings Street, Regent Road and Princess Road, while the Belgrave area of Leicester – which was a separate village in those days – also became popular as a residential suburb.

The reason for Leicester's expansion was to cater for the influx of people who became employed in the hosiery industry. One of the first factories built for cotton-spinning appeared on Northgate Street in 1792, and over the following decades, the area of St Margaret's just south of the mill between Humberstone Gate and the wharves of the Soar Navigation developed into the industrial area of Leicester, expanding in tandem with many Victorian terraces to house the workers; indeed, between 1801 and 1901, the population of St Margaret's parish grew from around 6000 to 100,000, while in the previously-mentioned Belgrave area, hosiery soon overtook agriculture as the number one occupation of its inhabitants.

Part of today's Oakham School (left) and Uppingham School (right), both founded in 1584 by Archdeacon Robert Johnson. However, both remained small until the 19th century, with Uppingham in particular expanding rapidly under Edward Thring, headmaster from 1853 to 1887.

The original 16th-century school buildings at Oakham (left) and Uppingham (right). The latter is still used by the school today.

Quirk Alert: *Poets' Corner*

The title hardly does this snippet justice. Because throughout the incumbency of Sir George Howland Beaumont (1753-1827), Coleorton Hall was subject to regular and lengthy visits from William Wordsworth and Samuel Taylor Coleridge, as well as brief visits from Scott, Byron, Constable and Sir Humphrey Davy. Himself an accomplished painter, Beaumont hosted the entire Wordsworth family from autumn 1806 to autumn 1807 during which time the great poet wrote some of his finest work.

The 17th century had seen the foundation of a number of schools, such as the ones at Osgathorpe and Billesdon, the latter having been attended by both George Villiers (close advisor to both King James I and King Charles I), and George Fox, the Quaker. Also in this category, but founded slightly earlier in the 16th century, was the school at Market Bosworth, where Samuel Johnson taught in the 18th century. And it was also in the 18th century that education gradually became available to the masses – although it was certainly true that Leicester Grammar School catered for the children of the more prosperous. However, St Mary de Castro church supported a school from 1785 that was open to children from all backgrounds. Nevertheless, all of these important Leicestershire schools were eclipsed by two much more famous grammar schools in Rutland. Remarkably, both Oakham School and Uppingham School were founded in the same year, 1584, by Archdeacon Robert Johnson. Both were free grammar schools, funded by Johnson's income from four church positions that he held. A strong Puritan, Johnson stipulated that "the schoolmaster shall teach all those grammar scholars ... freely without pay, if their parents be poor and not able to pay, and keep them constantly to school". The reality was, though, that although the schooling was free, permanent attendance meant the loss to a family of an income, and this kept many of the poor from attending. At Oakham, the original school building was restored in the 18th century and remained the sole classroom for 300 years. Meanwhile, the original 1584 schoolroom in Uppingham churchyard is still owned by the school and is a Grade I listed building. As for the first recorded schoolboy at Uppingham, this was Henry Ferne from York, who went on to become chaplain to Charles I. However, in the 17th, 18th and early 19th centuries both Oakham and Uppingham remained small schools of 30 to 60 pupils, with just two teachers, although then (as now), those pupils regularly secured places at Oxford and Cambridge. However, during the second half of the 19th century, Uppingham numbers began to expand rapidly when Edward Thring became headmaster in 1853, and he transformed the school from a small, high-quality local grammar school into a large, well-known public school, with 330 pupils; Thring also remained headmaster until his death in 1887.

In the previous chapter, we briefly spoke of the evidence of medieval coal mining in north-west Leicestershire. Of course, this industry was destined to explode in the 19th century, but what of the three centuries in between? Certainly there is evidence of pits being worked during the reign of Elizabeth I, with a series of surviving manuscripts providing a fascinating insight, including two that detail operations during the last two months of 1572. Of these, the *Collpit Book* reveals how miners worked in groups of up to 20 and were paid at the end of the week, while the *Synkinge Book* describes details of the extension of the mine at Coleorton. A further manuscript from November 1577 is a statement of accounts and reveals that 7000 *rooks* had been extracted in the previous twelve months (although they're not certain, historians believe that a *rook* weighed between one and two tons). As for that mine at Coleorton, it was controlled by Sir Francis Willoughby who owned a number of mines across the Midlands and built the magnificent Wollaton Hall in Nottingham from his profits, with his Coleorton mine alone outputting around 10,000 tons of coal a year in the 1570s, with much of that destined for Leicester.

Moving forwards two centuries, and by 1779, John Prior's map of Leicestershire shows there to be 37 pits scattered across the Leicestershire coalfields. The 1760s had also seen the sinking of deeper pits, such as those

Quirk Alert: *"No Pie, No Parson!"*

One of Leicestershire's most ancient customs – hare pie and bottle kicking – takes place in the village of Hallaton each Easter Monday. Local folklore offers several origins for the custom, one stating that it dates back to pagan times when it was traditional to sacrifice hares to the goddess Ēostre. However, the favoured story is that of two ladies of Hallaton who were saved from a raging bull when it was distracted from its charge by a startled hare. They showed their gratitude to God for sending the hare by donating money to the church on the understanding that every Easter Monday, the vicar would provide a hare pie, twelve penny loaves, and two barrels of beer for the villagers – who would then fight each other for the food and drink! However, on one occasion, the residents of the neighbouring village of Medbourne joined the fray and stole the beer, thus beginning the village rivalry that continues to this day.

Today, the event starts with a parade through both villages, with locals carrying a large hare pie and the three "bottles", which are actually small kegs or barrels. Two of the bottles are filled with beer while the third, known as "the dummy", is made of solid wood and painted red and white. The pie is blessed by the Hallaton vicar before being cut apart and thrown to the crowd for "the scramble". The rest is placed in a sack to be carried up nearby Hare Pie Hill where the hare pie is spread on the ground ready for the later contest. Meanwhile, the bottles are taken to the Butter Cross on the village green to be dressed with ribbons, at which point the penny loaves are then handed out. The parade then proceeds to the bottle-kicking field where the main event begins – a best-of-three contest, where the aim of the game is to move the three bottles across two streams about a mile apart, by any means possible. The only rules are that there is no eye-gouging, no strangling, and no use of weapons! The contest starts when each bottle is tossed in the air three

times. The teams then literally fight each other to move the bottles over fields, ditches, hedges, and even barbed wire; injuries clearly ensue, and the emergency services are always on standby!

After the game, participants and spectators return to the village, where the star players are helped up onto the top of the 10-foot-tall Butter Cross, and the opened bottle is passed up for them to drink from before being passed around the crowd. These traditional games have certainly taken place every year since records began in the late 18th century, apart from 2001 due to the Foot and Mouth outbreak – although in 1790, the rector of Hallaton attempted to ban the contest due to its pagan origins – at which point, the words "No pie, no parson" were scrawled across the vicarage wall one night, and its incumbent subsequently relented!

The Butter Cross at Hallaton, which was once used for keeping butter and cheese cool, and today, remains an integral part of the annual traditional bottle-kicking contest.

on Swannington Common that deployed gin wheels with pulleys powered by horses, while a lawsuit of 1794 reveals that the Silver Hill pit at Swannington had a sough deployed for drainage purposes. Of course, it was also at this time that the canals started to appear, giving a massive boost to the transportation of coal, with the aforementioned Charnwood Forest Canal and the Ashby Canal providing the initial outlets that eventually linked north-west Leicestershire coal to the nationwide canal network. Essentially, the wheels of the Industrial Revolution were now freely turning, and industry was poised to explode in the 19th century.

The Industrial Explosion of the 19th Century

The previous chapter ended with coal, and that's where we will start in the 19th century, too. The Ashby Canal had opened up the Moira coalfields to the nationwide canal network in 1804, which was also the same year that the Earl of Moira began the sinking of Double Pits

on Ashby Woulds. This time, the winding mechanism had moved on from gins and horses to a steam engine – the first usage of steam power for winding in Leicestershire. The Furnace Pits were then opened two years later, and by 1812, they were being mined to a depth of 600 feet, while the following year saw the opening of the Bath Pits. This western side of the coalfield was also developing a tramway network, linking the canals to the collieries at Heather, Lount, Normanton-le-Heath and Staunton Harold. As the century wore on, ever-deeper pits were sunk as the "hidden coalfield" beneath the Triassic layer of rocks began to be mined – although interestingly, the first person to breach this layer was a farmer from Ibstock who sank a 200 foot shaft in 1825! The following year, a large new colliery was opened by Viscount Maynard at Bagworth at the southern end of the Leicestershire coalfield. At around the same time, the Whitwick Colliery was opened and was sunk to a new record depth of 350 feet, and it was this colliery, in conjunction with the later railways, that led to the birth of Coalville.

As it also did in neighbouring Derbyshire, the lure of

The original colliery winding wheel from Whitwick Colliery stands as a memorial to the pit's former miners on Leicester Road, Whitwick. When Whitwick Colliery opened in the late 1820s, its mine became the deepest in Leicestershire at that time, at a depth of 350 feet.

The pits at Moira were given a huge boost when the Ashby Canal opened in 1804, thus opening up their product to the rest of England via the national canal network. The above shows the terminus of the canal alongside Moira Furnace, a blast furnace that was also built in 1804 alongside the coal mines.

coal brought the great George Stephenson to Leicestershire, and he directed the sinking of the mine at Snibston in 1831. He and his partners also oversaw the build of the new *village* of Snibston which was located on the turnpike road from Leicester to Ashby-de-la-Zouch. The timing was perfect, too, as Snibston, like all of the other collieries in north-west Leicestershire was about to receive a massive boost with the opening of the Leicester and Swannington Railway in 1832, and which was soon shipping coal from the Leicestershire coalfields to Leicester (more on the railways shortly). As for Snibston Colliery, it had expanded to four shafts by the mid-1840s, one of which went to a depth of 700 feet, while the village population had grown to around 1200. The growth of the Whitwick and Snibston collieries and the influx of people and house building in the area, eventually brought about the birth of Coalville, and the name first appeared in the mid-1840s on a County Rate Return as "Whitwick-Coalville". Then in 1847, the railway station that opened in the area was named as Coalville and the place-name had become established.

Quirk Alert: *Giving It Large*

Daniel Lambert (1770-1809) was a Leicester gaoler and animal breeder, who also owned the largest waistcoat in the world – largely due to the fact that at his death, he weighed 52 stone 11lb! During his lifetime, he had been remarkably active, despite his size, and taught swimming in Leicester – where he was able to stay afloat with two grown men sitting on his back! He also once punched a dancing bear in the head and floored it, after it had attacked his dog. Alas, as he grew older, his weight continued to increase, and he was forced to give up hunting by 1801, by which stage he had reached 40 stone. On his death in 1809, his huge coffin was built with wheels, but it still took 20 sweating men almost half an hour to lower it into his grave.

The remainder of the 19th century saw the coal industry in north-west Leicestershire boom, and by 1874, output had topped 1,000,000 tons for the first time. Two years later, and a trio of new pits were opened at Ellistown, Hugglescote and Nailstone, while 1877 saw the Whitwick Colliery reach a depth of 915 feet via a seam that was nicknamed "The Roaster". Throughout these times, the Coalville and Whitwick populations were expanding and new houses were being built, while the year 1900 saw the Leicestershire coal industry reach its zenith when the last mine of the "hidden coalfield" was sunk at Desford.

Although not quite to the same extent as its northern neighbours, Leicestershire also saw iron founding develop in the early 19th century, with James and Benjamin Court establishing the Britannia Iron Works at Belgrave Gate Wharf. By the 1840s, another Leicester company, Pegg and Mason, was also producing machinery and tools for the granite quarries of Charnwood Forest, while the Phoenix Foundry was producing heavy castings for bridge building, particularly those used on the by-now flourishing railways. By 1878, the Vulcan Works was founded on a 3-acre site, while by the turn of the century Leicester's largest engineering works had been established when Pearson and Bennion, who manufactured boot and shoe machinery, merged with an American company to form the British United Shoe Machinery Company in 1899. Other Leicestershire-based engineering of the late 19th century included crane manufacture, steam boilers and steelworks, while Loughborough's John Taylor Bellfounders continued to prosper, and in 1881, cast the largest bell in Britain, "Great Paul", for St Paul's Cathedral in London. From slightly earlier, Norman & Underwood began making sand-cast sheet lead roofing and stained glass in 1825 and their work can be found in many of England's major cathedrals and historic buildings, including Chatsworth House, Hampton Court Palace, Salisbury Cathedral, Westminster Abbey and Windsor Castle.

The Grade II listed Wymondham windmill was built in 1814, originally with six sails known as a Six Arm Lincolnshire Cross. Today it has an ogee cap and fantail, restored in 1985. The windmill ceased grinding corn in 1952.

This cast-iron mine seam marker at Moira, records the depths of several seams worked alongside the Ashby Canal, ranging from "Little" at a depth of 163ft to "Kilburn" at 392ft.

The Grade II listed Whissendine windmill was built in 1809 and, unlike neighbouring Wymondham, it is still milling today.

The construction of the Leicester and Swannington Railway was of immense importance to Leicestershire as, prior to this, the Derbyshire and Nottinghamshire mining industry had held an advantage, courtesy of their access to the Erewash Canal and the Soar Navigation. As covered in the previous chapter, the Charnwood Forest Canal briefly opened up trade with Leicester, but due to a series of setbacks, it soon fell into disuse. The idea for the railway came from William Stenson, the owner of Whitwick Colliery, and who was supported by a wealthy Quaker from Leicester called John Ellis. Ellis also happened to be a friend of George Stephenson, who was subsequently invited to visit Leicester to discuss this new railway line which was to service the Leicestershire collieries. Stephenson agreed to help supply a third of the costs via financier friends in Liverpool (the other two thirds – around £90,000 – was raised locally), and his son, Robert Stephenson became the engineer assisted by Thomas Miles. The line obtained Royal Assent in 1830 and the first part of it was opened in the summer of 1832. The Leicester and Swannington Railway became only the sixth line in Britain that employed steam locomotives and transported passengers, and its construction also required tunnelling techniques that at the time were virtually untried.

The line's start point was from a station and coal wharf alongside the Soar Navigation in Leicester, and within a mile of its northward journey, it passed through a tunnel at Glenfield of 1796 yards (1642m). The tunnel alone is thought to have cost around £97,000, and which went over-budget due to sections having to be brick-lined following the encountering of unexpected sandstone. From the tunnel exit, the line

This tribute to Loughborough's bell-founding tradition can be found in Queen's Park, Loughborough. It is actually the casting case of the 17 ton Great Paul that John Taylor Bellfounders cast for London's St Paul's Cathedral in 1881.

turned first westwards to Desford, then headed north-westwards to Bagworth Station before immediately climbing a short 1 in 29 incline of around 100 feet; this particular section was worked by a cable around a pulley at the top of the incline. The next section of the line saw it pass through a cutting at Battleflat, after which it passed Long Lane (Coalville by 1835) with its new mines. The final stretch of the line involved a half-mile 1 in 17 descent of around 150 feet to the established pits at Swannington, and this section was worked by a stationary steam engine at its head, designed by Robert Stephenson – and which, remarkably, remained in use until 1948. Back in the 1830s, though, the terminus at Swannington was then linked to further coal mines and limestone quarries by what was called the Coleorton Tramway.

The remains of the engine house that once stood at the top of the Swannington Incline, lowering engines down the final stretch of the Leicester and Swannington Railway. Below: The top of the 726 yard, 1 in 17 incline, today.

The line opened from Leicester to Bagworth in July 1832, but difficulties with the cutting at Battleflat delayed the opening of the final stretch to Swannington until the end of 1833. By this stage, though, the line was delivering coal from Whitwick, Ibstock and Bagworth, and these Leicestershire collieries were now able to compete with the Derbyshire and Nottinghamshire collieries in terms of efficiency. The line also found itself transporting around 60 passengers a day, too, once a carriage had been added to the standard goods train of 24 wagons, and the Glenfield Tunnel became only the second tunnel in the world on a passenger railway – although bars had to be fitted to the windows to prevent passengers sticking their heads out in what was a very narrow tunnel! In the early days, passengers also had to walk the 1 in 29 incline beyond Bagworth station due to safety concerns. Interestingly, the passenger element wasn't especially lucrative, with receipts for the first six months of 1843 showing that passenger fares only accounted for 5.1% of the railway's income; the other 94.9% was largely thanks to the delivery of 3000 wagons of coal during the same period!

> ## Quirk Alert: *Lucky Cheney!*
> *The chap in question is Colonel Cheney, and who is immortalised in marble in Gaddesby church astride his horse … while the horse in question is one of five poor beasts that were shot from underneath him in 1815 as he rode into battle at Waterloo!*

The effect of all this on the Erewash Canal-using coal-masters was severe, reducing the price of their coal by seven shillings per ton. They therefore decided to build their own line to Leicester, although this wasn't completed until much later, but which became one of the triggers for the formation of the Midland Counties Railway which, in turn, became one of three founding partners in the Midland Railway in 1844. But even before the 1844 merger, the Midland Counties Railway had built a line from Leicester to Nottingham along the Soar Valley, with passenger services commencing in the summer of 1840. This line was then later extended southwards to Rugby, enabling it to link up with the London to Birmingham line that had been constructed in 1838. It was also to the Midland Railway that the directors of the Leicester and Swannington Railway eventually sold out to in 1845. The reason for the purchase was because of an independent proposal to link up with the London and York Railway (later the Great Northern running from King's Cross) via Bedford, and thus supply Leicestershire coal to London, but which would have then threatened the profitability of the Midland's own line to London via Rugby. That scheme didn't become a reality, though, until 1857 when a route from Wigston on the Leicester to Rugby line opened to Bedford and thus on to King's Cross, but it still wasn't until 1868 that Leicester's first main line to London arrived when the Midland Railway completed the stretch from Bedford to St Pancras. As for the Leicester and Swannington line, one of the Midland Railway's first improvements was to deviate the track to avoid the Bagworth Incline and, as a result, the original Bagworth Station at the bottom of the incline was closed and a new station called Bagworth and Ellistown was opened beyond the summit. The line was also extended westwards from Coalville to Burton upon Trent, thus linking the line to the train network in the West Midlands and also leaving the Swannington Incline as a branch line. A station was also opened at Coalville in 1848 as the Victorian new town began to increase in importance, while a line from Desford to Knighton provided direct access to Leicester Campbell Street.

As for railways in eastern Leicestershire and Rutland, that was a whole different proposition, thanks to the difficult terrain of scarped ridges, watersheds and large countryside estates ... plus this was also traditional fox hunting country. Hence it wasn't until the latter part of the 19th century that the area became significantly served by railways, although the 1840s did see a route develop out from the Soar Valley line to Melton Mowbray, Oakham and then onto Stamford. But it was 1879 before a joint venture from several railway companies saw a line opened from Market Harborough to Newark, and which required expensive tunnels, cuttings, embankments and viaducts as it cut through eastern Leicestershire. A branch line north of Melton Mowbray also linked this route to the iron ore fields of Eaton and Holwell, while another branch line that was completed in 1882 headed off to a terminus at Belgrave Road in Leicester, and which included five platforms under a twin-arched roof. The final act in the 19th century saw the birth of the Great Central Railway, which in 1899, linked Manchester to Marylebone via Nottingham, Loughborough, Leicester and Rugby, with the Nottingham to Leicester section alone requiring a mile-long viaduct of 96 arches and 16 girder bridges.

In the 1860s, the declining hosiery industry was grad-

The Haymarket Clock Tower in Leicester City Centre was built by Joseph Goddard in 1868 by the site of the medieval East Gate. Each corner is adorned with a stunning statue of famous Leicesterians, Simon de Montfort, William Wyggeston, Sir Thomas White and Alderman Newton.

ually superseded by the boot and shoe industry, although even by 1846, there were 200 boot and shoe makers listed in White's *Directory of Leicestershire and Rutland*, for the Borough of Leicester alone. The most prominent of these was Thomas Crick of Highcross Street, and in 1853, he patented a machine for riveting the soles of shoes to their uppers, which along with other innovations of the day led to mass production, and the appearance of boot and shoe factories by the early 1860s. By this stage, Crick's factory employed 300 men and 420 women along with some children as young as twelve. By 1900, there were 225 boot and shoe companies in the borough, employing 24,000 people. Production also spread to rural areas as early as the 1860s thanks to an innovation called the "basket-work system", where the uppers were finished in the factories, but the attachment of the soles to the uppers by wax-thread sewing was completed in small village workshops. Naturally, this industry developed in the same villages where framework knitting had so recently become defunct, such as Anstey, Barwell, Earl Shilton and Sileby. Over the next three decades, the village practise evolved into the whole process and by 1896, there were 17 boot and shoe manufacturers at Anstey, 15 at Hinckley, 12 at Earl Shilton, 11 at Barwell and 4 at Shepshed. The basket-work system was also gradually phased out, particularly when the Boot and Shoe Operatives Union gained numbers and strength following its founding in 1874. This culminated in a demand in 1895, for an end to the link between the city factories and the rural workers with the slogan: "all work cut in Leicester shall be made and finished in Leicester".

Previously, we've talked about how Leicestershire's population began to expand rapidly in the late 18th century, particularly in those communities where the coal mining and hosiery industries were connected. However, the overall population of Leicestershire throughout the 19th century far outstripped anything that had been seen before. Starting with Leicester, the town had a population of around 17,000 in 1801, and which had risen to around 40,000 by 1841. By the end of the 19th century, though, the 1901 census revealed Leicester's population to be around 212,000, a 12-fold increase in just 100 years, with the decade between 1861 and 1871 alone seeing a 40 per cent increase. Throughout the 19th century, therefore, the town expanded outwards, particularly eastwards and southwards, and former villages around its rural rim – such as Aylestone, Belgrave, Evington, Knighton and Wigston – had all been absorbed into the borough by the close of the century. In 1827, St George's church was built in the former medieval parish of St Margaret's and became the first new church in Leicester since the early Middle Ages. However, it was soon followed by a number of others, and by the end of the 19th century, St Margaret's had been split into 10 separate parishes as the masses became ever-more tightly packed in. Of course, this brought with it increasing problems of sanitation which wasn't helped by more than half of the streets lacking sewers by the middle of the century, and the water supply being contaminated by those streets that *did* have them. Cholera, typhus and smallpox were rife, and Leicester's death rate of 30 in every 1000 ranked fourth worst in the British Isles.

Rutland, being largely rural, didn't have the same overcrowding or sanitation issues. In fact, the entire population of the county rose by a staggeringly small 329 between 1831 (19,380) and 1901 (19,709), and it hasn't even doubled since then, either, with the 2011 census revealing a population of 37,400.

One other significant development of the 19th century was the introduction of municipal government. The majority of English towns had been subject to the same local governmental framework since medieval times, but changes brought about by Lord John Russell in the 1830s changed urban life forever. Leicester became one of 183 towns in late 1835 for which town councillors were to be elected for a period of three years by ratepayers. As a recent Commission had pointed out, the corporations "had great wealth, yet did little to ease public burdens". This exposure, as well as a growing national conscience that was being championed by the various nonconformist religious denominations of the previous 200 years, saw the Liberal party land a huge majority in the election of 1835. The new incumbents were largely industrialists and/or members of dissenting chapels, and their intentions were largely philanthropic; indeed, the first seven Leicester mayors all

The Victoria Coffee House on Granby Street, Leicester, was built in 1888 and was originally known as The Temperance Coffee House. It was designed by Edward Burgess, a friend of Thomas Cook.

came from the local Great Unitarian Meeting. The new regime also inherited a £20,000 debt from their predecessors, and the new corporation immediately set about eradicating that debt by removing a number of medieval posts, abolishing civic feasts and auctioning off other former extravagances such as the town's great mace that dated from the 17th century, along with a large stock of cutlery, plates, glass and linen. The debt was paid off in five years.

The 19th century also saw slight changes made to Leicestershire's county boundaries, although neither Leicestershire nor Rutland were affected by the Counties (Detached Parts) Act 1844 where a number of exclaves were tidied up – exclaves being areas of land belonging to one county but which were completely surrounded by another county. However, in 1884, the three separate detached parts of the parish of Packington, including the chapelry of Snibston were transferred from Derbyshire to Leicestershire, where they formed part of the new parish of Ravenstone with Snibston. Finally, the last Derbyshire exclave in Leicestershire, known as the Donisthorpe-Measham exclave, was transferred to Leicestershire in 1897, including the parishes of Appleby Magna North,

Historic Melton Mowbray. Here we have the Half Moon Inn (near-side), and the former Corn Exchange building (farside) which was built in 1854. However, in the middle is Melton's famous Ye Olde Pork Pie Shoppe, and which has been the home of Dickinson & Morris since 1851 – the oldest pork pie bakery in the world.

Chilcote, Measham, Oakthorpe and Donisthorpe (partly in Leicestershire), Stretton en le Field and Willesley. At the same time the parishes of Netherseal and Overseal were transferred from Leicestershire to Derbyshire.

Rutland, meanwhile, was still divided into the ancient hundreds of Alstoe, East Rutland, Martinsley, Oakham and Wrandike. However, following the Poor Law Amendment Act of 1834, which allowed parishes to form unions which would be jointly responsible for the administration and funding of poor relief in their area, Rutland was covered by parts of three poor law unions and rural sanitary districts: those of Oakham, Uppingham and Stamford. The resulting *registration* county of Rutland (Registration Districts were based on Poor Law Unions which, in turn, were based on groups of parishes, some of which straddled historic county borders) contained the entirety of the Oakham and Uppingham rural sanitary districts, plus those parishes of these two rural sanitary districts that were over the border in Leicestershire and Northamptonshire. Meanwhile, the eastern part of the historic county of Rutland, and which was covered by the Stamford rural sanitary district, was included in the registration county of Lincolnshire. These examples amply demonstrate why the boundaries of the *registration* counties were very different from those of the *historic* counties!

The end of the 19th century also saw Leicestershire and Rutland follow suit with most other English counties, as the Local Government Act 1888 heralded the modern era of local government. Thus it was that in 1889, both Leicestershire and Rutland were formalised as *administrative* counties, which were based very closely on their *historic* county boundaries. Leicestershire County Council controlled almost the entirety of the administrative county area with the exception of Leicester, which was declared a county borough in 1889, while Rutland County Council controlled the entire county of Rutland. A couple of years later and the Leicester Extension Act of

Swithland Reservoir constructed between 1894 and 1896 by the newly-formed Leicester County Borough Council.

1891 expanded the boundaries of the County Borough of Leicester, trebling the area under the new corporation's control by totally absorbing the areas of Aylestone, Belgrave and Knighton, and part-absorbing Braunstone, Evington and Humberstone; Belgrave, alone, had a population of around 12,000. The corporation running the county borough soon made an impact, too, widening roads, creating parks, constructing Swithland Reservoir, and rebuilding a vastly improved sewage system in the town. They also vastly improved the town's flood defences against the River Soar, spending around £300,000 on deepening the river bed, cutting new channels, and removing problematic weirs.

In Rutland, as elsewhere, the Local Government Act 1894 saw the existing rural sanitary districts (RSDs) become partitioned along county boundaries to form three rural districts. So, the parts of the former Oakham and Uppingham RSDs *within* Rutland's county boundary formed the Oakham Rural District and the Uppingham Rural District; the two parishes from the former Oakham RSD that were in Leicestershire then became part of the Melton Mowbray Rural District, the nine parishes of Uppingham RSD previously in Leicestershire became the Hallaton Rural District, while the six parishes of Uppingham RSD previously in Northamptonshire became Gretton Rural District. At the same time, that part of the Stamford RSD that was in Rutland (the rest having been in Lincolnshire) became the Ketton Rural District. Then in 1911, Oakham itself was split out from Oakham Rural District to form the Oakham Urban District! And that is largely how things remained right up to 1st April 1974 when the Local Government Act 1972 was implemented – but much more on that a little later.

From Edwardian England to Present Day

Throughout the 19th century, coal mining had become the most significant of Leicestershire's industries. Alas, the year 1900 pretty much marked the peak of the industry in the area when Desford pit was sunk, and thereafter, the industry went into decline. It particularly suffered during the depression years of 1927 to 1933, with annual output falling by a staggering 1,000,000 tons. One minor highlight was the opening of a new pit at Lount on the exposed coal measures, only for it to suffer closure after World War II following its takeover by the National Coal Board in 1948, while all of the surviving north-west Leicestershire pits were closed in the 1980s and early 1990s due to cheaper coal being imported from abroad.

The hosiery industry was still strong at the start of the 20th century, with 50,000 workers still employed in the industry in 1911. However, by this time, engineering was starting to grow as an industry and already employed 7000 workers in 1911. Fast-forward to 1967, and a survey revealed that almost 70,000 workers were employed in engineering, which had now overtaken textiles (56,000) and footwear (16,000). Those engineering companies that had begun to flourish at the turn of the century, such as the British United Shoe Machinery Company, went from strength to strength in the 20th century, and by the 1930s, the company was employing 5000 workers. The growth of engineering in Leicester also meant that the city was much better placed than many others to weather the severe economic challenges of the 1920s and 1930s; in fact, the Bureau of Statistics identified Leicester in 1936 as the second richest city in Europe! Also at around this time, the Co-op became an important employer and landowner and when Leicester played host to the Jarrow March on its way to London in 1936, the Co-op provided the marchers with a change of boots!

The railways continued to prosper in Leicestershire and Rutland until the infamous Beeching Axe was wielded in the 1960s. Passenger trains on the extended line from Leicester London Road to Burton upon Trent ceased in 1964, while coal and oil traffic on the industrial line survived until 29th April 1966, including three veteran 19th century locomotives that worked the line until 1964. The winding engine at the Swannington end of the line is now at the National Railway Museum at York, while the site of the Swannington Incline is now owned by the Swannington Heritage Trust. Meanwhile, Robert Stephenson's wooden lifting bridge that originally carried a short branch over the Soar Navigation at West Bridge in Leicester has been reconstructed next to the entrance of Snibston Discovery Park in Coalville. Nevertheless, despite the demise of coal mining in the 1980s, the central part of the railway from Desford to Bardon Hill continues to serve two granite quarries. Other parts of the line have been re-used as walking and cycling trails.

As for the amazing Foxton Locks, they were complemented between 1900 and 1926 by an incline plane which enabled boats wider than the narrow boat to be raised up the 75ft incline. Up to two boats at a time were conveyed up and down the plane in one of two tanks or caissons, both full of water and counterbalancing each other, and taking around twelve minutes to complete the journey. Unfortunately, the need to main-

The Snibston Mine, Coalville – an exceptionally rare and privileged sight today, but hugely prevalent in the British coalfields throughout the 19th and 20th centuries.

The 75ft incline plane at Foxton Locks was in use between 1900 and 1926. Up to two boats at a time were conveyed up and down the plane in one of two counterbalancing tanks.

tain a constant supply of steam for the plane's engine proved expensive, and so despite its obvious effectiveness, its usage was stopped in 1911 to save money. Thereafter it saw occasional use, but was eventually dismantled in 1926 and sold for scrap in 1928 for a measly £250 – particularly measly since current plans to restore what has now been recognised as a Scheduled Ancient Monument are estimated at around £9 million! As for the Foxton Locks, they were eventually designated as part of the European Route of Industrial Heritage in 2008.

A number of significant events occurred in Leicester in the early decades of the 20th century. First and foremost, Leicester was granted city status in 1919. Eight years later, Leicester also became a cathedral city for the first time in over a thousand years, when it was allocated its own bishopric again, prising away a former part of the bishopric of Peterborough in the process. And then in 1935, the area of the city was doubled when it was expanded to include Beaumont Leys, Braunstone Frith, Gilroes and New Parks, as well as large parts of Braunstone, Evington and Humberstone. All this time, the city council were adding housing, starting with the Coleman Road estate in North Evington which was purchased in 1919 and which was followed in the 1920s by large housing projects to the south and west of the city; in fact, 12,000 city houses were built between 1920 and 1939 of which around 8000 belonged to the city council. Meanwhile, to the south-east of the city, the population of Oadby

Quirk Alert: *Double Heartbreak*

In the graveyard of St Luke's church at Newton Harcourt, there is a beautiful carving of a miniature church (below left). However, it is a poignant memorial for eight-year-old Christopher Gardner, and which was carved by his heartbroken father and stonemason, George Gardner. It was carved because Christopher had always said that when he grew up, he would like to be a vicar and "have his own church". And so his father gave one to him.

Meanwhile, the war memorial in Braunston-in-Rutland (right) has recently had an extra name added to it. Gladys Walter, from Braunston, worked as a rigger for the Women's Royal Air Force, and was one of only three women from Rutland who

died during service in World War I. It is thought that her omission from the war memorial was due to the fact that she died of pneumonia as opposed to being killed in action. Tragically, she was only twenty years of age. But even more heart-breaking, her tombstone in the churchyard of All Saints' church, embossed with the crest of the RAF, names the date of her death – 11th November 1918.

increased from 6200 to 15,300 between 1951 and 1966, with 40 per cent of the working population having professional or managerial roles. And back in the centre, large parts of Victorian Leicester – factories and terraced housing – were demolished and rebuilt, with structures like new bus stations and municipal car parks taking their place. The start of Leicester's inner ring road was begun as early as the late 1920s, although it wasn't until the 1960s that the outer ring road was completed. By the 1970s, the Haymarket shopping mall had also transformed the area just to the north-east of the city centre which, in turn, had become largely pedestrianised.

The first half of the 20th century was, of course, dominated by war, and World War II in particular was to shape parts of the Leicestershire and Rutland countryside. This was due to the heavy aerial warfare element of the conflict, which necessitated airbases in the east of England. Rutland, being closest of the two to the North Sea saw the establishment of military aerodromes at Cottesmore and North Luffenham. RAF Cottesmore opened in March 1938, initially for training, but by September 1943 the airbase was in the hands of the Americans under the designation USAAF Station 489; it was handed back to the RAF on 1st July 1945. Meanwhile, RAF North Luffenham opened as a training base in 1940, but was soon taken over by RAF Bomber Command. A little further back and behind the offensive bases, were four airfields in Leicestershire: at Bitteswell, Castle Donington, Ratcliffe and Rearsby. Castle Donington was originally established as a training centre, while Ratcliffe was used for ferrying aircraft between factories and the offensive bases further east; the airfield at Rearsby was established adjacent to a factory that built light military aircraft and the airfield

at Bitteswell was used for the testing of Lancaster bombers built in the West Midlands.

Alas, all but one of these bases has now closed. Of these, RAF North Luffenham lasted until 1998, and RAF Cottesmore only recently became a victim of defence cuts. However, it is worth noting that in 1981, the Tri-national Tornado Training Establishment (TTTE) was opened at Cottesmore, undertaking the training of Panavia Tornado pilots from the RAF and, in a somewhat telling development of time, the training of pilots from the Italian Air Force and the German Luftwaffe, too! The TTTE closed in 1999, while today, like the former RAF North Luffenham, the base is in the hands of the British Army. Of the Leicestershire-based airfields, Castle Donington became the most significant, because although RAF Castle Donington was decommissioned in 1946, the site eventually evolved into East Midlands Airport and which was opened as a passenger service in April 1965. Today, East Midlands Airport is the 11th busiest passenger airport in the UK, peaking in 2008 with 5.6 million passengers, while it is actually the UK's second busiest airport for freight.

In terms of agriculture, pastoral farming continued to outstrip arable farming in Leicestershire and Rutland at the start of the 20th century, with 85 per cent of agricultural land under permanent pasture by the 1930s. However, that number had dropped to around 35 per cent by the 1970s as methods for the intensive farming of cereal crops developed. All this time, the road network across Leicestershire and Rutland was improving. The old Fosse Way became the A46, with much of it converted to dual carriageway in the 1960s. The A50 and the A6 also became much improved, but the biggest revolution was the construction of the M1, with the Leicestershire section laid between 1965 and 1968.

St Martin's church, Leicester, which became Leicester Cathedral in 1927, as Leicester became a bishopric again for the first time in more than a thousand years.

The 151ft Carillon Tower, Loughborough, was built after World War I to commemorate the men of the town who gave their lives.

This war memorial sits high up at Bradgate Park and commemorates those who gave their lives in South Africa (1900-02), and during World War I.

A model of a Gloster E.28/39 at Lutterworth. The engine for this, the UK's first jet aeroplane, was developed by Frank Whittle at Lutterworth in 1939.

Quirk Alert: *Ring Of Honour*
Loughborough was the first town to set up a carillon in memory of the fallen of World War I, and with its 47 bells, ranging from 20 pounds to 4 tons, the Carillon Tower became the first of its type to broadcast bell music. Meanwhile, a few years earlier in 1909, Loughborough's All Saints' church was the scene of a world record, when ten bell ringers rang a peal of 18,027 Stedman Caters in just over 12 hours.

The motorway cuts a swathe right through Leicestershire from Lutterworth in the south to Kegworth in the north, cutting through Charnwood Forest in between and actually reaching the highest point on the motorway just east of Bardon Hill. The M69 was also added in 1977 to link the M1 with the M6, running from just west of Leicester to Hinckley before exiting Leicestershire for Warwickshire. Motorways, however, don't put in an appearance in rural Rutland, with only the A1, which skirts the county's eastern flank, offering any heavy traffic.

One bonus for Leicestershire of the expanding road network, though, meant that its central position and good road transport links to the rest of the country, attracted many new businesses in both the service and manufacturing sectors. The same reasons make it a favoured spot for distribution centres and warehouses, and many large retail companies today have huge warehouses at the Magna Park complex near Lutterworth.

Like most of the other counties in the East Midlands, today's Leicestershire and Rutland county boundaries are very close to those of their historic counterparts, bar the 19th century exclave reclamation, while the late 19th century urban expansion of Market Harborough also saw the area to the east of the town known as Little Bowden annexed from Northamptonshire in 1888. However, in the 20th century, there was certainly a major boundary impact between 1974 and 1997, thanks to the controversial changes brought about by the Local Government Act 1972, and which came into force on 1st April 1974. Many historic English counties were drasti-

Quirk Alert:
Mange Tout, Mange Tout!
The Beaumonts, formerly of Coleorton Hall until its sale to the National Coal Board in 1948, can be traced all the way back to the Norman Conquest. However, one of the Hall's final incumbents became renowned in the area for being a door-to-door vegetable seller! For when he discovered that local salesmen were buying his lettuces for 1d and selling them for 3d, he decided to take the matter into his own hands. Circulating the neighbourhood in his van, he would then call out his wares and his gardener would collect the money! Accounts do not specify what he charged, though, nor do they confirm whether or not his van was a yellow three-wheeler!

cally reduced to accommodate brand new metropolitan counties, and some unfortunate historic counties disappeared altogether. Leicestershire, though, fared particularly well, as not only did it not *lose* any territory, but one of the many radical changes introduced by the Act was to enlarge Leicestershire to include all of Rutland's county area, making the latter merely a non-metropolitan district of the former. To clarify, poor Rutland had joined Cumberland, Westmorland and Huntingdonshire on the English county scrap-heap.

Unsurprisingly, loss of county status caused outrage in Rutland. It may well have been England's smallest county – indeed Rutland County Council embraced this in 1950 by adopting the motto *Multum In Parvo* ("much in little") – but it was also one of England's 39 historic counties that dated back to the 11th and 12th centuries, and its removal from the modern county map was considered sacrilegious by many locals. Alas, many of the changes brought about in 1974 were based on population, and even today, Rutland is still by some distance the smallest unitary authority in mainland England, this owing to the fact that it is largely rural and only contains two towns, Oakham and Uppingham, which are both relatively small. In fact, if we break England down into distinct districts, Rutland comes 348th out of 354, population-wise. Even more ominous for Rutland back in 1974, was the fact that it didn't quite meet the minimum population criteria for a *district*, either – this being 40,000 back then. So initial proposals were to pair Rutland with Leicestershire's new Melton district, but the Rutland outcry soon saw the Act of 1972 amended in favour of a standalone non-metropolitan district to take the place of the now-abolished late-19th century administrative county; Rutland had survived, in part, to fight another day.

One other point of interest regarding late 20th century boundary changes, are the potential changes that could have happened had other commissions had their say. For example, the Local Government Commission for England ran from 1958 to 1967, and Rutland was part of the Commission's General Review Area for the East Midlands. And initially, Rutland would have disappeared completely, with draft recommendations proposing the county be split, with Ketton Rural District going along with Stamford to a new and larger administrative county of Cambridgeshire, and the western remainder going to an enlarged Leicestershire. The final proposals were less radical, though, and instead proposed that Rutland become a single rural district within the administrative county of Leicestershire – which is similar to what actually happened in 1974. However, happily for Rutland, that particular Commission never got the support that it needed. But then hot on its heels we had the even more controversial Redcliffe-Maud Report of 1969, which would also have severely impacted the county. This report marked the culmination of the Royal Commission on Local Government in England, which had run from 1966 to 1969 under the chairmanship of Lord Redcliffe-Maud, and which had been looking at restructuring local government in England. Regarding Rutland, its proposals were to create a new unitary area of Leicester and Leicestershire that would have included most of Rutland's area, except for the south-eastern part which would have gone to another proposed new county/unitary authority known as Peterborough-North Fens. Once again, Rutland as any type of local governmental entity would have completely vanished. This is demonstrated in the 2nd of the following sequence of maps, which show Leicestershire and Rutland's boundary proposal and evolution over the last fifty years or so.

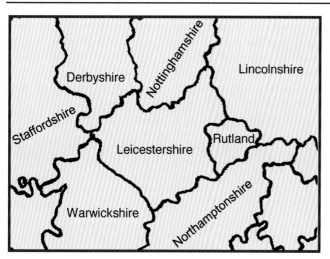

1. Historic Counties – Pre 1974

2. Redcliffe-Maud Proposals – 1969

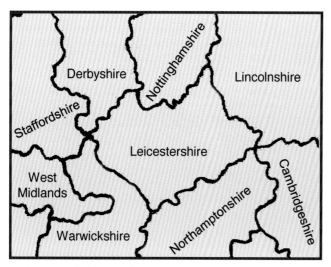

3. Ceremonial Counties – 1974-1997

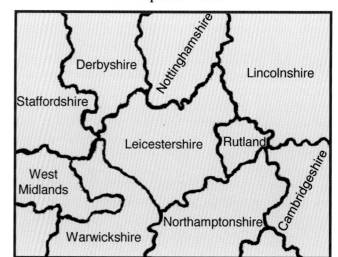

4. Ceremonial Counties – 1997-2015

However, in 1970, the incoming Conservatives rejected the Redcliffe-Maud Report and its subsequent Labour-issued White Paper, and created their own White Paper instead. The subsequent Local Government Act 1972 was then based upon the Conservatives' 1971 White Paper proposals, which in most cases were less radical, but in Rutland's case, still resulted in the disappearance of the county, anyway (see map 3 above).

Nevertheless, the folk of Rutland did not give up their fight, and after a twenty-three year battle to have their independence restored, this duly arrived on the 1st April 1997, when their county was reinstated as an English *ceremonial* county, whilst also becoming a unitary authority, too (*map 4*). This all happened off the back of the Local Government Commission for England, which was set up in 1994 and which was committed to conducting a structural review of English local government. Thus it was that as well as becoming a ceremonial county and unitary authority, Rutland regained its Lord Lieutenant and shrievalty as well as its council regaining control of county functions such as education, main roads, public transport and social services. That said, other functions, such as the emergency services, quite understandably remained under the control of Leicestershire, via the Leicestershire Constabulary and Leicestershire Ambulance Service.

One final victory for the people of Rutland was the reinstatement of their county by the Royal Mail as a *postal* county. This had also been a bone of contention because commencing in 1974, the Royal Mail had included Rutland as part of the Leicestershire postal county – and quite understandably, too, given the new county map that had been created that year. But after a lengthy campaign, and despite a code of practice which excludes amendments to former postal counties, the Royal Mail agreed to create a postal county of Rutland in 2007. This came to fruition in January 2008 by amending the postal county to "Rutland" for all of the Oakham (LE15) post town and for a small part of the Market Harborough (LE16) post town, too.

Sticking with the late 20ᵗʰ century boundary changes, Maps 3 and 4 *(opposite)* also demonstrate that the reinstatement of Rutland as a county in 1997 is the only boundary change in this part of the Midlands since 1974, as all of those county boundaries around Leicestershire and Rutland remained the same. Furthermore, maps 1, 3 and 4 also demonstrate that Leicestershire's bounding counties have pretty much stayed the same for around 1000 years, with the exception of 1974 to 1997, when the acquisition of Rutland meant that Leicestershire briefly shared a tiny border to the east with Cambridgeshire!

The only other county-related change since 1974 is that the city of Leicester was converted to a unitary authority in 1997, and thus now has its own City Council which runs its own affairs from offices in Leicester. The other seven districts of the county are

administrated via the standard two-tier "shire county" system. In Leicestershire's particular case, the upper tier (education, roads, public transport, policing, fire services, etc.) is controlled by Leicestershire County Council from County Hall in Glenfield, which is situated just outside the north-western boundary of the City of Leicester. Meanwhile, the seven District Councils are responsible for their own local planning, council housing, environmental health, refuse collection and so on. Of course, the seven districts *plus* the City of Leicester still collectively form the *ceremonial* county of Leicestershire and have the same Lord Lieutenant.

Shifting left slightly onto parliamentary constituencies, and Rutland had its own until 1918, after which it became part of the Rutland and Stamford constituency, along with Stamford in Lincolnshire. Since 1983, though, it has formed part of the Rutland and Melton constituency along with Melton borough and part of the Harborough district of Leicestershire. The constituency therefore closely mirrors the original intentions for the area local government-wise back in 1972.

It was also during the 1970s that Rutland's most famous modern feature, Rutland Water, was constructed – although it was somewhat ironically completed when Rutland *wasn't* a formal county any more. During what must have been a period of complete outrage for the people of Rutland, the

Rutland Water from the south shore, near Normanton's partly submerged church of St Matthew.

The pleasure cruiser Rutland Belle *berthed at Rutland North Shore, near Whitwell.*

construction of Rutland Water – or Empingham Reservoir as it was then known – was also heatedly opposed as the proposal was to drown more than 3000 acres of beautiful countryside in the Gwash Valley. This was particularly painful as the reservoir was being constructed to service the non-Rutland towns of Peterborough, Corby, Northampton and Milton Keynes. Nevertheless, the project went ahead, and when construction began in 1971, it became Europe's largest man-made lake at that time. It is roughly the same size as Lake Windermere, but in terms of artificial lakes, it is the largest reservoir in England by surface area, although Kielder Water in Northumberland is deeper and has a greater capacity.

LEICESTERSHIRE'S HERITAGE RAILWAYS

Some of the Heritage Railway engines still plying their trade around Leicestershire. On the top row are two shots of the diesel DMS No 51321, built in 1960 and now running on the Battlefield Line between Shackerstone and Shenton in south-west Leicestershire. The diesel serves alongside several steam locomotives. Meanwhile, on the middle and bottom rows are shots of some of the beautiful steam engines still running on the Grand Central Railway between Leicester North and Loughborough Central. Centre left at Rothley Station is an LMS Class 2 2-6-0 originally built in 1953 and which spent most of its working life in Wales, while bottom right at Quorn and Woodhouse Station is a Stanier LMS 8F Class 2-8-0, built in 1943 for the Southern Railway.

During the building of Rutland Water, a Roman farmstead was discovered complete with an iron-smelting hearth and furnace – but alas, this is now buried under one of Rutland Water's car parks! The construction also meant that Nether Hambleton and most of Middle Hambleton were demolished, while their neighbouring village of Upper Hambleton survived on the now-distinctive Hambleton Peninsula, as it had been located on a former ridge between two valleys. As for the village of Normanton, this just avoided being submerged, but the lower half of its church did not (see *Quirky Leicestershire and Rutland [Edith Weston]* for more). Construction of the reservoir was eventually completed in 1975, although it took a further four years to fill the lake.

Today, the opposition is long-forgotten and the reservoir is a magnet for tourists and locals alike, including visitor centres, the *Rutland Belle* pleasure cruiser, and a 25-mile track around the reservoir that is popular with walkers and cyclists. Naturally, Rutland Water is also very popular with water-sport enthusiasts and anglers. It is also an important nature reserve serving as an overwintering site for wildfowl and a breeding site for ospreys.

A number of other tourist attractions appeared in the late 20th century, including some impressive heritage railways. One of these, the Battlefield Line, runs from Shackerstone to just east of Shenton, terminating at the site of the Battle of Bosworth Field. The railway runs on part of the former line jointly operated by the London and North Western Railway and the Midland Railway, and which was initially opened in 1873. Passenger services ended in 1931 and freight in the 1960s, but the Shackerstone Railway Society formed in 1969 and by 1992 had realised their dream of reopening the line to

steam and diesel trains, with the inaugural journey performed by the aptly-name 0-6-0 tank engine "Richard III". A little further north-east is the preserved Great Central Steam Railway, a heritage railway running from Leicester North Station to Loughborough Central, and calling at Rothley and Quorn & Woodhouse Stations in between. The Great Central Railway underwent numerous transitions in the 20th century, amalgamating with the London and North East Railway in 1923, becoming part of British Rail (Eastern Region) in 1948, but moved across to the Midland Region in in 1958. The ex-GCR was inevitably wound down in favour of the former Midland route and was eventually closed in 1966. However, once again, a group of enthusiasts restored the line and, at present, the GCR is the only double track mainline heritage railway in Britain. Finally, Rutland also gets in on the heritage railway act, courtesy of the Rutland Railway Museum – or "Rocks by Rail: The Living Ironstone Museum", as it is now known. Situated a few miles north-east of Oakham, this open-air site has recreated an ironstone tramway system in its entirety, based on a typical mid-20th century quarry system when both steam and diesel power was used.

Also appearing from a tourism perspective in the late 20th century was the National Forest, a 33,000 acre area covering north Leicestershire, south Derbyshire and south-east Staffordshire, and aimed at linking the ancient forests of Needwood and Charnwood. This environmental project is run by The National Forest Company, a not-for-profit organisation founded in 1995, but supported by DEFRA. Their aim is to convert one third of the land in the National Forest to woodland and, so far, around 8 million trees have been planted, tripling the woodland area from 6% to around 18%, and thus offering an additional tourist area to Leicestershire.

It was also at around this time that two other tourist attractions appeared in the new National Forest area. Snibston Discovery Park, with Robert Stevenson's wooden lifting bridge on show alongside its entrance, focuses on technology and design and how it affects

One of a number of houses in Market Bosworth decorated with arms celebrating the quincentenary of the Battle of Bosworth Field, in 1985.

The Curve Theatre on Rutland Street, Leicester, designed by architect Rafael Viñoly and engineered by Adams Kara Taylor, and which was opened in 2008.

everyday life, offering high quality and interactive exhibitions. It also includes such diverse aspects as a tour around an old coal mine and the largest fashion gallery outside of London! Meanwhile, 6 miles to the east is Conkers, a 120 acre children's theme park offering multiple indoor and outdoor attractions, and which was built on the site of the former Rawdon Colliery. And not too far away, also in western Leicestershire, is Twycross Zoo. Opened in 1963, it has the largest collection of monkeys and apes in the Western World, and attracts over half a million visitors every year.

Moving into the 21st century and Leicestershire still plays host to the brewing industry (Everards), plus the production of cheese, (Stilton and Red Leicester), Melton Mowbray pork pies and Walkers crisps. Leicestershire food producers also include Claybrooke Mill one of the very few commercially working watermills left in Britain producing a range of over 40 flours. Then there is Brockleby's who produce meat from rare and minority breeds, whilst the nicely named Seldom Seen Farm produces Christmas turkey and goose. Food processing also includes popular British fish and chip shop pie Pukka Pies who are based in Syston, whilst the Masterfoods UK factory at Melton Mowbray produces pet food for brands such as Cesar, Kitekat, PAL, Pedigree, Sheba, Whiskas, Aquarian and Trill. Furthermore, some 15 major Indian food manufacturers are based in Leicester including Mayur Foods, Cofresh Snack Foods Ltd, Farsan, Apni Roti, and Spice n Tice.

One remarkable constant of the last 500 years or so has been the Rutland title. The first Earl of Rutland was created as far back as 1385 for Edward Plantagenet, (1373–1415), son of Edmund of Langley, Duke of York, and grandson of King Edward III. However, when Edmund of Langley died in 1402, Edward Plantagenet became Duke of York. He held the title jointly with Earl of Rutland, but the latter fell into disuse when Edward was killed at the Battle of Agincourt in 1415. The title was then resurrected when Thomas Manners was created Earl of Rutland in 1525. His mother, Anne St Leger, was Richard Plantagenet's granddaughter, and Richard was the first earl's nephew and father of King Edward IV. The earldom then stayed within the Manners family up to the 9th earl, John Manners (1638-1711), who was then made *Duke* of Rutland and Marquess of Granby in 1703 by Queen Anne. Remarkably, we are now onto the 11th Duke of Rutland and the title is still held by the Manners family after just under half a millennium.

However, the last word in this history section has to go to Leicestershire's most famous resident. Earlier, we discussed a number of accounts and legends surrounding the question of what happened to the body of King Richard III after his death at Bosworth Field. It is fairly well established that he was draped naked over a horse which carried him to Leicester, before eventually being interred at Greyfriars in the town centre. Thereafter, there are several rumours, one of which turned out to be true – and which was proven thanks to the collaboration

in 2012 of the University of Leicester, Leicester City Council and the Richard III Society. Led by the University of Leicester Archaeological Services (ULAS), the team resolved to locate the lost site of the former friary known as Greyfriars, but which was demolished during the Dissolution of the Monasteries – with the intention of finding Richard's remains. Using a combination of ancient maps and modern techniques, the team identified the friary's foundations beneath a 20th century car park. The excavators then moved in, and by September 2012, they had identified the location of the garden reputed in the early 17th century to be the location of a memorial to Richard – and lo and behold, they discovered the human skeleton of an adult male who had severe scoliosis of the spine. Furthermore, there was an object that appeared to be an arrowhead embedded in the spine along with catastrophic injuries to the skull, including a shallow orifice most likely caused by a rondel dagger, and a scooping depression to the skull inflicted by a bladed weapon, most probably a sword. Additionally, the bottom of the skull presented a gaping hole, where a halberd had cut away and entered it. The initial signs that this was Richard were very strong.

Of course, none of these findings provided proof that the body was Richard III. However, genealogical research was used to trace matrilineal descendants of Anne of York, Richard's elder sister. A British-born woman who emigrated to Canada after the Second World War, Joy Ibsen (née Brown), was a 16th-generation great-niece of the king in the same direct maternal line. And although Joy died in 2008, her son, Michael, donated a mouth-swab sample to the research team. When compared to the mitochondrial DNA of the body from Greyfriars, a match was found. The team were thus able to announce on 4th February 2013, that the skeleton was beyond reasonable doubt that of King Richard III.

At this point, the Mayor of Leicester announced that the king's skeleton would be reinterred at Leicester Cathedral in early 2014, thus triggering a year or so of controversy. The decision to reinter at Leicester was challenged by an organisation known as the Plantagenet Alliance who actually filed a court case, claiming that the king should be buried at York Minster instead. However, a ruling in May 2014 decreed that there are "no public law grounds for the Court interfering with the decisions in question". In other words, the reinterment was free to go ahead. And so on Sunday 22nd March, thousands turned up to witness the funeral procession which proceeded from Leicester University out into south-west Leicestershire to tour Bosworth field, Market Bosworth and other villages linked to the events of 1485, and then back to Leicester Cathedral, where the University formally released Richard's remains to the church. A funeral ceremony was then held for Richard, including contributions from both the Church of England and the Roman Catholic Church (the former didn't exist in 1485, and Richard was a member of the latter faith), and then Richard was

---

Quirk Alert:

The Fertile Fields of Rutland

In 2006 it was reported that Rutland has the highest fertility rate of any English county – the average woman having 2.81 children, compared with only 1.67 in Tyne and Wear.

THE LAST PLANTAGENET

Quirk Alert: *The Barwell Meteorite*

On Christmas Eve 1965, the Leicestershire village of Barwell was hit by a meteor, the fragments of which, when combined, were about the size of a traditional Christmas turkey. Fortunately, no one was hurt, although some minor damage to buildings and property occurred. Furthermore, one large fragment went through a car destroying the engine. When the owner attempted to claim on his insurance company, they deemed it to be an "Act of God", and therefore wouldn't cough up. Chancing his arm, the outraged owner subsequently sent the claim onto the priest of the local church. Alas, compensation was not forthcoming!

The coffin of Richard III, now maintained in this glass case in Leicester Cathedral.

Statue of Richard III outside Leicester Cathedral, decorated with many of the white roses that were thrown at his coffin during the funeral procession.

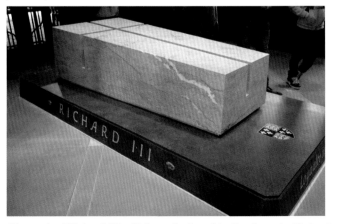

The tomb of Richard III which can be found in the chancel of Leicester Cathedral.

---

formally interred in a magnificent new tomb in the chancel of Leicester Cathedral, four days later.

Some Quirky Leicestershire and Rutland Stats

To complete the *Conventional Leicestershire and Rutland* section, here are some unique, unusual and quirky statistics! For starters, despite being land-locked, Leicestershire's borders actually include 70 miles of water! Then there is Appleby Parva, home to the only known school built by Sir Christopher Wren (in 1697), while Ashby-de-la-Zouch is the scene of a tourney in Sir Walter Scott's classic, *Ivanhoe*.

As for churches, Gaddesby's has a very rare equestrian statue (one of only four in English churches), while Sibson and Sheepy Magna churches have very unusual heart shrines. Meanwhile, Tickencote's church has a magnificent Norman shrine, while the carved vaulting of its chancel roof is only matched by that at Canterbury Cathedral, and the outermost of the magnificent chancel arch's five recesses is a unique foliage pattern. Leicestershire and Rutland's tallest spire is at Bottesford (210ft), while Oakham's parish church is crowned by Cock Peter, a weather vane dating from the 14th century and therefore one of the oldest in the country. Meanwhile, Scalford's parish church is the only one in the land dedicated to the 7th century saint, Egelwine, while Wigston Magna's is the only one dedicated to Wolstan, the 11th century bishop of Worcester.

Somewhat more quirkily, Cosby had a rector named Samuel Pepys, while the longest-serving Leicestershire servant was Birstall's Hannah Bond (over seventy years). In the 19th century, Parson Adams of Ashwell church became the first clergyman to receive the Victoria Cross for bravery in India and Afghanistan, while a memorial to Henry Rawlins and his five wives at Brooke St Peter's church demonstrates that the five wives died within thirteen years of each other!

Next, Little Dalby was the birthplace of Stilton cheese, created by Mrs Orton in around 1730, while a brass at Wanlip, dated 1393, contains the oldest prose inscription in English on any brass in the country. Meanwhile, the parish of Knaptoft can truly be described as the "watershed of England", as here rise three streams, one which flows into the Welland and which heads eastwards to the Wash, another which flows into the Soar and thus northwards towards the Trent and the Humber, and the third which flows into the Swift, which is a tributary to the Avon which flows westwards into the River Severn and the Bristol Channel. As for the county of Rutland, it would take more than 300 of them to fill the entire area of England and 40 just to fill up the historic county of Yorkshire!

Finally, not a fact, but a fine Leicestershire phrase to define something as impossible: "You might as well thatch Groby Pool with pancakes!"

Market Harborough Grammar School dates from 1614, and must be the quirkiest in the country!

Quirky Leicestershire and Rutland

Introducing the Shire-Ode

A Shire-Ode tells the story – in rhyming verse – of fictitious, eccentric inhabitants of the county in question. However, in so doing, it also incorporates into the flow of the verse, many place-names that can be found within that county – places which then go on to form a county almanac, of sorts. Each place appears in roughly alphabetical order, although some of the smaller places are batched up into trios known as a "Three's Up" or feature in "The Best of the Rest". The location of all of the places is also pinpointed in the maps on the pages following the Shire-Ode.

As for the *Leicestershire and Rutland* Shire-Ode, this tells the tale of *The Signing of Magna-Parva*, with the dynamic striking duo in question doubling up as the Harborough village of Great Glen (also known as Glen Magna), and the Leicester suburb of Glen Parva. And what signings they prove to be…

Leicestershire and Rutland Shire-Ode: The Signing of Magna-Parva

This is a tale of two Leicestershire Glen's
Who in youth played for **Coalville** and soon became friends
Glen Magna, a striker; struck the ball with some zing;
Glen Parva, a speedster, who played on the **Wing**.

By eighteen, Glen Magna was a **Burley** six-two
On a weird diet of **Tonge**, **Quorn** and **Branston** stew!
He worked part-time for **Sketchley**; got **Freeby**'s for **Cotes**;
Cleaned the full youth team's kit for a couple of notes.

At nineteen Glen Parva signed for **Preston North End**
Where his **Eye** for a goal became more than a trend
While Glen Magna, at **Stoke**, used to **Battram** all game
Despite **Belton** the nose, he'd score all the same.

At twenty, the boys met their wives – cue a quirk:
They were both called Ashby, and both quite berserk
For **Ashby Magna** was the world **Frisby** champ;
Ashby Parva, a **Care Village** worker who glamped!

As they turned twenty two, home-town **Leicester** did call
For the boss, **Earl Shilton**, craved their skill with the ball
Their debuts: **The Valley**: they bagged a brace each
And one **Blaston** the volley was an absolute peach.

Between them, the Glen's **Birstall** records for goals
They were **Hoton** the break, each assured in their roles
Acquired on the cheap, no **Coston** the side
And yet week after week, they would not be denied.

In time, for Glen Magna, **Scotland** did call
Since **Moira**, his Gran, was born north of the wall
So aptly, in time, he was known as **Great Glen**
Got his **Bagworth** each season, time and again.

Meanwhile, Glen Parva's aunt, **Edith Weston** she was called
Was involved with the club; had a **Seaton** the board
On match-days, the punters, she'd **Greetham** with **Teigh**;
They'd soon **Eaton** her scones, too, of jam, marg' and brie.

As for Leicester, things started to **Tixover** well
A great cup run saw all the boys put it **Tinwell**
Though Earl tweaked with the line ups, he'd always **Pickwell**
A boss with a brain who used his **Whitwell**.

And **The Brand** of football the Earl used to play
Was pure showmanship worthy of a **West End** play
Glen Magna kept scoring; Glen Parva on his day
Was as skilful as **Worthington**, fans used to say.

For the FA Cup semi, the pair were immense
Plus they'd bought **Carlton Curlieu** to shore up defence
Then a **Swift** break from Parva with his license to roam
And a cross aimed at Magna who would **Soar** to head home.

With the scene set for Wembley all looked **Welland** good
But the other side spoiled things as best as they could
They'd **Belvoir** away and then stick the boot in
Plus they'd trips 'em and **Clipsham;** anything to win.

And so losing one-nil with ten minutes to go
The Earl **Broughton Astley**, a good seasoned pro
He then **Broughton Lodges**, a winger with speed
When he crossed with precision, those Glen's each did feed.

The two-one success was hailed wide and far
The ale flowed from **Aylestone** to <hic> **Belcher's Bar**
And as fans drank their **Kegworth**, plus **Stoughton** the side
Glen's Magna and Parva were toasted with pride.

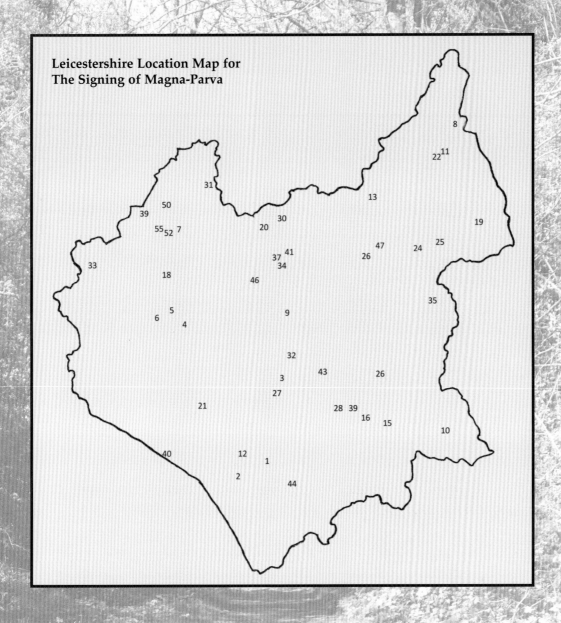

Leicestershire Location Map for
The Signing of Magna-Parva

PLACE-NAME TABLE FOR THE SIGNING OF MAGNA-PARVA

1	Ashby Magna	2	Ashby Parva	3	Aylestone	4	Bagworth	5	Battram
6	Belcher's Bar	7	Belton[2]	8	Belvoir	9	Birstall	10	Blaston
11	Branston	12	Broughton Astley	13	Broughton Lodges	14	Burley	15	Care Village
16	Carlton Curlieu	17	Clipsham	18	Coalville	19	Coston	20	Cotes
21	Earl Shilton	22	Eaton	23	Edith Weston	24	Eye[2]	25	Freeby
26	Frisby[2]	27	Glen Parva	28	Great Glen[1]	29	Greetham	30	Hoton
31	Kegworth	32	Leicester	33	Moira	34	North End	35	Pickwell
36	Preston	37	Quorn	38	Seaton	39	Scotland[2]	40	Sketchley
41	Soar	42	Stoke Dry	43	Stoughton	44	Swift	45	Teigh
46	The Brand	47	The Valley	48	Tinwell	49	Tixover	50	Tonge
51	Welland	52	West End	53	Whitwell	54	Wing	55	Worthington

[1] Also known as Glen Magna.
[2] Place appears twice in Leicestershire and Rutland.

**Rutland Location Map for
The Signing of Magna-Parva**

PLACE-NAME TABLE FOR THE SIGNING OF MAGNA-PARVA

1 Ashby Magna	2 Ashby Parva	3 Aylestone	4 Bagworth	5 Battram
6 Belcher's Bar	7 Belton[2]	8 Belvoir	9 Birstall	10 Blaston
11 Branston	12 Broughton Astley	13 Broughton Lodges	14 Burley	15 Care Village
16 Carlton Curlieu	17 Clipsham	18 Coalville	19 Coston	20 Cotes
21 Earl Shilton	22 Eaton	23 Edith Weston	24 Eye[2]	25 Freeby
26 Frisby[2]	27 Glen Parva	28 Great Glen[1]	29 Greetham	30 Hoton
31 Kegworth	32 Leicester	33 Moira	34 North End	35 Pickwell
36 Preston	37 Quorn	38 Seaton	39 Scotland[2]	40 Sketchley
41 Soar	42 Stoke Dry	43 Stoughton	44 Swift	45 Teigh
46 The Brand	47 The Valley	48 Tinwell	49 Tixover	50 Tonge
51 Welland	52 West End	53 Whitwell	54 Wing	55 Worthington

[1] Also known as Glen Magna.
[2] Place appears twice in Leicestershire and Rutland.

The Signing of Magna-Parva –
A Leicestershire and Rutland Shire-Ode Almanac

NAME (STATUS):	**ASHBY MAGNA** (Village)
POPULATION:	347
DISTRICT:	Harborough
EARLIEST RECORD:	*Essebi Magna*, 1086 (Domesday Book)
MEANING:	Farmstead or village where ash-trees grow
DERIVATION:	From the Old English word *æsc* (ash-tree), plus the Old Scandinavian word *bý* (farmstead, village or settlement). The *Magna* affix derives from the Latin for "great", as opposed to *Parva* (little).

Ashby Magna Church: St Mary's

St Mary's church was built in around 1220 by Robert Esseby – a family who took their surname from the place that they owned, but who were also descendants of William Peveril, one of William I's illegitimate sons. The church has been much restored and therefore the only 13th century remains can be found in the north aisle and arcade along with a medieval piscina in the chancel. The tower dates from the 14th century, while the nave was restored in 1860 and the chancel in 1907. Interestingly, this latter restoration included tiles embossed with the City of Cardiff's motif!

Ashby Magna Historic Trivia: Population and Railway

Ashby Magna – as its name suggests – was large by medieval standards, with a constant population of between 300 and 400 and is therefore unusual in not having expanded at all, with the 2011 census listing the population as 294. Meanwhile, the late 19th century saw the village provided with a station on the Great Central Railway. Completed in 1899, the GCR was the last main line to be constructed from the north of England to London. Ashby Magna's station comprised a single island platform with tracks on either side, with access provided by a stairway which led down from the road bridge on Station Road. The GCR later became part of the London and North Eastern Railway in 1923, while following the nationalisation of British Rail in 1948, the station passed to BR's London Midland Region. It was then closed by the British Railways Board in 1969. Little of it remains today, since the construction of the M1 motorway to the east of the station resulted in the demolition of the stationmaster's house and the loss of the goods yard.

Ashby Magna Quirk Alert: Crossings

Today, Ashby Magna lies almost as far from the sea as is possible in Britain. It is located near to the North Sea and Bristol Channel watershed, near the crossing of two of Britain's longest Roman Roads (the Fosse Way and Watling Street), near the junction of two of its longest modern motorways (the M1 and the M6), and beside one of Britain's finest former railways (the Great Central).

St Mary's church, Ashby Magna.

View down Peveril Road, Ashby Magna.

NAME (STATUS):	**ASHBY PARVA** (Village)
POPULATION:	233
DISTRICT:	Harborough
EARLIEST RECORD:	*Essebi Parva*, 1086 (Domesday Book)
MEANING:	Farmstead or village where ash-trees grow
DERIVATION:	From the Old English word æsc (ash-tree), plus the Old Scandinavian word *bý* (farmstead, village or settlement). The *Parva* affix derives from the Latin for "little", as opposed to *Magna* (great).

Ashby Parva Pub and Church:
The Holly Bush and St Peter's

Ashby Parva has just the one pub, the Holly Bush on Main Street. Meanwhile, St Peter's church is Grade II listed and dates from the 15th century, although the tower and chancel were restored in the 19th century. The church's oldest possession is its font, dating from Norman times and sporting typical Norman cable moulding below the bowl.

Ashby Parva Historic Trivia:
Counting the Cost

At the start of the English Civil War in May 1642, around one hundred Parliamentarian troops from the Coventry garrison visited Ashby Parva, where they stole horses and then spent three hours availing themselves of "free quarter"; basically, they helped themselves to "meat, drink and provender". Then in 1644 Ashby Parva was re-visited for two days, during which time sixty men from Warwick quartered in the village, led by a Captain Wells. During this time, they consumed "diet and horsemeat" worth an estimated ten pounds, which led the inhabitants to claim back ten pounds from the Warwickshire County Committee in 1646!

Moving forwards a generation, and William Paul was born in Ashby Parva in 1678. He grew up to become a clergyman of some prospect, but alas, he found himself drawn into the Jacobite movement, supporting the Old Pretender (James Francis Edward Stuart). So when the Jacobite standard was raised he joined other sympathis-

The Holly Bush, Ashby Parva.

ers from Lutterworth in what was tantamount to open rebellion. Inevitably, he was captured, tried and sentenced to death for treason. He did actually abjure the Jacobite cause in the hope that it would save him, but when it became clear that it wouldn't, he reverted his stance and took his Jacobite allegiance to the grave.

Ashby Parva Quirk Alert: One of a Kind

Ashby Parva is the home of the Midlands Roller Arena, a purpose-built, international-sized covered skating rink designed for inline hockey and roller sports. Opened in January 2012 on the former grounds of the Ashby Parva Plant Centre, it is the only purpose built inline hockey arena in the UK that is solely for the use of this one sport.

St Peter's church, Ashby Parva.

View down Main Street, Ashby Parva.

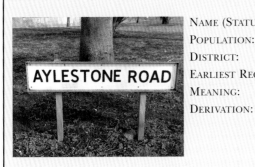

NAME (STATUS):	**AYLESTONE** (Suburb)
POPULATION:	11,151 (Aylestone ward)
DISTRICT:	City of Leicester
EARLIEST RECORD:	*Aileston*, 1086 (Domesday Book)
MEANING:	Farmstead or village of a man called Ægel
DERIVATION:	From the Old English personal name *Ægel*, plus the Old English word *tūn* (farmstead).

Aylestone Pub: The Black Horse

The Black Horse is situated within the Ayelstone Village Conservation Area. It is popular with walkers and cyclists thanks to the fact that it is located just 100 metres from the Grand Union Canal and Aylestone Meadows Nature Reserve.

Aylestone Church: St Andrew's

Although there was almost certainly a predecessor to St Andrew's church, the oldest parts of the current church date back to the 13th century – these being the tower and the north aisle. The large chancel dates from the 14th century and is actually taller, longer and wider than the nave, while the clerestory was added in the 15th century along with the south aisle. However, St Andrew's – which sports a fine figure of the saint above the porch – is more famous as being the location of the marriage of eloping Dorothy Vernon of Haddon Hall.

Aylestone Historic Trivia: Elopement and Cricket

At the time of the Norman Conquest, Aylestone belonged to Alveva, Countess of Mercia, but was shortly afterwards re-apportioned to Norman nobles. By the time of Domesday Book (1086), the manor belonged to Robert de Beaumont, 1st Earl of Leicester. From here, it passed through four generations of his family, eventually ending up with the Pembrugge family of Tong in Shropshire. However, on the death of Fulke de Pembrugge IV in 1409, the manor passed to his wife Isabel and eventually to the grandson of Fulke's sister Juliana, Richard Vernon III. Aylestone then remained in the hands of the Vernon family until the death of Sir George Vernon in 1565.

It is at this point that we find Aylestone's most significant historic trivia, and which is linked to a family who would hold two of the finest manors in the country, Belvoir Castle in Leicestershire and Haddon Hall in Derbyshire and it is all related to the succession of the aforementioned Sir George Vernon. For legend has it that in 1563, Dorothy Vernon, Sir George's daughter and heiress, eloped to Aylestone church where she married John Manners, second son of the first Earl of Rutland. The legend has it that John Manners used to frequently visit Dorothy at Haddon Hall in the guise of a forester, and that the elopement occurred during a

The Black Horse, Narrow Lane, Aylestone.

St Andrew's church, Aylestone.

ball to celebrate her sister's wedding. As it happens, though, the legend was spawned in the 19th century and has since been woven into novel, opera and play. The reality is, that although Sir George may have had her lined up to marry someone else, he clearly forgave her as she inherited Haddon Hall, and through her marriage the estate passed to the ducal house of Rutland and has remained there ever since. Dorothy Vernon and John Manners actually made their home at Aylestone Hall, though, as did their eldest son, George, while the Parish Registers also record the baptisms of John and Dorothy's grandchildren at St Andrew's, too. As for Aylestone Manor, this also remained in the possession of the Dukes of Rutland until June 1869, when the estate was sold by the 6th Duke of Rutland. Alas, much of the medieval fabric of the hall was destroyed during 19th century renovations, although some remaining timber framing has been dated by dendrochronology to 1333-35. The hall eventually became a ladies boarding school in the 19th century, but was requisitioned by the army during World War II. Thereafter, it was purchased by Leicester City Council who turned the hall and grounds into a public park and which were opened in 1954 along with a restaurant and a clubhouse for the local bowling club.

Almost a century after the Vernon-Manners union, the year 1645 saw King Charles I stop at Aylestone Hall during the first siege of Leicester. Of course, back in those times, Aylestone was largely an agricultural settlement, and remained so until the end of the 19th century when the Leicester Extension Act of 1891 incorporated Aylestone into the Borough of Leicester. Meanwhile, between 1875 and 1920, the housing area known as Aylestone Park was developed, and which adjoins Aylestone to the north-east. This resulted in the village population soaring from 450 in 1871 to 2546 in 1881 and 5,381 in 1891.

In the first half of the 20th century, Aylestone Road cricket stadium hosted Leicestershire County Cricket Club. It was first used in 1901 after it was decided that the previous (and current) ground, Grace Road, was too far from the city centre – and which, ironically, is located on the outskirts of Aylestone! During its time, Aylestone Road hosted 401 first-class cricket games, albeit 398 of them before World War II. However, the ground was damaged during the war and was also partially used for industrial development, so when cricket resumed in 1946, Leicestershire returned to Grace Road and have remained there ever since – although Leicestershire did play two Championship matches at Aylestone Road in 1957. Aylestone is also home to Aylestonians RFC, founded in 1921.

Aylestone Quirk Alert: A Unique Name

The aforementioned cricket ground on Aylestone Road is still used for cricket and is home to a sports and social club, while across the road, is Leicester City FC's impressive King Power Stadium … and a few yards up the road is Filbert Street, former home to Leicester City FC from 1891 to 2002. However, the "road" in question that links all of these places is a uniquely named road known as Raw Dykes Road. It is named after the remains of a Roman aqueduct found just to the west of Aylestone Road. The surviving stretch of the Raw Dykes is about 100 metres of linear earthworks comprising two parallel earthen banks with a channel measuring about 6 metres between them, although this stretch is but a fragment of very much larger works. The height of the bank varies between 4 and 7 metres.

Aylestone Old Bridge, an 11-arched 15th century packhorse bridge that crosses the River Soar at Aylestone. Inset: *Part of the earthen banks of Raw Dykes, all that remains of a Roman aqueduct.*

NAME (STATUS):	**BAGWORTH** (Village)
POPULATION:	1472
DISTRICT:	Hinckley and Bosworth
EARLIEST RECORD:	*Bageworde*, 1086 (Domesday Book)
MEANING:	Enclosure of a man called Bacga
DERIVATION:	From the Old English personal name, *Bacga*, plus the Old English word *worth* (enclosure, enclosed farmstead or settlement).

Bagworth Church: Holy Rood

Bagworth's church is known as Holy Rood and various guises of the church have been known as that for centuries. The current incarnation of prefabricated concrete panels was built in 1968 when its Victorian predecessor was demolished following subsidence caused by mining. This, in turn, was built in 1873, replacing all but the tower of its medieval predecessor, a granite-built edifice with limestone dressings, and buttresses banded with red brick and blue vitrified brick. We do still have some insight into that medieval church, though, as in 1848, Holy Rood was described as having a Saxon door and that its walls bore the date 1637. It also consisted of a nave and north aisle, separated by three arches built of local stone while the short tower housed three bells and the church was entered through the south door with its Norman arch.

As for today's church, it consists of a square building of two tiers and a covered walkway which leads to the separate tower which houses two bells. Inside, the nave is, naturally, rather square, and which is accompanied by two "aisles" – all nicely symmetrical, and rather pleasing to the eye.

Bagworth Historic Trivia:
Succession, Railways and Coal

During the early 13th century, Bagworth belonged to the Earl of Leicester but around 1238 it passed to Stephen de Seagrave. By 1347, Robert Holland was lord of the

Bagworth no longer has a pub, but it does have a Bier House! The plaque on the above building states that: "The building and the funeral bier which it houses were gifted by Thomas Morton Bloxsom a local farmer in memory of his wife Lucy, who died on 25th October 1930..." and was for the use of all the inhabitants of Bagworth.

manor, but after his death his wife Maud granted the manor to the Bishop of Durham. By 1474, William Hastings had enclosed the manors of Bagworth and Thornton and built a moated fortified house to the east of the current village after which the area became known as Bagworth Park. During the early 17th century, Sir Bryan Cave owned the manor but in 1629 he owed so much money that the property became forfeit. The manor then came into the possession of Frances Manners who resided there during the English Civil

The southern entrance to Bagworth announcing its Anglo-Saxon name that was also recorded in Domesday Book (1086). The northern entrance to the village has a similar structure but celebrates "BAGWORTH: OVER 160 YEARS OF MINE & RAIL".

Holy Rood church, Bagworth, built in 1968 of prefabricated concrete panels.

War when it was garrisoned for the Royalists with around 50 men. After the fall of Leicester on 31st May 1645, though, the garrison quit Bagworth Park and the house was demolished to be eventually replaced by a farmhouse in 1769.

When the Leicester and Swannington Railway opened in 1832, it passed within half a mile of Bagworth and provided a railway station for the village. The Midland Railway took over the route in 1845 and in 1849, opened a new Bagworth railway station one mile north of the centre of the old village. The new station was re-named Bagworth and Ellistown in 1894 to include the nearby colliery village that had developed following the sinking of Ellistown Colliery in 1873. British Railways eventually withdrew passenger services from the line and closed the station in September 1964.

Meanwhile, Bagworth Colliery had been opened in 1825, and the mining of coal in the village soon saw its population begin to increase. In its heyday of the mid-20th century, the colliery produced more coal per man-shift than any other pit in Europe, and is entered as such in the *Guinness Book of Records*. However, between 1976 and 1984, as coal mining began to decline, one in three people left the village – although this was also partly due to the subsidence that had also claimed the Victorian church. Bagworth Colliery finally closed in February 1991, having survived just long enough to be the last pit in Leicestershire. The other pit within the village boundaries – Desworth Colliery – had been closed seven years earlier.

Bagworth Quirk Alert: A Tale of High Stakes

This tale takes place in around 1707, and was triggered by Matthew Bott, a Bagworth smith who would later be executed at Leicester for forgery. However, on this occasion some iron had been stolen from his shop, and on tracking down the thief, a remarkable set of events began to play out. The thief turned out to be a chap called Glass, who had apparently lived incestuously for many years with his sister. On searching his house for the iron, two children were found in a basket with a cloth sewed over them, and shortly afterwards, two more infants were found. Shockingly, bones of further children were also found … in the dunghill! On discovery of the first children, the sister apparently struck a penknife into her throat and died, while Glass fled the scene, but was believed to have been picked up for theft at a later date and was transported to Australia. The sister was then buried at a crossroads, which was not uncommon for suicides as they were not generally allowed to be buried in churchyards … but at her burial, a stake was also driven through her heart!

Statue of a coal miner in the centre of Bagworth. Inset: *The former pit winding wheel from Bagworth Colliery.*

NAME (STATUS):	**BELTON** (Village); **BELTON-IN-RUTLAND** (Village)
POPULATION:	734; 348
DISTRICT:	North West Leicestershire; Rutland
EARLIEST RECORD:	**LEI:** *Beltona,* c.1125; **RUT:** *Belton,* late 11th century; *Bealton,* 1167; *Belton-in-Rutland,* 1982 (to distinguish from Belton, Leicestershire)
MEANING:	"Farmstead in a glade or on dry ground in a marsh" or "farmstead near a beacon or funeral pyre"
DERIVATION:	Either from the Old English words *bel* (glade or dry ground in marsh) and *tūn* (farmstead) or from the Old English words *bēl* (fire, funeral pyre or beacon) and *tūn*.

Belton Pubs: The Queens Head and The Sun Inn

The Queens Head at the Leicestershire Belton is a former coaching inn built in the early 18th century, but has been trading as a village pub since the early 19th century. The pub looks out onto the church and also the market place where you will find one of the last remaining maypoles in England. The maypole is still danced around by local children every May Day. Meanwhile, The Sun Inn at Rutland's Belton goes back a further two centuries, having been a coaching inn in the 16th century.

Belton Churches: St John the Baptist and St Peter's

The church at Belton in Leicestershire is known as St John the Baptist. It dates from the 14th century, although its tower and clerestory are from the 15th century, while its font is the oldest element, dating back to the 13th century. The church also contains numerous relics from the nearby Grace Dieu priory, which was a victim of the Dissolution in the late 1530s. The tomb of the priory's founder, Lady Roesia of Verdun, also lies in the church.

St Peter's church at Belton-in-Rutland is slightly older, dating back to Norman times, although the oldest remaining part of the church is the late 12th century south arcade along with a trefoil window in the nave. The font dates from the 13th century and the limestone ashlar tower from the 15th, including its distinctive frieze running along all four sides below the battlements and corbel table. The chancel is also largely 15th century, too, while the west end of the south aisle and much of the south porch date from the late 16th century. Local tradition has it that

The maypole at Belton, Leicestershire, one of the last remaining in England. Note the Leicestershire fox at the top.

there used to be a north aisle but that this was destroyed by fire in the 14th century.

Belton Historic Trivia: Grace Dieu Priory

A mile south-west of Belton are the ruins of Grace Dieu Priory. The priory was founded by Lady Roesia of Verdun sometime between 1235 and 1241 as a house for Augustinian canonesses, and was dedicated to God, the Holy Trinity and St Mary. Roesia belonged to the family who were lords of Belton manor and she endowed the priory with *"all my manor of Belton … the park, warren and mills"*, as well as the manor of Kirby in Kesteven, Lincolnshire. The priory name originates from its charter of 1241 which describes the priory as *"the church of the Holy Trinity of the Grace of God at Belton dedicated to God and St Mary"* – and hence the moniker *Gratia Dei* or Grace Dieu. As for the canonesses or nuns, they became known as "the White Nuns of St Augustine", a unique order in medieval Britain. Meanwhile, Roesia was initially buried in the priory chapel, but her tomb and effigy were later removed, possibly at the Dissolution, to Belton's church, where it can still be viewed today.

As for the priory, its first prioress was Agnes de Gresley, while John Comyn, Earl of Buchan and the Lord of Whitwick added another 100 acres of land at Whitwick and Shepshed to the priory estates in 1306. By 1377 the priory had 16 nuns, with a hospital for 12 poor people attached. Remarkably, early 15th century ledgers from Grace Dieu survive, detailing rent values, product sales and stock controls – and hence we know that the land at Belton was valued at £21 17s 9d while sale of fish from the mill at Belton brought in £6. By 1535, the priory's net income was £92 per annum

The Queens Head, Belton, Leicestershire.

St Peter's church, Belton-in-Rutland.

but, alas, its days were numbered. Because of its relatively low value, what was seen as a "lesser monastery" actually survived the initial cull meted out by Henry VIIIs Dissolution, but it eventually succumbed in 1538. Rather more pleasingly, around 300 years later, William Wordsworth stayed at nearby Coleorton Hall where he wrote the following verse:

> *"Beneath yon eastern ridge, the craggy bound,*
> *Rugged and high, of Charnwood's forest ground,*
> *Stand yet, but, Stranger, hidden from thy view*
> *The ivied ruins of forlorn Grace Dieu,*
> *Erst a religious House, which day and night*
> *With hymns resounded and the chanted rite."*

After Dissolution, the priory was purchased by John Beaumont who converted it into a private manor house. Ironically, he had been one of the commissioners who had undervalued the property in 1536, thus earning it that two-year reprieve. Whether that was ruthless profiteering we know not. However, Beaumont later became Master of the Rolls in 1550, but was soon found guilty of "abusing his position for gain", and his estates were thus seized by the crown! Beaumont's descendants did actually hold on to the property for another hundred years or so, but by 1696, most of the manor buildings had been demolished, leaving only a

St John the Baptist church, Belton, Leicestershire.

few fireplaces and a set of three Tudor chimneys still standing. Today's ruins include the east end of the 13th century church, parts of the east range, and the exterior wall of the south range. The most impressive feature is the chapter house, entered via a stone arch while several 16th century fireplaces have survived, too.

Finally for Leicestershire's Belton, mention must be made of two of John Beaumont's descendants, another John Beaumont and his brother Francis. For both brothers became published writers and poets and were friends with William Shakespeare and Ben Jonson and both were interred in Westminster Abbey. But it was Francis Beaumont in collaboration with John Fletcher who, after their deaths, would have 52 "Beaumont and Fletcher" plays published.

Moving onto Belton-in-Rutland, and in 1153, a certain Ralph de Freney donated land here to the Priory of St Mary at Brooke. The Freney family owned the manor

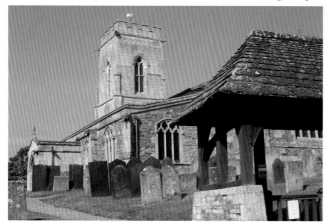

Another angle on St Peter's church, Belton-in-Rutland.

Some of the remains of Grace Dieu Priory, which lies a mile or so to the south of Belton, Leicestershire.

until 1252 when it passed to the Crown and then onto Richard, Earl of Cornwall. In 1270 a William de Blount held the manor and then it passed to the Haselwood family.

In 1776, the village was the victim of a terrible fire which destroyed 27 dwellings. The fire actually reached the church, and even today you can see discolouration from the fire on some of the church's stone pillars. A servant girl throwing out hot ashes at the house now known as Ivydene was thought to have started the fire. A few cottages which remain today on Littleworth Lane are said to be those saved from the fire, hence the name! Moving on to 1942 and a Dornier 217 dropped four large bombs on Chapel Lane, damaging a few houses along with the former pub known as The Black Horse. Amazingly, no one was hurt. Finally, it is rumoured that Charles I rested on the King Stone on Belton's market cross following his defeat at Naseby.

Belton Quirk Alert:
The Ghost of Grace Dieu

Records survive that suggest that during the early years at Grace Dieu, the spiritual state of the priory was questioned! The records don't elucidate, but as a result, a rule was brought into play requiring the nuns of Grace Dieu to never leave the priory precincts!

More recently, the priory has earned a reputation as one of the most haunted places in Leicestershire. Legend has it that a 16th century prioress named Agnes Litherland bore an illegitimate child at the priory. The story goes that her reward was the drowning of her child in the priory fishpond, while she was walled up inside the priory – and thus she still inhabits the ruins, searching for her poor baby. A comprehensive record has been compiled by locals dating back to 1926, with many of the sightings sharing similar traits, often referring to white or grey apparitions, robed, with no hands or feet, hovering or gliding above the ground and appearing on the opposite side of the road to the priory. One other explanation for the so-called "White Lady" is that manifestations such as these are actually rare but naturally occurring phenomenon brought about by fault-lines generating unusual electromagnetic fields. And indeed, research has shown that the site of Grace Dieu Priory is located directly above the Thringstone Fault, while the site is also located close to a standing stone a few yards west of the priory, examples of which are often found close to geological faults or ancient ley lines!

The war memorial, Belton-in-Rutland. Inset: *The house shown nearside has a plaque commemorating the re-naming of Belton to Belton-in-Rutland in 1982 – to differentiate the two Beltons.*

NAME (STATUS):	**BELVOIR** (Village, Vale, Castle, Hunt)
POPULATION:	263 (Belvoir parish)
DISTRICT:	Melton
EARLIEST RECORD:	*Belveder*, 1130
MEANING:	Beautiful view
DERIVATION:	From the Old French words *bel* (beautiful) and *vedeir* (view).

Belvoir Etymological Trivia: No Lodges Here!

As stated above, the word Belvoir is derived from Old French meaning beautiful view. And if you pronounced it in French, it would sound exactly as it looks – *bel–voir*. However, although we English tend to twist pronunciations a little, this one takes top prize – for the locals pronounce the place *bee-ver* – like the oversized rodent! It makes the view not sound quite so enticing or the castle quite so romantic ...

Belvoir Geographical Trivia: Vale of Secrets

As well as its village, civil parish and castle, this whole area of north-east Leicestershire along with a small slice each of Nottinghamshire and Lincolnshire is known as the Vale of Belvoir, and which is now officially classified as an area of natural beauty. It is comprised mainly of sedimentary mudstone and thin limestone, with its south-eastern margin the most clearly defined, as it is formed by a noticeable scarp slope, about 100 metres higher than the valley floor – this being where Belvoir Castle is located. Somewhat remarkably, the Vale of Belvoir used to once play host to the River Trent, which cut a gap through the limestone ridge at Ancaster and then headed eastwards to the North Sea. However, around 130,000 years ago, a mass of stagnant ice left in the vale forced the river to divert north along the old Lincoln River, while it took its present course northwards towards the Humber around 70,000 BC, again following changes brought about by glaciation.

View across the Vale of Belvoir looking west towards Belvoir Castle.

The Vale of Belvoir is also home to two world renowned brands: Stilton cheese, and Melton Mowbray pork pies, with both brands covered by European Protected Designation of Origin orders. And of the six dairies currently allowed to produce true Stilton cheese under the terms of its protected origin status, only one is not located in the area; indeed until the end of the 19th century all Stilton cheese was being produced within 20 miles of Melton Mowbray. That said, Stilton "the village" was located in Huntingdonshire (now Cambridgeshire) where it was served at the coaching inns on the Great North Road. As for Melton Mowbray pork pies, these are produced by traditional methods using uncured pork and hand-formed pastry and served cold.

The Chequers Inn, Woolsthorpe by Belvoir.

The Manners Arms, Knipton.

Finally, the vale is renowned fox hunting country and has many historical ties to the sport.

Belvoir Pubs:
The Chequers Inn and The Manners Arms

The village of Belvoir is too small for a pub, but the Belvoir parish also includes Woolsthorpe by Belvoir and Knipton where you will find The Chequers Inn and The Manners Arms, respectively. Of these two, The Manners Arms is a former hunting lodge built for the 6th Duke of Rutland, but which today is a luxury AA 4-Star country restaurant – and which is still owned by the current Duke and Duchess of Rutland!

Belvoir Church:
St James' of Woolsthorpe by Belvoir

The village of Belvoir doesn't have a church, but once again, the parish has a handful. The nearest is St James' at Woolsthorpe by Belvoir. This Grade II listed church was built of ironstone between 1845 and 1847 by G. G. Place of Nottingham, and replaced an earlier church built in 1793. However, there was an even earlier church here that was burned down in 1643 by the Roundheads during the English Civil War, and only a few stones survive in the old graveyard. Between 1643 and the build of the 1793 church, the Chapel of St Mary served worshippers in the centre of the village.

Belvoir Historic Trivia: Belvoir Castle

Belvoir Castle is a Grade I listed building which occupies a prominent position overlooking the Vale of Belvoir and has been the ancestral home of the Dukes

St James's church, Woolsthorpe by Belvoir.

of Rutland for almost 500 years. Prior to that, Belvoir had been a royal manor until it was granted to Robert, 1st Baron de Ros in 1257. The manor passed to the Manners family in 1508 when George Manners inherited the castle and barony through his mother. His son was created Earl of Rutland in 1525, but it was 1703 before John Manners, the 9th Earl of Rutland became the 1st *Duke* of Rutland. Belvoir Castle is currently the family home of the 11th Duke and Duchess!

As for the present castle, this dates from the early 19th century, and is actually the fourth to have stood on the site since Norman times, with earlier incarnations suffering either complete or partial destruction. These events occurred during the 15th century Wars of the Roses, the 17th century English Civil War – as it had been a notable Royalist stronghold – and finally, due to a catastrophic

The stunning Grade I listed Belvoir Castle.

fire in 1816. The castle was then re-built in its present Gothic style by the wife of the 5th Duke of Rutland who engaged the talents of architect James Wyatt.

Like many other country houses, Belvoir Castle is now open to the public and is *the* tourist focal point of the area, whilst at the same time it remains a family home, albeit now only in one "corner" of the castle. The interior is certainly stunning with its elegant Elizabeth Saloon (named after the wife of the 5th Duke), the Roman-inspired State Dining Room and the delightful Regents Gallery, while the Guard Room, the Old Kitchen and the Bakery provide an insight into a life of service in the 19th century. The castle also contains many notable pieces of art including paintings by Gainsborough, and possesses many outstanding collections of furniture, porcelain, silks, tapestries, and Italian sculpture, too, while the outdoor statue collection terraced into the hillside includes work by Caius Cibber, sculptor to Charles II. Meanwhile, the vast estate of almost 15,000 acres offers the public a range of outdoor activities, including shooting, fishing, quad biking and four-by-four driving. The estate also hosts sheep, duck and dog exhibitions throughout the year.

In recent years the Belvoir name has also become more widely known through the national and international sale of various cordials and other produce, a scheme introduced by the present duke's father to raise funds for the continued upkeep of the castle, and to provide employment in an otherwise farm-dominated local economy.

Finally, several films and television programmes have featured Belvoir Castle, such as the film *Little Lord Fauntleroy* starring Sir Alec Guinness while it also represented Castel Gandolfo as the Pope's summer residence in *The Da Vinci Code*. It also featured in the 1985 film *Young Sherlock Holmes* and 2007's *The Young Victoria* as well as the 2001 Jim Henson production of *Jack and the Beanstalk: The Real Story*, and the 1999 version of *The Haunting*.

Belvoir Quirk Alert: The Birth of Afternoon Tea and a Case of Mistaken Identity

In the 1840s, Belvoir Castle served breakfast in the morning, a light luncheon at midday and dinner between 19:00 and 20:30. And so it was that when the Duchess of Bedford visited, she recognised the need to fill the long hours between luncheon and dinner with additional refreshment. Her preference was for a light meal of tea (usually Darjeeling) and cakes or sandwiches, and she soon began inviting her friends to join her. Thereafter, the concept of Afternoon Tea became quickly established amongst many middle and upper class households!

Meanwhile, in August 2010, Belvoir Castle's website was hacked into by a group of Algerians who removed a number of pages about a quintessentially English stately home and replaced them with anti-Semitic texts in Arabic. Alas, the hackers had mistaken Belvoir Castle for Belvoir Fortress, the ruins of a Crusader fortress in northern Israel that dates back to 1168!

Belvoir Castle gardens.

NAME (STATUS):	**BIRSTALL** (Village)
POPULATION:	12,216
DISTRICT:	Charnwood
EARLIEST RECORD:	*Burstele*, 1086 (Domesday Book)
MEANING:	Site of a stronghold
DERIVATION:	From the Old English word *burhstall* (fortified place or stronghold).
PHOTO:	The symbol of Birstall is a cedar tree as demonstrated left. The original tree stands today in Roman Road, but was once in the grounds of the now-demolished Birstall Hall.

Birstall Geographical Trivia

Birstall is definitely the largest village in Leicestershire, but it has also claimed to be the largest village in England and indeed Europe. This wasn't always the case, though, as the village population was only 611 back in 1901. However, the arrival of the Great Central Railway in 1899 triggered a rapid population expansion and the village had exceeded 11,000 by the turn of the 21st century. The "village" continues to expand today, with major new housing developments in progress. Meanwhile, location-wise, Birstall lies on the northern outskirts of Leicester and is part of the Leicester Urban Area, but does not lie within the area covered by the unitary authority of the City of Leicester.

Birstall Pubs: The Old Plough and The White Horse

The Old Plough is the oldest pub in Birstall, dating back to 1789 and is located on the narrow and quaint Front Street. Just around the corner, and even narrower, is White Horse Lane where you will also find the White Horse Inn. Both pubs are situated close to the River Soar, the Grand Union Canal and on the edge of Watermead Country Park, with the latter a haven for wildlife and a peaceful stretch of countryside comprising over 12 lakes and smaller ponds, wildflower meadows, woodland, grassland and reedbeds.

Birstall Church: St James's

The church of St James's at Birstall dates mostly from the 13th century although an original Saxon window was discovered in the north wall of the chancel during major restoration work carried out in 1869. This clearly demonstrates that a much older church once existed here; the circular font is thought to be pre-Norman, too. Of other interest is the 13th century tower which once supported a steeple, but which was so badly damaged by lightning in 1823 that it had to be removed. As for that 1869 restoration, it was carried out by Sir Charles Gilbert Scott, and involved the re-modelling of the sanctuary and chancel along with an extension to the nave.

In 1926 Birstall became an ecclesiastical parish in its own right, and by this stage, the population of what was now a popular commuter village had increased to such an extent that the church wasn't able to accommodate everyone. However, the Second World War intervened and the 20th century extensions – which involved a new nave and vestries running from north to south at right angles to the original church building – weren't completed until 1963. Nevertheless, the extension increased church seating from 170 to 500 and also brought about a fascinating amalgam of old and new architecture. It was also during this time that a piece of ancient Saxon stonework depicting a heraldic beast was placed in the south wall of the nave, and which has become known in the village as "The Birstall Beast".

Birstall Historic Trivia: Families and Growth

As happened almost unilaterally in Britain, the Norman Conquest of 1066 saw the replacement of the local Saxon lord with a Norman equivalent. Birstall was

The Old Plough, Birstall.

The White Horse, Birstall.

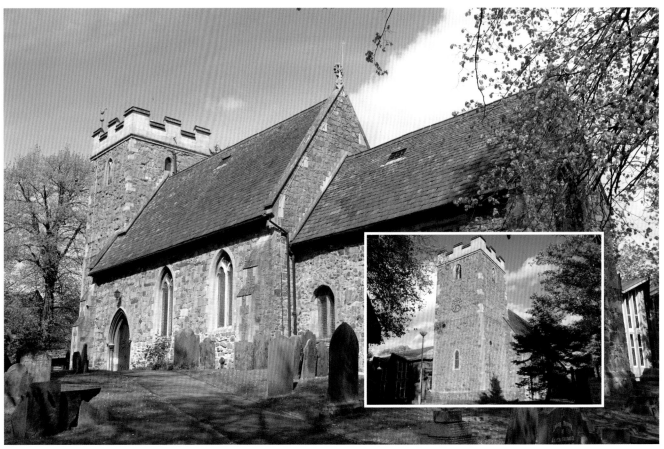

St James' church, Birstall, showing the largely 13th century "old church". Inset: St James' church from the west, showing the 13th century tower alongside part of the 20th century "new church".

no exception, to the loss of poor Alwin Phochestan and the gain of Hugh de Grandmesnil. Over the following centuries the manor passed to various families, including the De La Warres, the Villiers, the Brokesbys and the Giffords. In the 16th century, two families – the Whiles and the Tuffleys – established themselves as landowners in Birstall, and their prominence continued until the early 19th century for the Tuffleys and 1907 for the Whiles when Elizabeth, last of the family, died without an heir. Also prominent were the Sibsons, originally a family of farmers who were first recorded in 1327, and who still have a presence in the village today.

It was during the Gifford tenure in 1751, that Lady Mary Gifford sold the entire Birstall estate of 1000 acres to John Bass, a wealthy Leicester businessman for £21,000. It was Bass who built Birstall Hall alongside the old Leicester to Derby turnpike road, enclosed the fields and modernised the estate's agriculture. By the end of the 18th century, Birstall had become a fashionable place for Leicester businessmen to live while the 19th century saw even more elevated persons setting up residence. These included John Mansfield, a banker, MP, and mayor of Leicester who lived at Birstall Hall, Benjamin Payne, a local politician who was also an estate agent and newspaper owner who moved into Goscote Hall in 1841, and John Coupland, shipping magnate and master of the Quorn Hunt who succeeded Payne at Goscote Hall which he proceeded to expansively renovate. This was the heyday of landed gentry,

but that was all to change in the 20th century as a result of a fall in land values, an increase in wages, and the crippling imposition of death duties. Village folk were no longer tied to their lord of the manor on basic wages, and by 1901 only 4% of the population were agricultural labourers and only one framework knitter remained (there had been 67 fifty years earlier). Instead, the village boasted 45 shoe manufacturers, 11 teachers, 12 market gardeners, 6 managers, 4 commercial travellers and 4 engineers. Others just hopped on the tram to work in factories in Leicester.

However, the biggest changes to the village were brought about by the railways, which actually arrived late in Birstall in 1899, but triggered significant population growth. The Great Central Railway built a station at Birstall and passenger services saw an influx of even more Leicester businessmen and professionals. As a result, new housing sprang up west of Loughborough Road on Birstall Hill, while the 1930s saw the addition of many new semi-detached houses to accommodate Leicester families moving out of 19th century town centre terraces. Conversely, both Birstall Hall and Goscote Hall had to be sold to builders and were subsequently demolished.

Birstall Quirk Alert: Pegasus Parasols

Birstall is also home to a rather unusual Grade II listed building – this being the Red Hill petrol filling station on Loughborough Road. The petrol station is an

Beautiful Birstall buildings.

example of the Pegasus design created by modernist architect Eliot Noyes for Mobil in the mid-1960s. The design comprised six over-lapping circular canopies or parasols, illuminated from below and supported by single slender columns. Each canopy was comprised of 28 segments, meeting at a ring in the middle, and forming the junction between parasol and column, and they originally covered cylindrical steel and black petrol pumps on the garage forecourt, accompanied by a simple brick office and minimal signage other than Mobil's red Pegasus logo. It was designed to be instantly recognisable as a Mobil garage and was used on nearly 20,000 new and refurbished filling stations around the world until the 1980s. The plain edge of the canopy also accommodates the branding for the petrol company which runs the filling station – i.e. BP's green with yellow highlights or Esso's red and white. However, gradual changes in ownership meant that new companies phased out the Mobil design, and so by 2015, as well as receiving their listing status, the six circular canopies and their supports at Birstall are among the last surviving examples in the UK.

Red Hill filling station, perhaps the UK's last Pegasus!

NAME (STATUS):	**BRANSTON** (Village)
POPULATION:	c.150
DISTRICT:	Melton
EARLIEST RECORD:	*Brantestone*, 1086 (Domesday Book)
MEANING:	Farmstead of a man called Brant
DERIVATION:	From the Old English personal name, Brant, plus the Old English word *tūn* (farmstead).

The Wheel Inn, Branston.

Branston Pub: The Wheel Inn

The Wheel Inn dates from the 18th century and is Branston's only pub. As well as its beamed ceilings, it also offers such delights as crispy pig's cheek salad, and pheasant, bacon and prune pie. Now that's a country pub!

Branston Church: St Guthlac

The unusually named St Guthlac church at Branston is Grade II listed, and dates largely from the 13th century, with the steeple added in the 14th century and the clerestory along with further alterations added in the 15th century. The south porch was then added in 1872 and both the chancel and the nave were re-roofed in 1895-96 by local architects George Frederick Bodley and Thomas Garner. However, its oldest possession is its 12th century Norman font, while it also has a stone in the chancel floor that contains an engraved portrait of John Perkyn, a 14th century priest; there are also engravings of bagpipes carved into the 15th century pews situated in the centre aisle. As for St Guthlac (c.673-713), he was a Christian saint from nearby Lincolnshire.

Branston Historical Trivia: George's Porphyria

The most famous person connected with Branston is Francis Willis (1718 – 1807), as he was a 18th century physician, famous for his treatment of George III. After an undergraduate career at Lincoln College, Oxford and St Alban's Hall, he was elected a Fellow of Brasenose College, Oxford in 1740 and was ordained as a priest, but resigned his Fellowship in 1750 when he married Mary Curtois, daughter of John Curtois, Rector of Branston, on 23 December 1749, at Branston church.

However, as well as having been a priest, he also later graduated as a Bachelor and Doctor of Medicine from Oxford in 1759. He then served as a hospital physician in Lincoln, where his success with the mentally ill led to him treating such patients in his own home. So when George III had his first attack of porphyria in 1788 (often referred to as to as "the madness of King George"), Willis was recommended to the Queen by the daughter of one of his former patients.

Branston Quirk Alert: The Final Curtois

Branston's St Guthlac church was subject to a remarkable family connection for 240 years between 1680 and 1920. For on the 16th December 1680, the Reverend John Curtois became the Rector of Branston and held that position until his death in 1719. His son, also John, took over until 1767, after which he was succeeded by his son Peregrine Harrison Curtois, and who held the post until 1814. It was also Peregrine who built the Grade II listed Old Rectory, while the final Curtois in the early 20th century was the Reverend Algernon Curtois.

St Guthlac church, Branston.

Branston Village.

NAME (STATUS):	**BROUGHTON ASTLEY** (Village)
POPULATION:	8940
DISTRICT:	Harborough
EARLIEST RECORD:	*Broctone*, 1086 (Domesday Book); *Broghton Astele*, 1322
MEANING:	Farmstead by a brook
DERIVATION:	From the Old English words *brōc* (brook) and *tūn* (farmstead). The Astley part is a manorial affix from the *de Estle* family, who lived here in the 13th century.

The Bull, Broughton Astley. Check out the pies!

The Red Admiral, also Broughton Astley. Folk music or chess here!

Broughton Astley Pubs:
The Bull and the Red Admiral

Both of these pubs are owned by Everards and their website informs you that Monday night at The Bull is Pie Night. What more does a bloke need to know? Other "Events" listed on the website present a dilemma for Thursdays: live folk music at the Red Admiral, or a curry at The Bull? Or what about Wednesday's: chess at the Red Admiral or Steak Night at The Bull? The answer is obvious, of course: meal at The Bull followed by entertainment at the Red Admiral!

Broughton Astley Church:
St Mary the Virgin

St Mary's is first referenced in 1220, although it is likely that a church had occupied this position as far back as the early 12th century with the existing nave walls potentially dating from then, too. However, the chancel is probably late 13th century, although much of it has since been restored, while the nave, north aisle, tower and clerestory probably all date from the early 14th century. As for the original spire, this dated from the 15th century – although it didn't fare too well, being ruinous by 1771 when it was completely rebuilt along-side extensive re-roofing. The church clock was installed much later in 1887 to celebrate Queen Victoria's Golden Jubilee, while the north porch followed ten years later to commemorate her Diamond Jubilee; the Lady Chapel was then added in 1925. Much of the glass is also 19th century although fragments of 14th century glass can be found in most of the windows in the nave and the north aisle.

Broughton Astley Historic Trivia:
Mergers, Quakers and Murderers

Today, the parish of Broughton Astley consists of the villages of Broughton Astley and Sutton-in-the-Elms. However, the *village* of Broughton Astley is actually comprised of two formerly separate villages: Primethorpe and Broughton. Back in 1086 when Broughton Astley was recorded as *Broctone*, Primethorpe was recorded as *Torp* – meaning "outlying farmstead or hamlet". It wasn't until 1316 that it became known as *Prymesthorp*, with the name now meaning "outlying farmstead or hamlet of a man called Prim", and deriving from the Old English personal name, *Prim*, plus the Old Scandinavian word *thorp*, meaning "secondary settlement, dependent outlying farmstead

The church of St Mary the Virgin, Broughton Astley.

The war memorial in the centre of Broughton Astley.

or hamlet". For completeness, Sutton-in-the-Elms is recorded as *Sutone* – meaning "south farmstead or village" – this being presumably before any elms grew in the vicinity! Anyway, the villages of Broughton Astley (as it became known after the 13th century arrival of the *de Estle* family) and Primethorpe eventually converged in the 20th century, with the latter losing its identity – although until recently there were still pointers to its past, such as Primethorpe Post Office, and which continued to trade with that name decades after the two villages merged. Should the former *Sutone* also succumb in the future, they really ought to preserve all three places in the merged super-village and stake a claim for longest English village name: something like Broughton Astley-by-Primethorpe-with-Sutton-in-the-Elms!

The population of Broughton Astley began to increase significantly in the 19th century when the village became known for framework knitting, climbing from 450 people in 1800 to 1200 by 1900. However, it was the 20th century which saw the real population explosion, culminating in around 9000 inhabitants today, and obviously absorbing Primethorpe along the way.

Moving back to 1647, Broughton Astley was the location of the first public outdoor address delivered by George Fox, the famous Quaker who founded the Religious Society of Friends. Born in 1624 in Drayton-in-the-Clay to a Leicestershire weaver, he travelled throughout Britain as a dissenting preacher and later also undertook tours of Holland and North America. It is thought that his address in Broughton Astley was close to where the two bridges cross the stream and lead onto St Mary the Virgin church.

Finally, we will move forward to 1907, for this was the

year that seventeen year-old domestic servant Annie Haynes was murdered and her body dumped in a ditch at Broughton Astley. Two days later, her boyfriend, Archibald Page from nearby Sapcote confessed to her murder. He had apparently met Annie off a train at Croft (a mile north of Broughton Astley), but then strangled her after they quarrelled before dumping her body in the ditch. Page was sentenced to death, but then had his punishment changed to life imprisonment. Even more fortunate for him, was that he was later offered and took the option of fighting in World War I, and was allowed to go free. Furthermore, he survived the Great War, but when he tried to return to Sapcote, he was "stoned out of the village". It would appear from this juncture that he headed south for West Sussex, married, had children and eventually died aged sixty-two.

Looking towards the two bridges that cross over to St Mary's church. Is this perhaps where the Quaker George Fox addressed his first outdoor assembly?

NAME (STATUS):	**BURLEY** (Village)
POPULATION:	325
DISTRICT:	Rutland
EARLIEST RECORD:	*Burgelai*, 1086 (Domesday Book)
MEANING:	Woodland clearing by or belonging to a fortified place
DERIVATION:	From the Old English words *burh* (fortified place or stronghold) and *lēah* (wood, woodland clearing or glade).

Burley Church: Holy Cross

The church of Holy Cross at Burley is Grade II listed, but because it was declared redundant in 1984, it was taken under the wing of the Churches Conservation Trust in 1988. The church dates from the 12th century, and originally consisted of a nave, chancel and north aisle, with the south aisle added during the 13th century and the tower during the 14th. The church was restored in 1796 when square-headed windows were inserted, and box pews were added. However, it was restored more extensively between 1868 and 1870 by the acclaimed Victorian architect, J. L. Pearson, with the restoration including a rebuild of the entire east end of the church, replacing all but one of the windows, and adding a new porch. Survivors from the 12th century include the north arcade with its Norman-style round arches, while the south arcade is 13th century Gothic with pointed arches.

Burley Historic Trivia: Burley-on-the-Hill Hall

Located alongside the church is the Baroque stately home of Burley-on-the-Hill. The mansion was built in the 1690s by Daniel Finch, the 2nd Earl of Nottingham, who consulted Sir Christopher Wren before commencing the build of what was one of the most ambitious of the late 17th century – an H-plan with a central block and slightly projecting end pavilions, plus symmetrical wings and outbuildings forming a *cour d'honneur* (a three-sided courtyard). Later, in 1778, a new dining room was designed for the 8th Earl of Winchilsea, while in 1908 a fire broke out during a party attended by Winston Churchill, destroying the west part of the house. The mansion was eventually converted into six stunning homes between 1993 and 1998, with a further 22 built on the estate.

Going further back in time, there were two predecessor mansions on this site, and which hosted royalty on several occasions. The early 17th century house, when owned by Sir James Harrington, played host to James I on at least two occasions, including one in 1621 when Harrington commissioned Ben Jonson to write a masque for the occasion. Charles I and Queen Henrietta Maria were also hosted here – see *Burley Quirk Alert* for more on that!

Finally, in the 1920s, the Old Smithy on the village green was used in advertisements for Cherry Blossom shoe polish!

Burley-on-the-Hill Mansion, former seat of the Finch family but recently converted into six exclusive homes.

The centre of the tiny village of Burley.

Burley Quirk Alert: Jigsaws, First Class Cricket and a Dwarf in a Pie!

Holy Cross church also contains a beautiful 1820 memorial by the famous sculptor Sir Francis Chantrey to Lady Charlotte Finch (1725-1813). As well as being the governess to George III's children for over thirty years, Lady Charlotte was also reputed to be the inventor of the wooden jigsaw and dissected maps!

Lady Charlotte's son was George Finch (1752-1826), the 9th Earl of Winchilsea. He lived at Burley Hall in the late 18th century and used its grounds – known as The Park – to stage a number of cricket matches, including six first-class matches between 1790 and 1793 while it also staged a match in 1814 between Rutland and Nottinghamshire. The first first-class match in 1790 was between an all-England team and Hampshire with the fixture repeated the following year. Also in 1791, The Park hosted a match between the Old Etonians and the Marylebone Cricket Club (MCC) while in 1793 England played Surrey there. More recently, the grounds of the mansion has been used for occasional cricket matches, such as that between the Lord's Taverners and a Rutland XI in 1994 to mark the 300th anniversary of the house.

However, Burley's most obscure story revolves around Sir Jeffrey Hudson. Born in 1619 to a tall broad-shouldered drover in the employ of the Duke of Buckingham, Hudson was allegedly still only 18 inches tall by the age of nine. However, he was also perfectly proportioned and the Duchess took to dressing him up in fine silks and satins in their stately home at Burley-on-the-Hill. Then, during a visit from King Charles I and Queen Henrietta Maria in 1626, the climax of the lavish banquet was the presentation to the Queen of a large pie – at which point, Jeffrey burst out of the crust with a flourish, possibly dressed in a miniature suit of armour. The Queen was so taken with Jeffrey that she

decided to keep him in her court. He thus became widely-known as the "Queen's dwarf", as "Lord Minimus" and as "one of the wonders of the age". During his time at court, he was painted by Van Dyck and accompanied the queen's dancing master to her French Court in 1630 where he received £2500 of presents – only to have them stolen by Flemish pirates on his way home!

Probably the victim of congenital hypopituitarism, this certainly didn't prevent Hudson from living a long and extraordinary life. His adult exploits included fighting with the Royalists during the English Civil War where he was made Captain of Horse, fleeing with the Queen to France, but then expulsion from her court in 1649 for killing a man in a duel – this being the unfortunate Lord Crofts who didn't take Hudson seriously and was consequently shot through the head during a duel on horseback. Alas, on his return journey to England, Hudson was captured by Barbary pirates and spent twenty years as a slave in North Africa before being ransomed back to England in 1669 – along with one extraordinary fact: he claimed to have grown to 45 inches during this time, his height allegedly doubling after he reached thirty years of age. In 1676 Hudson returned to London, perhaps to seek a pension from the royal court. However, having been brought up as an ardent Catholic at the court of Queen Henrietta Maria, he had the misfortune to arrive during turbulent times of anti-Catholic activity, which included the "Popish Plot" of Titus Oates – another famous Rutlander of the age. Hudson was thus detained at the Gatehouse prison for nothing more than "being a Roman Catholic", and was not released until 1680. He died about two years later on an unknown date, in unknown circumstances, and was buried in an unknown grave.

NAME (STATUS):	**CLIPSHAM** (Village)
POPULATION:	166
DISTRICT:	Rutland
EARLIEST RECORD:	*Kilpesham*, 1203
MEANING:	Homestead or enclosure of a man called Cylp
DERIVATION:	From the Old English personal name, *Cylp*, plus either of the Old English words *hām* or *hamm* ("homestead" or "enclosure").

Clipsham Pub: The Olive Branch

Historically, the Olive Branch was originally three farm labourers' cottages which were knocked together to make a pub in 1890. For the next 107 years it was a typical village pub at the heart of the community, but was forced into closure in 1997. Fortunately the current owners lovingly restored this traditional village pub, and then added luxury accommodation to move it into a different league, also encouraging a friendly and informal atmosphere with open fires on which chest-nuts are indeed roasted in the winter! As a reward for their hard work, the pub was then awarded a Michelin star in 2008 when it also won the Michelin Pub of the Year award along with The Good Pub Guide Inn of the Year 2008. It has also been the Leicestershire and Rutland Dining Pub of the Year, every year since 2003, with the exception of 2012.

Clipsham Church: St Mary's

The arches of the north aisle of Clipsham St Mary's date back to Norman times, as does its font. It's distinctive broach spire dates from the 14th century and is adorned at its base with castellated battlements, while at three different levels of the tapering spire are sets of four crosses. However, the church's most precious posses-sion is the heraldic glass in the north chapel, and which found its way here from Pickworth All Saints when the

St Mary's church, Clipsham.

church was damaged during the Wars of the Roses. The church is Grade II listed.

Clipsham Historic Trivia: Clipsham Stone

Clipsham is well-known for its limestone quarries and indeed, Clipsham stone can be found in many of Britain's most famous buildings including King's College Chapel, Cambridge, the Examination Schools in Oxford and York Minster. It was also used in repairs to the Houses of Parliament while the earliest recorded use of Clipsham Stone was for Windsor Castle between 1363 and 1368.

The Olive Branch, Clipsham.

Clipsham Quirk Alert: A Hundred and Fifty Shades of Green

The shades in question can be found on Yew Tree Avenue, which largely occupies the former carriage drive to Clipsham Hall – for this 500 metre stretch is now adorned with lots of fine examples of topiary, and which is now maintained by the Forestry Commission. In total there are around 150 shaped yew trees leading towards the 18th century Hall, and which are shaped into birds, animals and many other different kinds of weird and wonderful objects. Many of them are also over 200 years old, and don't seem to be any worse off for having been trimmed in this way since 1870. But before you ask: no, the topiary has no bearing on the village name; that goes back many centuries!

Some of the c.150 examples of yew topiary on Yew Tree Avenue, Clipsham.

NAME (STATUS):	**COALVILLE** (Town)
POPULATION:	5988
DISTRICT:	North West Leicestershire
EARLIEST RECORD:	Coalville, 19th century
MEANING/ DERIVATION	So-named because it was situated where coal mining exploded in the 19th century. Another theory is that the place-name is derived from Coalville House, the home of the owner of nearby Whitwick Colliery – although the house was presumably so-named for the same reasons!

The Vic Bikers, Coalville.

Coalville Pub: The Vic Bikers

Originally called The Victoria, and therefore presumably dating from the second half of the 19th century, this particular pub became a meeting point for bikers from all over the British Isles in the late 20th century, and hence changed its name to the Vic Bikers. The pub has its own Vic Anthem (available with words to sing along to on their website), has its very own *YouTube* video, and is the venue for numerous rock bands throughout the year. However, the annual focal point is the two-day Friday/Saturday festival closest to the June summer solstice, and which is known as The Moxters of Rock – the perfect name for a festival dominated by tribute bands, and a nod to the annual Monsters of Rock festival that was first staged at nearby Donington Park in 1980 and which is now the Download Festival.

The Vic Bikers also hosts numerous other events, like the annual Brass Monkey Run around Charnwood Forest at the beginning of January – plus a number of charity events throughout the year, too. The pub website plays heavily on the fostering of friendship, and it doesn't discriminate, either: Monday night is 3-wheeler night, Tuesday is car club night (any classic make and model), Wednesday is for vintage cars, and Thursday night is bike night, with lambrettas as welcome as Harley Davidsons.

Unsurprisingly, the pub has featured on television programmes, such as *Holiday Showdown* and as Pub of the Week on *The Al Murray Show*, while famous patrons have included England's Rugby Union World Cup-winning captain Martin Johnson, world superbike

champion James Toseland, Chas and Dave, and the Hairy Bikers! In fact, the pub is so unique and famous, that it became the first pub in the UK to be flagged by a brown tourism sign!

Coalville Church: Christ Church

Coalville's parish church is known as Christ Church and, like the town it serves, it dates from the 19th century. The church was built between 1836 and 1838 in the Early English style by the architect H. I. Stevens of Derby, with the chancel added in 1853 and vestries for the clergy and choir added on the north side of the chancel in 1936. Meanwhile, the churchyard contains the gravestone of James Stephenson, the brother of the famous George Stephenson, and who worked as an official at nearby Snibston Colliery. It had once been suggested that the construction of Christ Church was funded by George Stephenson himself, although this theory has been questioned by more recent historians. Also at rest in the graveyard is Amos Clarke (d.1930) who, although blind, was organist at Christ Church for around fifty years.

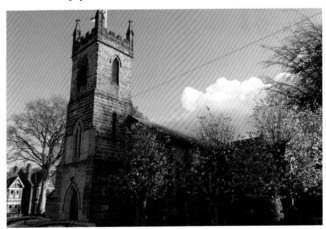

Christ Church, Coalville.

Coalville Historic Trivia: The Railways and Coal … Naturally

As stated above, Coalville only dates from the 19th century thanks to the coal mining industry which exploded in the coalfields of north-west Leicestershire at that time. Prior to that, the area was little more than a few isolated buildings on an east-to-west track known as Long Lane, and which divided the parishes of

Swannington and Whitwick to the north, from the parishes of Snibston and Ibstock to the south. A north-to-south track from Whitwick to Hugglescote crossed Long Lane at the point where the Clock Tower War Memorial now stands, and a few yards from The Red House, one of those very rare 18th century buildings that existed BC – Before Coalville! However, coal had actually been mined for centuries in the area and hence place-names like Coleorton just to the north of Coalville, while traces of ancient mine workings have been found at Swannington where the coal seam is actually at ground level. However, the seam gets gradually deeper as you head south-eastwards towards Bagworth, and this accounts for why this area became such a hotbed of coal mining in the 19th century, as it wasn't until this period that mining technology developed to the point of enabling the sinking of deeper shafts. Deep coal mining was pioneered by local engineer William Stenson, and it was he who sank the first deep shaft in the area at Whitwick in 1824 – and thus earned himself the nickname of the "Father of Coalville". Whitwick was followed by another colliery at Snibston in 1831, and sunk by none other than the great George Stephenson who was in the process of creating the Leicester and Swannington Railway at that time – Leicestershire's first railway. Opened in 1832, it reached Coalville in 1833, opening a small station on the aforementioned Long Lane and which, by this stage, had become Coalville's first street; indeed some of those initial miners' cottages still survive on what is today called Ashby Road. By 1845, the railway had been extended to Burton upon Trent, thus placing Coalville on an important route between Burton and Leicester, while further railways linked the town to Nuneaton and then to Loughborough via the Charnwood Forest Railway.

Other industries such as engineering, quarrying and textiles flourished throughout the 19th century alongside coal mining, and Coalville's population grew exponentially. The darkest moment occurred in 1898, though, as a result of what became known as the Whitwick Colliery Disaster following a catastrophic fire in No. 5 pit. It happened in the early hours of 19th April when there were 42 men working down the mine at the time. Of these, 39 men were the wrong side of the fire, although five managed to escape underneath the fire on the main roadway. That left 34 consigned to their horrible fate, but the number of deaths was 35 because the gallant Charles Clamp returned to the scene to attempt to help his fellow colliers and succumbed himself. There is still a small memorial garden to the 35 on the site of what is today known as the Whitwick Business Park.

Of course, although still strong in the first half of the 20th century, both the railways and coal mining were to suffer in the second half. Both railways to Nuneaton and Loughborough were closed and dismantled while passenger services were withdrawn from the Leicester to Burton line in September 1964 – although it still

The Red House, Coalville, one of very few buildings which pre-date the town!

Coalville Rotary Club.

remains open for freight. Coal-mining survived a little longer, but went the same way as the rest of the country in the 1980s when it became cheaper to import coal from abroad. The Snibston Colliery site has since been developed into Snibston Discovery Park, a museum focused on transport, mining and engineering, plus technology and design, while Whitwick Colliery site has been redeveloped as the Whitwick Business Park.

During the 20th century, Coalville was also the home of the former British toy company, Palitoy. The company manufactured some of Britain's most popular toys of the 20th century, including Action Man, the Care Bears, Tiny Tears, Pippa, and Star Wars figures. Originally founded by Alfred Edward Pallett in Coalville in 1909, his Cascelloid Company produced their first toy in 1920 and the first doll in 1925, whilst the word "Palitoy" was created as a trademark in 1935 for their toy division. Palitoy was sold to General Mills in 1968, but became the Palitoy Company in 1980 when Palitoy, Denys Fisher, and Chad Valley broke away from General Mills. However, it closed as a business only four years later in 1984, and the factory, toy moulds and copyrights were all bought by US toy manufacturer Hasbro from whom they had been a major licensee.

Finally, no great surprise, this one, but the town's motto is *Ex Terra Opres* which means "From the earth wealth".

Memorial Square and the 68ft high Clock Tower which was built in 1925 in memory of those Coalville residents who gave their lives in World War I.

Another memorial in the centre of Coalville, this one to all of its coal miners.

Coalville Quirk Alert: Lies, Damned Lies … and Sacrificial Bells

Poor Coalville features on the www.ilivehere.co.uk website under the "Britain's Worst Places to Live" section, and where there are some depressingly forthright opinions on the locals. Perhaps even more startling is the Coalville statistic for people with "No qualifications" on the North West Leicestershire Council's document under the "Qualifications and students" bullet. On a brighter note, the vicar at Christ Church back in 1936 was certainly a canny man, for this was the year that a certain gentleman called Dr Francis E. Knowles ordered three bells from John Taylor's foundry at Loughborough for his church back in America. Unfortunately, in the interim period, the church was destroyed by a tornado … so the local vicar, no doubt full of heart, persuaded Dr Knowles to donate the bells to Christ Church – which up until then

only had one bell in its tower! As for the vicar in question, his name would perhaps have been more appropriate for the generous Dr Knowles, for he was the Reverend W. A. J. Martyr!

Finally, local legend has it that the 18th century Red House has had something of a bloody history. It is alleged, for example, that in 1799 the landlord, William Wisdom, was shot in the chest and which resulted in the hanging of a sweep from nearby Thringstone. However, several years later, another man confessed to the shooting. It is also asserted that the Red House was once known as The Cradle and Coffin, this based on a tale about a former landlord discovering his wife's infidelity and then murdering both his wife and his child and burying them both in the yard behind the pub. And then during the 20th century, it is known that two Red House landlords also committed suicide on the premises …

NAME (STATUS):	**COSTON** (Village)
POPULATION:	c.75
DISTRICT:	Melton
EARLIEST RECORD:	*Castone*, 1086 (Domesday Book)
MEANING	Farmstead of a man called Kátr
DERIVATION:	From the Old Scandinavian personal name, *Kátr*, plus the Old English word *tūn* (farmstead).

Coston Church: St Andrew's

Coston is dominated by St Andrew's church, which dates back to the 13th century and was built in the Late Norman and Early English style. The tower – or perhaps turret is a better description for this slim structure – still dates from the 13th century, but the spire that it supports is 15th century. Some of the windows date back to the 14th century including one portraying Mary standing at the foot of the cross, while the other interesting feature of the church is a stone frieze of foliage which runs around the south wall.

Coston Quirk Alert:
A Most Melancholy Tragedy

St Andrew's church also contains a brass plaque commemorating Temple Edgecumbe Crozier, the son of the then rector who was tragically stabbed to death, aged only twenty-four, at the end of a play at the Novelty Theatre in London in 1896. This calamitous accident occurred during the last moments of a melodrama called *The Sins of the Night*. It was being performed for the first time (and presumably the last, too), in which an actor called Wilfrid Moritz Franks was playing the part of a Creole called Pablo looking to avenge the seduction and supposed murder of his sister; Temple Crozier was playing a Spaniard, Manuel Ramez, the archetypal villain of the piece. Right at the end of the play, Pablo confronts the goading Ramez and stabs him through the heart, with the words: "I have kept my oath – my sister is avenged – die, villain, die!" He then makes his exit from the stage to rapturous applause. At the time, the audience had no idea that a fatal blow had been struck in real life, as the curtain also fell at that point. It was later revealed that Franks was not using the standard dagger prop but, perhaps out of a young man's vanity, was using a real jewelled stiletto that he had recently received as a gift and which looked more authentic than the shabby prop he had been offered. It was later thought that the two ambitious actors, who were also good friends and had rehearsed the scene many times with the same stiletto, had just become so carried away with their intoxicating performances that Crozier had placed himself into the wrong position at the moment of the dagger thrust. The coroner thus summed up what was "a most melancholy tragedy" and returned a verdict of "Death from misadventure".

St Andrew's church, Coston, demonstrating the fact that the steeple is built more from a turret than a tower!

Approaching the ford at the northern entrance to Coston, and…

…the ford itself.

NAME (STATUS):	**COTES** (Hamlet)
POPULATION:	c.40
DISTRICT:	Charnwood
EARLIEST RECORD:	*Cotes*, 12th century
MEANING	The cottages or huts
DERIVATION:	From the Old English word *cot*, and Middle English plural of *cotes*, meaning "cottage, hut or shelter".

Cotes Pub: Cotes Mill

Cotes Mill is located on the western side of Cotes Bridge over the River Soar. This former 17th century watermill is Grade II listed, but was converted into a pub and restaurant a few years back, while more recently it was converted once again, this time into an English Kitchen Showroom! Back in the day, though, it would appear that anyone unfortunate enough to be taking corn to the mill, and who approached from the north, would have to pay a toll to cross the bridge!

Cotes Mill, a former watermill, then a pub and restaurant, but now a kitchen showroom.

Cotes Historic Trivia: Passengers!

Cotes is a tiny hamlet and very small civil parish a mile or so east of the outskirts of Loughborough. It is thought that the medieval village of Cotes was abandoned, possibly because of plague, although a hall remained at Cotes for several centuries. As for today, the hamlet lies just to the east of the River Soar and is crossed here by Cotes Bridge which takes the A60 away from Loughborough and on towards Nottingham. The bridge has marked an important river-crossing point for centuries, and the current bridge contains the tip of what is thought to be a medieval arch at the eastern end. Certainly, this was the likely medieval route from Nottingham to Leicester and then on to Coventry, so it is likely that it was constructed in the 13th century, although the first written reference to it appears in the early 14th century when its upkeep was the part-responsibility of Garendon Abbey. How-

ever, Nikolaus Pevsner's *Buildings of England* dates the remaining medieval arch to the 15th century, thus suggesting a number of incarnations of Cotes Bridge. Interestingly, a reference to the bridge from 1619 lists it as having thirteen arches, while the rebuild of 1795 had eight arches.

There have also been a number of fatalities relating to travel at Cotes over the centuries, but usually related to flooding rather than the fault of the bridge. This was because the eastern approach to the bridge was three feet lower than the bridge itself, and the approach wasn't raised to the same height until 1880. So before that, even when the road was dry, high-sided vehicles had difficulty negotiating the sharp bend. And indeed, between the years 1713 and 1776, twenty five people buried in Stanford-on-Soar churchyard, were identified simply as "passengers"! Meanwhile, an account from 1830 stated that "one of the twelve or more daily coaches running between Nottingham and London was coming off the bridge towards Cotes, when – although the coachman (an old veteran) had driven many hundred times with safety – the coach swayed in turning the corner, and fell over, killing poor Pearson, the driver". It is also likely that the bridge claimed a few more casualties in 1644, as it was the site of a minor skirmish in the English Civil War known as the Battle of Cotes Bridge, which ended with the Parliamentarians chasing the Royalists through Loughborough and back to their garrison at Burleigh House.

Cotes Bridge, an important crossing point over the River Soar for centuries, and which now takes the A60 over the river.

NAME (STATUS):	**EARL SHILTON** (Town)
POPULATION:	10,047
DISTRICT:	Hinckley and Bosworth
EARLIEST RECORD:	*Sceltone*, 1086 (Domesday Book); *Erle Shilton*, 1576
MEANING	Farmstead on a shelf or ledge
DERIVATION:	From the Old English words *scylf(e)* meaning "shelf of level ground or ledge", and *tūn* (farmstead). The affix stems from its early possession by the Earls of Leicester, whilst the shelf refers to the original village that was perched on top of a hill. Also, and for the benefit of non-football fans, England's most capped player is Peter Shilton. Peter was also born in Leicester, and started his career at Leicester City, therefore the Earl was a *must* for manager of the club in the Shire-Ode – particularly as Leicester also had a striker called Steve Earle in the 1970s, too!

Earl Shilton Church: St Simon and St Jude

The Grade II listed St Simon and St Jude's church was almost completely rebuilt between 1855 and 1856, at a cost of £3500, although it kept its 15th century tower and spire. The rebuild followed Earl Shilton earning parish status in its own right, having been tied to Kirkby Mallory as a chapelry for many centuries prior to that. The former chapel had also gone by a different name, being dedicated to St Peter.

Earl Shilton Historic Trivia: Earls, Kings and a Drunken Curate …

The Earl Shilton area was settled as far back as the Iron Age, when Shilton Hill was a well-known landmark, whilst in Roman times evidence of a pottery industry evolving on Shilton Heath has been discovered. By the time the place was recorded as Sceltone in 1086, though, it was yet another area of land owned by Hugh de Grandmesnil, and had been since 1068 after William the Conqueror had attacked and destroyed Leicester. Later on, the medieval manor at Earl Shilton became the subject of a power struggle between the Grandmesnils and another Norman aristocratic family, the Beaumonts. Subsequent reconciliations through a marriage pledge were betrayed by Robert Beaumont, and when Hugh's son, Ivo de Grandmesnil, died on his crusade to Jerusalem in the early 12th century, Beaumont seized control of most of Leicestershire and dispossessed Ivo's children adding all of the de Grandmesnil estates to his own, including Earl Shilton. Shortly afterwards, Robert Beaumont was given the title of the first Earl of Leicester.

Subsequent Earls of Leicester also featured in royal and political struggles, such as that in the 12th century between Stephen and Matilda, which led to the fortification of Shilton Hill by a later Robert Beaumont in the 1130s. The motte and bailey castle lasted for around forty years before its destruction in 1173 this time due to the Beaumont's opposing the King (Henry II) in yet another royal power struggle.

Moving into the 13th century, and Shilton Park was

St Simon and St Jude's church, Earl Shilton.

created as a hunting estate by Simon de Montfort, 5th Earl of Leicester, and it was he who added the "Earl" affix to village name. Following his death in 1218, King Henry III held Shilton manor and park, before giving it to his son Edmund Crouchback in 1272, as well as making him the next Earl of Leicester and Lancaster. By the end of the 13th century, Edmund had installed Richard de Schulton as Lord of the Manor and he became the first person to actually live and work at the estate.

By the late 14th century, the manor was held by John of Gaunt, the fourth son of Edward III. As for Shilton Park, its forest laws were rescinded in the 1460s by Yorkist King Edward IV, presumably because the land had formerly belonged to Lancastrians, while his younger brother, Richard III, was thought to have passed via Shilton Hill on his fateful march to Bosworth Field in 1485. And sure enough, shortly after his victory at Bosworth, Henry VII reinstated the forest laws for Earl Shilton! His successor, Henry VIII then granted part of the Earl Shilton estate to Trinity Hospital, Cambridge, while land disputes in the manor continued throughout the reign of Elizabeth I, with at least five families claiming a stake.

In the mid-17th century, Earl Shilton found itself embroiled in the English Civil War. Clergymen who openly sided with the Parliamentarians were taken prisoner by the Royalists, while the local curate, William Holdsworth, was hauled before the County Committee in 1646 for "reviling" Parliament. His offences included ignoring the enforcement of puritan reforms, refusing sacraments to those not kneeling, allowing Sunday games and reading a Royalist Protestation in the middle of a sermon. He was also accused of being "several times drunk" and using "old notes as new sermons for the past twenty years"!

The mid-17th century was also the time that framework knitting took off in the area and which continued to flourish into the 19th century. By 1844, there were 650 stocking frames recorded in Earl Shilton while the village was home to numerous shoe, hosiery and knitwear factories and generally thrived as a result. One period of exception, though, was during the American Civil War (1861-1865), when the Northern States blockaded the ports to prevent the export of cotton from the Southern States, and the knock-on effect to Earl Shilton was severe. By World War I, though, business was booming and the village factories supplied the government with thousands of pairs of socks and army boots, as well as providing for the Russian Cossacks, too.

Finally, during World War II there were 192 air raid alerts in Earl Shilton. One of these occasions saw a lone German bomber drop three stick bombs at around 07:00 one morning, after which he opened up his machine gun on those going to work and school. One boy on diving for cover lost his scarf, and when he retrieved it, he found that it contained a bullet hole!

Earl Shilton Quirk Alert: A Genuine Witch, Dangerous Wigs and Peg-leg Watts

In 1776, a woman from Earl Shilton claimed that she had been bewitched by an eighty-year-old woman from Aston. The drama then unfolded as the accuser, her husband and son went mob-handed to confront the frail old woman, threatening to kill her unless she agreed to give the "afflicted" woman a blessing and remove her disorder. And so, under threat from the son's drawn sword, the old lady proceeded with an

Earl Shilton Castle was originally built in the 12th century by Robert Beaumont. It was destroyed around forty years later and replaced with a hunting lodge. Only earthworks remain today in Hall Park alongside the church; the above gateway is a modern replica whilst the remains of the lodge were used to renovate St Simon and St Jude's church in the 19th century.

A nod to Earl Shilton's prolific shoeware industry of bygone days. Shoes were manufactured in Earl Shilton during the 19th and 20th centuries, including at Eatoughs Ltd, founded by Oliver Eatough in 1919, and which made children's slippers and sandals. They also made over 100,000 pairs of slippers for the RAF and the USAF which were attached to electrically heated flying suits for WWII bomber crews. The factory closed in 1989.

exorcism ceremony of sorts before they left her in peace. But, of course, the woman wasn't miraculously cured. And so they returned with many more people, stripped the old lady bare, tied her hands and legs together and threw her into the horse-pond. Thankfully, she didn't drown, at which point the enlightened mob concluded that she must be a genuine witch!

Two years later in 1778, it came to light that a house in Earl Shilton was haunted by a former resident who could not rest in his grave because he had been defrauded in life. The effect was that tables and chairs in the house were said to dance about the room, while pewter dishes jumped off the shelves. However, that was nothing to the alarm caused by the third phenomenon, which was that hats and (even better) wigs had taken to throwing themselves off the heads of their wearers!

Finally, it is recorded that the last ever person to be put in Earl Shilton's stocks, was a man called Peg-leg Watts. There is no more detail than that, but you have to wonder if they were leg stocks…

NAME (STATUS):	**EATON** (Village)
POPULATION:	648
DISTRICT:	Melton
EARLIEST RECORD:	Aitona, c.1130
MEANING:	Farmstead on a spur of land, or on dry ground in a marsh, or on well-watered land
DERIVATION:	From the Old English words *ēg* and *tūn*, meaning "island, land partly surrounded by water, dry ground in marsh, well-watered land, or promontory", and "farmstead", respectively.

Eaton Church: St Denys

St Denys (or St Denis) is the patron saint of Paris, one of seven bishops sent to convert Gaul in around 250 AD. He later became Bishop of Paris, but was martyred in connection with the Decian persecution of Christians. He is said to have picked up his head after decapitation and then walked 6 miles, preaching a sermon along the way – and hence his statue holding his own head outside Notre Dame today. As for Eaton's church, this is made of locally quarried ironstone which lends it a wonderfully warm feel, as it looks out over the beautiful Vale of Belvoir.

Eaton Historic Trivia: Sandstone and Iron Ore

The land surrounding Eaton has at least ten known springs and the village is also close to the source of the River Devon. Historically, an area just outside the village was quarried for sandstone, although that has now long-since closed while iron ore was also mined here, most notably in the 1880s. Between 1885 and 1958, the iron ore was shipped to two local iron works via the Eaton Branch line; indeed, the railway bridge under which the iron was transported still survives in Eaton.

Eaton Quirk Alert: Cats and Robbers

Eaton is one of many places claiming its own beast, this one a black panther courtesy of numerous alleged sightings, and backed up by evidence of dead herons and dead lambs found in trees.

Another older legend of Eaton relates to an organisation known as Ash Tree Operations – this being a band of local 17th century vigilantes formed to tackle criminals who, at that time, found the remote Eaton area to be ripe for loot and even murder. Ash Tree Operations were reputed to have built a huge underground hideout somewhere in the Eaton vicinity to which the entrance was via a hollow ash tree. The vigilantes certainly showed no mercy to anyone found guilty of committing a serious crime. As for today, local legend still has it that if anyone commits a serious crime in Eaton again and gets away with it, the site of Ash Tree Operations will be revealed, the finder will re-create Ash Tree Operations, and the group will track down and mete out justice to the perpetrator!

The Castle Inn, Eaton, along with Eaton Village Store.

St Denys' church, Eaton.

Church Walk, Eaton.

NAME (STATUS):	**EDITH WESTON** (Village)
POPULATION:	1359
DISTRICT:	Rutland
EARLIEST RECORD:	*Westona*, 1113; *Weston Edith*, 1275
MEANING:	West farmstead or village. The "Edith" affix is named after Queen Edith of Wessex (1029–1075), the wife of Edward the Confessor and sister of Harold Godwinson; Edward granted this part of Rutland to Edith.
DERIVATION:	From the Old English words *west* (west) and *tūn* (farmstead or village).

Edith Weston Pub: The Wheatsheaf

The Wheatsheaf is located on King Edward's Way in Edith Weston – the king in question being Edward the Confessor (1042-1066), and the Edith in question, his queen. More recently, the pub has become the lunchtime venue for a number of motorbike trips, including the Wrinkly Run, all organised by the South Lincolnshire and Peterborough branch of the Vintage Motorcycle Club.

Edith Weston Church: St Mary's

St Mary's church is Grade I listed and dates from the 12th century, although the pinnacle-adorned tower and recessed spire date from the 14th century – and both of which justify the inscription in the church:

> *Crown of all the neighbouring lands,*
> *High and lifted up it stands.*

Inside the church, much of it is still Norman, including the chancel arch with fine carvings on its capitals. The north arcade is also Norman, while the south arcade, although early 13th century, retains the Norman style; also 13th century is the arch to the tower. The church is an unusual shape in that it has both a south transept alongside a south chapel with the latter accessed from the chancel, which is also adjoined by an organ chamber and a vestry on its north side. The south

St Mary's church, Edith Weston.

transept and the clerestory probably date from the 14th century, while the chancel was re-built in 1865 along with the south chapel by Slater & Carpenter under the charge of Rev. Charles Halford Lucas – and to whom the reredos by Sir George Frampton is a memorial. The porch was either added or rebuilt in the 18th century.

Finally, the church has some fine memorials including one to Sir Gilbert Heathcote (d.1733), Governor of the Bank of England in the early 18th century. The inscription calls him "a great instrument in founding and governing the Bank of England". He was also Lord Mayor of London in 1711.

Edith Weston Historic Trivia: Aliens

Edith Weston Priory was a small "alien" house of Benedictine monks – "alien" because it was under the control of a religious house beyond English shores; in this case, the parent house was the French Abbey of Saint-Georges, Boscherville. It is thought that the church and manor at Edith Weston were donated to the Abbey in around 1114 by William de Tankerville, and a small cell of monks from Boscherville was set up close to the village at a position now probably submerged beneath Rutland Water. Like all alien houses, control and revenue passed to the crown in time of war with France and it was during one of these periods that the priory closed; certainly by 1394 the church and manor had been sold to the convent of St Anne in Coventry. As for the Prior from 1339-1355, Robert de Cunebaud, he was well-known as a delinquent whose abuses were used to justify widespread suspicion of alien cells!

Edith Weston Hall was built in 1830 in an Elizabethan style for the Rev. Richard Lucas. He was succeeded in 1846 by his son, also Richard Lucas, and High Sheriff of Rutland in 1847 who passed the Hall onto his brother George Vere Lucas, who took the surname of Braithwaite under the terms of a will. His son Major Ernest Lucas Braithwaite (also High Sheriff in 1902) sold the estate in 1904 to his nephew, Stafford Vere Hotchkin. Alas, the hall was destroyed by a catastrophic fire in 1920, so Hotchkin sold the estate lands by auction and then in 1922 sold the hall remains and the park. The hall was eventually demolished in 1954.

Edith Weston Quirk Alert: Submerged and Subsumed

The tiny hamlet adjoining Edith Weston to the north-east is called Normanton. When Rutland Water was created between 1971 and 1975, the handful of houses at Normanton was safe, but St Matthew's church had to be partially submerged. The lower part of the building was strengthened and supported to minimise the water damage so that its upper part could be used to present the story of the construction of the reservoir to the public. However, that still left the question of what to do with the graveyard! The macabre answer was to remove the bodies and cremate them, but to commemorate them with a plaque in St Mary's church at neighbouring Edith Weston. The plaque lists 22 people who were buried here between 1875 and 1966.

The Wheatsheaf, Edith Weston.

Well Cross, Edith Weston.

The church of St Matthew at Normanton, partially submerged between 1971 and 1975 when Rutland Water was created.

NAME (STATUS):	**EYE** (River, Brook, Reservoir)
DISTRICT:	River Eye: Melton; Eye Brook: Harborough, Rutland
LENGTH:	River Eye: 13 miles (21 km); Eye Brook: 10 miles (16 km)
SOURCE:	River Eye: Immediately south of Bescaby
	Eye Brook: Just south-west of Tilton-on-the-Hill
MOUTH:	River Eye: N/A – becomes the River Wreake
	Eye Brook: Confluence with the River Welland
NAME DERIVATION:	From the Old English word *ēa* (river)

An infant River Eye at Coston.

River Eye Geographic Trivia: From Bescaby to the River Wreake

The source of the main branch of the River Eye is immediately south of the tiny hamlet of Bescaby, and flows in front of Bescaby House. At this point, the infant river is only around 7 miles north-east of Melton Mowbray where it will ultimately end after a roundabout 13 mile course. But from Bescaby, the Eye flows east towards Saltby, where it then turns south, flowing past the villages of Sproxton and Coston. At Coston it flows under the B676 and then heads off south-west, past Garthorpe and Saxby. From just south-west of Saxby, the Eye then heads westwards towards Melton Mowbray via Stapleford, Wyfordby and Brentingby, entering Melton at a place known locally as Swan's Nest, and exiting via Egerton Park. A few yards further on, the Anglo-Saxon River Eye then changes its name to the Danish River Wreake! From here, the Wreake flows into the Soar which heads northwards towards the Trent, which ultimately empties into the Humber.

Eye Brook Geographic Trivia: From Tilton-on-the-Hill to the River Welland

The source of the Eye Brook is less than a mile to the south-west of Tilton-on-the-Hill. From here, it trickles under the B6047 and heads off in a south-easterly direction until it reaches East Norton. About a mile east of here, it passes eastwards under the A47 where road and brook divide the Rutland village of Belton-in-Rutland to the north and the Leicestershire village of Allexton to the south. The Eye Brook then begins a 6 mile stretch where it heads south-eastwards, marking the boundary between Leicestershire and Rutland. In the process, it passes the village of Stockerston after which it is damned to form the Eyebrook Reservoir before exiting at the other end and then flowing onto its junction with the River Welland just south of Caldecott.

River Eye/Eye Brook Historic Trivia: Danes and Dambusters

The upper reaches of the River Eye are close to a possible prehistoric site known as King Lud's Entrenchments. It is certainly thought that they may form some kind of territorial border, which is interesting given it lies just inside Leicestershire's county border with

A ford on the River Eye at the northern entrance to Coston.

The River Eye as it passes under the five arches of Lady Wilton Bridge in Melton Mowbray.

Lincolnshire. Today, the county boundary follows the watershed between the River Eye and the River Witham, and is marked by the ancient route-way from south-east England to the north, known as Sewstern Lane or The Drift.

Moving forward to the Iron Age, and the significant hillfort known as Burrough Hill, and which may have been the tribal centre for the Celtic *Corieltauvi* before they moved to Leicester (*Ratae Corieltauvorum*), lies about 6 miles south of the River Eye, and supplies the river with one of its tributaries. There is also evidence of a prehistoric track-way heading north from Burrough Hill to Melton Mowbray, where it then crosses the River Eye and heads north-eastwards towards the Vale of Belvoir.

Many of the villages bordering the River Eye have Danish names, most of them ending in *bý*, which was Old Scandinavian for "farmstead, village or settlement". However, the Eye itself is Anglo-Saxon, deriving from the Old English word *ēa* (river), while a handful of other places along its course such as Sproxton, Coston and Stapleford are also Anglo-Saxon, with the latter meaning "ford (on the River Eye) marked by a post". Perhaps these places resisted the Danish invaders, although it is more likely that their names reverted to their Anglo-Saxon originals after the Danes were finally booted out of Britain for good in the early 11th century. Throughout this time, though, Melton Mowbray was the Eye's main trading centre, and its market is one of very few listed in Domesday Book (1086).

When the Oakham Canal was built in the early 19th century, it stretched from Oakham to Melton Mowbray, and actually canalised a 6-mile stretch of the River Eye from Stapleford to Sysonby. However, in 1844, the Midland Railway bought the canal as part of the agreement to build the Syston and Peterborough Railway – and promptly allowed the canal to fall into disrepair – mainly because the canal was its only transport competitor in the area! Some vestiges of the canal do remain today, but the river has largely reverted to its natural state along this 6-mile stretch.

As mentioned earlier, the latter stages of the Eye Brook are dominated by Eyebrook Reservoir, created between 1937 and 1940 when the Eye Brook was dammed. The reservoir was created by Stewarts & Lloyds to supply water to their Corby steel works (now part of Tata Steel and formerly Corus). During the Second World War it was used in May 1943 to represent the Möhne Reservoir as a practice site for the Dambusters raids. Flying at night, the Lancaster Bombers would swoop down to a mere 60ft above the water and aim for canvas targets placed on top of the reservoir's dam. The operation proved to be a pivotal moment in the war, although 53 of the men who had practised at Eyebrook, died on the night of the raid.

River Eye/Eye Brook Natural History

Much of the land surrounding the Eye Brook is a Site of Special Scientific Interest. Indeed, a report by English Nature considered the river to be one of the most "natural" in the country due to the fact that there is no industry along its 10 mile course and very little human intervention at all. Furthermore, the Eye Brook Community Heritage Project, funded by the Heritage Lottery, ensures that all usage of land around the brook and its catchment is properly documented, as is the management and use of natural resources associated with the brook and its underlying ecology. As a result of its purity, the brook is home to a variety of fish species, including roach, dace and chub, while wild brown trout spawn in its lower reaches.

Similarly, the River Eye in north-eastern Leicestershire flows through gentle rolling countryside, farmland and fields bounded by hawthorn hedges. The farming is largely pastoral, which accounts for the Stilton and Red Leicester cheeses that originally came from the village and farm dairies in the Eye basin.

Eye Quirk Alert: 103

The River Eye lent its name to the UK's first community radio station in 2005. Since then, "103 The Eye" has been broadcasting to Melton Mowbray, the Vale of Belvoir and surrounding areas.

The River Eye as it heads west out of Melton Mowbray where it becomes the River Wreake. Inset: Eyebrook Reservoir at dusk. The reservoir was created between 1937 and 1940 when the Eye Brook was dammed.

NAME (STATUS):	FREEBY (Village)
POPULATION:	244
DISTRICT:	Melton
EARLIEST RECORD:	*Fredebi*, 1086 (Domesday Book); Frieby, 1816
MEANING:	Farmstead or village of a man called Fræthi
DERIVATION:	From the Old Scandinavian personal name *Fræthi*, plus the Old Scandinavian word *bý* (farmstead, village or settlement).

Freeby Church: St Mary's

St Mary's church is a Grade I listed building of iron-stone and limestone ashlar, built largely in the Early English style. The church dates from the 14th century although the aisles were added some time later, and the tower is 16th century and also built of limestone. However, the church has been restored many times throughout its history, largely due to the fact that the hill upon which it sits is not solid rock. Furthermore, as Dr Anthony Streeten, the English Heritage Regional Director states in a brief BBC video: "The foundations of the church are quite simply, crumbling away".

Unsurprisingly, therefore, services haven't been conducted at St Mary's for around fifteen years, and now take place over the road in the tiny United Reform Chapel that dates from around 1880. As for St Mary's church, it would ordinarily seat 200, but the chances of it ever doing so again are slim, due to its small congregation and the sheer cost of repairing something that isn't going to remain intact indefinitely. Following a survey of the church, English Heritage stated that: "The church serves a small community, who have maintained it extremely well over the years, but some of the stonework needs urgent repairs". They acknowledge that English Heritage and the Heritage Lottery Fund provide a scheme of repair grants to places of worship like St Mary's, and in cases like this, they would perhaps be looking to find another use for the church. But looking at it realistically, it is hard to imagine any organisation willing to take on the huge expense that this would incur. As Dr Streeten says: "Ultimately, if all

St Mary's church, Freeby. But for how many more years will it stand here?

avenues have been exhausted, ecclesiastical law requires that the church should be demolished".

Freeby Historic Trivia: In-Despenserble

In the 13th century, the Freeby estate was granted as a manor to Sir Hugh le Despenser (d.1238). His son was another Hugh le Despenser (1223-1265), and the 1st Baron le Despenser. This particular Hugh was an important ally of Simon de Montfort during the reign of Henry III, serving as Chief Justiciar of England from 1260 to 1261 and also as Constable of the Tower of London in 1263, before meeting his death fighting for de Montfort at the Battle of Evesham in August 1265. Continuing the line was his son, yet another Hugh Despenser (1261-1326), and who was also known as

The chapel where Freeby services are now held.

A slightly different angle…for potential posterity!

Hugh Despenser the Elder. This Hugh Despenser became Chief Advisor to Edward II in 1312 but political machinations and exposure of his own corruption led to his exile in 1321, along with his son – yep, you've guessed it – Hugh Despenser (1286-1326) – this one also known as Hugh Despenser the Younger. However, Edward II recalled them both, making Hugh Despenser the Elder the 1st Earl of Winchester. This enraged his queen, Isabella, who subsequently led a rebellion in 1326 against her husband along with her lover, Roger Mortimer. Both Elder and Younger Despenser were captured, and executed. Hugh Despenser the Elder was executed first; he was hung in his armour at Bristol and then beheaded. His body was then cut into pieces for the dogs while his head was sent onto Winchester, which had supported the king. However, the fate reserved for Hugh Despenser the Younger was much more gruesome. It appears that he was particularly hated by Isabella. Clearly a ruthless political player, he earned himself many enemies, but he is also known to have manoeuvred himself into the King's affections. Edward IIs sexuality has been the subject of much historical debate while the Bishop of Winchester was accused of having stated in 1326 that Edward was a "sodomite", the bishop later arguing his innocence by claiming that it was Hugh Despenser the Younger that he was actually accusing. Immediately after his trial, Despenser was dragged behind four horses to his place of execution, where he was stripped naked, and Biblical verses denouncing arrogance and evil were carved into his skin. He was then hanged from a gallows, but was cut down before he could choke to death. One account states that he was then tied to a ladder and had his genitals sliced off, followed by his entrails being slowly pulled out and, finally, his heart cut out. However, most accounts state that he was merely hanged, and beheaded after which his body was cut into four pieces and his head mounted on the gates of London. It is also alleged that both Isabella and Mortimer feasted with their main supporters, as they watched the execution take place!

As for the manor of Freeby, this continued to pass through many families including the Hartopps during the late 16th and 17th centuries. Sir John Hartopp, 3rd Baronet of Freeby, became MP for Leicestershire (1678-1681) and it was he who employed the non-conformist Isaac Watts – he being the writer of many well know hymns such as "O God our help in ages past" and "Jesus shall reign where ere the sun". Watts lived in the village as chaplain to the Lord of the Manor and tutored his children.

Today, all of the properties, except the United Reform Chapel, still belong to the Freeby estate.

Freeby Quirk Alert: Milking It

As mentioned above, St Mary's church is currently unsafe due to structural issues, and therefore services are now conducted over the road in a small chapel. But perhaps not always … because according to the Melton Mowbray Team Parish website, this actually depends upon "the milking schedules of the organist"…

Looking down Sykes Row towards St Mary's church... Inset: *...and further down the road alongside the church.*

NAME (STATUS):	**FRISBY** (Hamlet); **FRISBY ON THE WREAKE** (Village)
POPULATION:	Frisby: 26; Frisby on the Wreake: 557
DISTRICT:	Frisby: Harborough; Frisby on the Wreake: Melton
EARLIEST RECORD:	*Frisebie*, 1086 (Domesday Book) – applies to Frisby (Melton)
MEANING:	Farmstead or village of the Frisians
DERIVATION:	From the Old Scandinavian words *Frísir* (genitive *Frísa*) and *bý*, meaning "Frisians" and "farmstead, village or settlement", respectively. Wreake is an Old Scandinavian river-name meaning "twisted or winding".

Frisby Pub: The Bell Inn

The only pub in the two Frisbys is The Bell Inn on Main Street, Frisby on the Wreake, and which dates back to 1759. Interestingly, the pub website now names it as The Bell & Brasserie, and even offers a description of the new affix: *Brasserie: Noun, – An unpretentious restaurant, tavern, or the like, that serves drinks, especially beer, and simple or hearty food.* Meanwhile, the house today known as the Coach House was an old 18th century coaching inn known as the Black Horse, but closed as a pub in 1974.

Frisby Church: St Thomas of Canterbury

The Frisby in Harborough doesn't have a church, but Frisby on the Wreake has yet another beautiful Leicestershire ironstone church. St Thomas of Canter-

The Bell Inn, Frisby on the Wreake.

The church of St Thomas of Canterbury, Frisby on the Wreake.

bury is also a more common church name than you might think, with most named after the 12th century Archbishop of Canterbury, Thomas Beckett, who was brutally murdered in 1170 in Canterbury Cathedral allegedly on the instruction of Henry II. The church is Grade I listed and was built in stages between the 12th and 15th centuries, while the north aisle was rebuilt around 1820. The oldest part is the base of the tower which is probably Norman, while the most unusual feature is the large south transept.

Frisby Historic Trivia: The Plague and The Cross

The more northerly of the two Frisbys had its name suffixed with "on the Wreake" sometime after Domesday Book, in order to distinguish between the two Frisbys. As for the other Frisby down in the Harborough district, today's hamlet is situated close to the ancient village, which became one of the many deserted medieval villages courtesy of the plague that ravaged England in the 14th century. The ancient village site is now a Scheduled Ancient Monument. Meanwhile, Frisby on the Wreake still has its ancient medieval preaching cross and which later became the village's market cross. It dates from the 13th century when used by the Cistercians or Black Friars from Launde Abbey. The cross has recently moved to avoid traffic damage, with the original site marked, and which also pinpoints a buried time capsule containing various modern artefacts that should be of interest to future generations. Finally, the house today known as Zion House dates from 1715 and was once "an academy for young gentlemen". The tiny cottage attached to the main house is thought to have been the home of a notorious highwayman called George Davenport, who was eventually hanged at Red Hill, Birstall, in 1797.

The 13th century cross in the centre of Frisby on the Wreake.

Glebe Cottage, Frisby on the Wreake, one of the oldest properties in the village.

The Coach House, Frisby on the Wreake – a former 18th century coaching inn known as the Black Horse.

Frisby Quirk Alert: Skinner the Butcher and Leicestershire's Gretna Green

Frisby on the Wreake is also home to Skinner's Yard (*right*), once the location of the local butcher and his slaughter house, but which closed back in 1973. However, the road was named more after the butcher than his occupation, as he was also called Mr Skinner! Meanwhile parts of Glebe Cottage on Church Lane date back to medieval times, with the cottage extended in 1759 by Rev. William Brecknock Wragg. Incumbent between 1756 and 1796, Wragg also took to marrying couples without the obligatory banns, thus earning the village the moniker of "the Gretna Green of the Midlands". That said, both Peak Forest in Derbyshire and Fledborough in Nottinghamshire might question that title, both of which appear in this *Unusual & Quirky* series of books! And like both of those places, folks came from all over the country to be married at Frisby and probably against the wishes of their families, too.

Nevertheless, the number of weddings at St Thomas' was significantly higher during the Rev. Wragg's tenure when compared to earlier and later times!

Finally, the area of Frisby on the Wreake where medieval archery was practiced is still known today as Butt Hole!

The hamlet of Frisby in Harborough. Inset: *Frisby signal box – the only surviving manually operated signal box in Leicestershire.*

NAME (STATUS):	**GLEN PARVA** (Suburb and former village)
POPULATION:	6189
DISTRICT:	Blaby
EARLIEST RECORD:	*Parva Glen*, 1242
MEANING:	The smaller place in the valley
DERIVATION:	From the Old English word *glenn* (place at the valley). The "Parva" *affix* was applied to distinguish the place from Great Glen (aka Glen Magna), which means "the larger place in the valley".
FAMOUS RESIDENTS:	**Sue Townsend** (1946-2014), author; **Tom Ford** (b.1983), snooker player

Glen Parva Geographic Trivia: Absorbed

Formerly a village, Glen Parva was eventually absorbed into the Leicester Urban Area in the 20th century. However, it remains just outside the City of Leicester unitary authority, and is therefore part of the district of Blaby. Meanwhile, the River Sence which runs through the "glen" in question, was once called the River Glene, and probably derived from the Celtic word *glano*, meaning "clean or holy". The name-change to the Sence probably happened in the 16th century with the name first appearing on early maps around 1600. There is a ford over the River Sence at Glen Parva, while the fields around here often flood after heavy rainfall.

Glen Parva Pub: The Glen Parva Manor

Glen Parva Manor can be found just off Little Glen Road on what is known as The Ford, and it is indeed a former manor house. As for its age, documents from both 1240 and 1279 refer to this area as the manor of Glen Parva, but the oldest parts of the current house date from the 15th century.

Glen Parva Church: Glencroft/Blaby All Saints

It is recorded in 1220 that a small chapel stood in the Glen Parva area – probably on the site of what is now Glen Ford Grange. It is likely that in those days, a priest from Aylestone St Andrew's would have taken the services. As for today, the main church in the area is the modern 20th century, brick-built Glencroft Church on Knightsbridge Road, whilst the nearest traditional parish church is the 13th century Blaby All Saints, just down the road in Blaby.

Glen Parva Manor, a former 15th century manor house but today, one of Leicestershire's most attractive pub/restaurants.

Glen Parva Historic Trivia:
Moats, Bones and Prisons

There is strong evidence to suggest that not only the medieval village of Glen Parva, but an even older settlement was based around the River Sence and the area now known as Glen Ford that lies adjacent to the road called The Ford. Fragments of pottery found near the medieval Moat Site that lies adjacent to The Ford, have been dated to somewhere between 1000 BC and 500BC. Excavations carried out in the 1960s also revealed a cobbled area beneath the moat island and the field outside the moat with further evidence of an oven or kiln and 16 post holes in a roughly circular arrangement. As for the moat itself, it could have been dug anytime between the 13th and 15th centuries, although pottery fragments near the surface were dated to the 13th and 14th centuries. The rather striking post in the centre of the island – and which from a distance looks like a prehistoric standing stone – is reputed to have been placed there by Joseph Knight who lived at the manor house in the 1860s.

In 1866, workmen digging for gravel about a mile north-west of Glen Parva unearthed a perfectly preserved skeleton which was found to be the remains of a Saxon woman, who died in the first half of the 6th century. She became known as the 'Glen Parva Lady', and she is now on display at the Jewry Wall Museum in Leicester – including her actual skeleton, a facial reconstruction made using a cast of the Glen Parva Lady's skull, and a life-sized reconstruction model of how experts believed she would have looked. When discovered, she was also found to be buried with her possessions, most notably a number of brooches which also date to the early 6th century – and these are on display in the museum, too, alongside her skeleton in exactly the same positions as they were found in 1866. However, none of these objects appear to be ecclesiastical and this factor, combined with the fact that the Glen Parva Lady was clearly of an elevated status but was not buried near to any known church sites, suggests that this was a pagan burial.

Thanks to historic records, it is also known that Glen Parva was home to 11 households in 1327 and 14 in 1664, while the first ever census in 1801 records a population of 128 for the village. The late 19th century then saw Glen Parva Barracks opened in 1881 and Glen Parva attain civil parish status in 1884, while the 20th century saw the village extended to include a young offenders' institute – although HMYOI Glen Parva is separated from the main village by the Birmingham to Peterborough railway line and can only be accessed from Tigers Road in South Wigston. Still on the village side of the railway, the Knightsbridge Road estate was originally built as accommodation for the prison officers working at HMYOI Glen Parva, with a footbridge allowing access to the prison over the railway. However, most of those houses are now privately owned, and the footbridge has a locked security gate halfway across.

Glen Parva Quirk Alert: Mole Models

Sue Townsend, the author of the Adrian Mole books grew up in Glen Parva, and it is thought that a number of locations and characters in her books were based on local places and people.

The Moat Site, close to the Manor at Glen Parva. The post in the centre of the "island" is reputed to have been placed there by Joseph Knight who lived at the manor house in the 1860s.

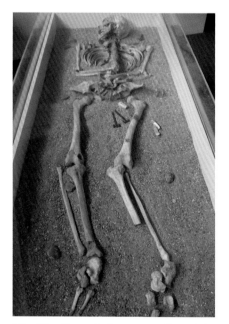

The Glen Parva Lady, now resting at the Jewry Wall Museum in Leicester.

Blaby All Saints' church, just down the road from Glen Parva.

NAME (STATUS):	**GREAT GLEN/GLEN MAGNA** (Village)
POPULATION:	3662
DISTRICT:	Harborough
EARLIEST RECORD:	*Glenne*, 849; *Glen*, 1086 (Domesday Book); *Magna Glen*, 1247
MEANING:	The larger place in the valley
DERIVATION:	From the Old English word *glenn* (place at the valley). The *"Magna"* affix was applied to distinguish the place from Glen Parva, which means "the smaller place in the valley".
FAMOUS RESIDENTS:	**Engelbert Humperdinck** (b.1936), singer; **Trevor Benjamin** (b.1979), footballer

Glen Magna Geographic Trivia

Great Glen is located a couple of miles to the south-east of the Leicester Urban Area and around 6 miles from the City Centre. Derived from the Old English word *glenne*, meaning "valley", the valley in question is that through which the River Sence flows and, rather appropriately, one of Leicestershire's two places called Scotland is located on the opposite side of the valley and river to Great Glen!

Glen Magna Pub: The Pug and Greyhound

The Pug and Greyhound (formerly the Old Greyhound Inn) is a Grade II listed, ex-coaching inn, parts of which date back to the 16th century, although it is largely 18th century. The name also dates back to the 16th century, as the Lords of the Manor from the 1550s to the 1640s were the Nele (or Neale) family, and John Nele's Coat of Arms included the heads of three greyhounds. Back then, the place was probably an Ale House of sorts, but it developed into an important coaching inn during the latter half of the 18th century, thanks to its position on an important route from London to the north (today's A6). The gates to the right of the building led to outbuildings which included stables for the horses and a blacksmith's workshop, and which were converted into seven bedrooms in the 1990s.

Glen Magna Church: St Cuthbert's

St Cuthbert's church was granted to Alcester Abbey in 1140 by Ralph Butler, with control moving to Evesham Abbey from 1465 until the Dissolution of the 1530s; thereafter it belonged to the Crown. The church lost its spire in around 1760, while much of the rest was restored during the 19th century. However, some ancient gems remain, such as its 12th century font, and also the Norman doorway with rare carvings of horses on its capitals, while at the east end of the north aisle are two pre-Norman carved stones, one depicting a mutilated crucifix and the other not so clear, but which has been suggested to portray Jesus healing a blind man.

Glen Magna Historic Trivia: Several Shades of Grey

After the Norman Conquest the manor of Great Glen passed through many hands including the de Zouche

The Pug and Greyhound Inn, parts of which date back to the 16th century, but which really came into its own as a coaching inn during the 18th century.

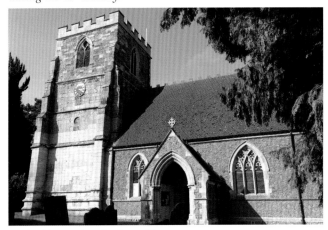

St Cuthbert's church, Great Glen.

and Martell families. It was also to Great Glen, that Henry Grey (1517-1554), became lord of the manor. He went on to become a key part of Henry VIII's court between 1533 and the King's death in 1547, but fell out of favour with Edward VI's government only to re-join the government and become part of the Privy Council in 1549 following a change in the position of Protector of England. Grey then became Duke of Suffolk in 1551, and used his position in Parliament and the Privy Council to push for protestant reforms. By 1553, Edward VI was dying and named Suffolk's daughter, Lady Jane Grey, as his successor. Thus it was that three days after Edward's death on 6th July 1553, Suffolk, the Duke of Northumberland and other members of the Privy Council proclaimed Lady Jane Grey queen. Alas, we all know the rest.

Following the Battle of Naseby in 1645, Great Glen was visited by a number of Parliamentarian soldiers who were pursuing some of the defeated Royalist Cavalry. They were later joined by the rest of the army who camped overnight before moving onto Leicester, but not before they'd camped in the church and broken all of the windows. As for today, there are five road names in the village that mark the events of the English Civil War: Cromwell Road, Naseby Way, Rupert's Way, Edgehill Close and Halford Close.

During the mid-18th century, the A6 was turnpiked through Leicestershire and included a turnpike bridge built over the River Sence at Great Glen in 1751. Naturally, the aforementioned Old Greyhound Inn

The Yews on London Road, Great Glen.

flourished as a coaching inn along with another inn called The Crown. Also built in the 18th century in the Great Glen parish was Stretton Hall, named after nearby Stretton Magna (now known as Great Stretton). The hall was converted into a hospital in 1932 but was closed in the 1990s. Finally, Great Glen Methodist church was built in the centre of the village in 1827, and is now a Grade II listed building, while Leicester Grammar School, founded in Leicester City Centre in 1981, opened a new campus at Great Glen in 2008.

Glen Magna Quirk Alert: K6's and K9's

On Great Glen's village green, you will find an old K6 telephone box and which is now Grade II listed. K6s were designed by Sir Giles Gilbert Scott in 1935, made of cast iron and are the type with a domed roof, and unperforated crowns on the top panels. Meanwhile, the Fernie Hunt (hint: hounds) used to meet on a small field in front of The Old Greyhound up until 1919 – which was the year that Lord of the Manor, Colonel E.C. Packe, left with his regiment for India. However, before he left, he gave the land to the village to be converted into a Village Green along with a War Memorial in honour of the men from the village who died in action during World War I.

Great Glen's pretty village green, complete with war memorial. Inset: *The Grade II-listed K6 telephone box on Great Glen's village green and which dates from around 1935.*

NAME (STATUS):	**GREETHAM** (Village)
POPULATION:	638
DISTRICT:	Rutland
EARLIEST RECORD:	*Gretham*, 1086 (Domesday Book)
MEANING:	Homestead or enclosure on gravel
DERIVATION:	From the Old English words *grēot* (gravel) and either *hām* or *hamm*, (homestead or enclosure).
FAMOUS RESIDENTS:	**John Senescall** (1853-1947), cricketer

The Black Horse.

The Wheatsheaf.

Greetham Pubs: The Plough Inn, The Black Horse, The Wheatsheaf

Greetham boasts three very attractive, stone-built pubs and which all lie within a few yards of each other on the same road. Entering Greetham from the west on the B668, the first pub is The Plough Inn followed by The Black Horse and then The Wheatsheaf, with the latter a Grade II listed building, dating from the end of the 18th century.

Greetham Church: St Mary's

St Mary's church is Grade I listed and still retains some of its original Saxon and Norman features, mainly carvings and mouldings, as well as a 12th century font. However, the tower was rebuilt in the 13th century as was the south wall of the chancel including two lancet windows depicting Matthew, Mark, Luke and John, while the spire, the north arcade and the clerestory date from the 14th century, as do the windows on the north side of the clerestory. The south

St Mary's church, Greetham.

porch was then added in 1673. The church was then restored in 1897 when the south clerestory was rebuilt, but more-or-less everything else was restored and replaced in its original position.

Greetham Historic Trivia: All's Well

It is thought that King Edward I stayed at the Old Manor House in Greetham in September 1290. The house was the hunting lodge of the Earl of Warwick, and was probably situated to the west of the church – although nothing remains of it today. Meanwhile, an ancient well can also be found on Church Lane (*shown right*) and which has the inscription:

> ALL YE WHO HITHER COME TO DRINK
> REST NOT YOUR THOUGHTS BELOW
> REMEMBER JACOBS WELL AND THINK
> WHENCE LIVING WATERS FLOW

Greetham Quirk Alert: The Ram Jam Inn

A little further along Stretton Road from Greetham, and still in the Greetham parish, is The Ram Jam Inn a former 18th century coaching inn on the Great North Road (now the A1). Originally known as the Winchelsea Arms, it was alleged to have changed its name to The Ram Jam Inn by the early 19th century, in line with a local legend. It is probably true that legendary highwayman Dick Turpin was a temporary lodger at the inn, and resided here at around the time he first became notorious. However, it is also said that he once gave a lesson to his landlady, a Mrs Spring, on how to draw mild and bitter ale from a single barrel. The story goes that he told her to "ram one thumb in here whilst I make a hole … and now jam your other thumb in this hole while I find the pegs". At which point, with Mrs Spring trapped with two thumbs in the barrel, Turpin apparently did a

runner without paying his bill! However, an alternative account suggests that another con-man pulled the same trick with the landlord while he had his wicked way with the landlady, whilst a third tale concerns the fact that by the 19th century "ram-jam" was a term that meant both eating to capacity and a place full of people – as in "ram-jam packed".

The Ram Jam Inn.

NAME (STATUS):	**HOTON** (Village)
POPULATION:	353
DISTRICT:	Charnwood
EARLIEST RECORD:	*Hohtone*, 1086 (Domesday Book)
MEANING:	Farmstead on a spur of land
DERIVATION:	From the Old English words *hōh* (heel of land or projecting hill-spur) and *tūn* (farmstead).

Hoton Pub: The Packe Arms

The Packe Arms dates back to the 18th century when it served as a coaching inn on the turnpike road from Loughborough to Nottingham (now the A60). However, its 18th century name was The Marquess of Granby, named after an 18th century Commander-in-Chief of the forces, John Manners, and who was also the eldest son of the 3rd Duke of Rutland. The current name is derived from another prominent local landowning family, this time from the 19th century. And in fact, it was Charles James Packe, of neighbouring Prestwold, who restored The Packe Arms in 1831, and which therefore explains both the change in pub name at that time, plus the inscription in stone above the door which reads: 1831, C.J.P.

The Packe Arms, Hoton.

Hoton Church: St Leonard's

St Leonard's church in Hoton dates back to medieval times although much of it was rebuilt in the 18th and 19th centuries, including the granite chancel which was rebuilt by the aforementioned Charles James Packe in 1834 – interesting that he restored the pub before the church, though! Following Charles James Packe's death in 1837, his son, Charles William Packe, continued the church restoration, taking down the spire, replacing the bells and the clock, while also paying the minister a small salary. It may also have been at this time that the church was re-dedicated to St Leonard – as it had previously been called St Anne's. Anyway, the original 14th century tower of St Leonard's church still survives,

The 14th century tower of St Leonard's church, Hoton, now a private residence.

which must make it a pretty exciting place to live – given St Leonard's church is now a private residence! When the church closed in 1987, many of its contents were given to other churches in Leicestershire, most notably the organ which went to St Michael and All Angels church at Wartnaby while the pews went to St Guthlac's church at Branston. Naturally, the bells went to St John the Baptist church at Belton!

Hoton Historic Trivia: A Packe of Restorers

Although St Leonard's church dates back to medieval times, there was actually a chapel of ease at Hoton that pre-dates it and which is recorded in 1225. Spinning forward four centuries, and the church suffered a much earlier financial crisis than its 20th century counterpart. This one, somewhat inevitably, was due to the English Civil War, and the fact that the Lord of the Manor, Sir Henry Skipwith, was a Royalist. As happened pretty much everywhere else, he had his properties sequestered and hence the church went into decline until the Parliamentarian, Sir Christopher Packe, took over the manor at neighbouring Prestwold in the 1650s. As his 19th century successors Charles James and Charles William Packe were also to do, he oversaw the necessary repairs … although that spirit of community service didn't stop the Packe's from enclosing the local land in the 18th century following the Hoton Enclosure Act of 1760!

Several decades later in 1821, the Packes finally purchased the Manor of Hoton, thanks to Charles James Packe. Many of the Prestwold villagers were rehoused at Hoton, and by 1827, the population of the village included the mandatory farmers and labourers, but they were now joined by a carpenter, tailor, baker, miller, butcher, shoemaker, blacksmith and framework knitters. Twenty years later in 1847, the population had grown to 460 and had been joined by a windmill and a Wesleyan chapel.

Moving into the 20th century, and yet another Packe, Sir Edward, got in on the church restoration act, completely refurbishing it in 1926, while the 20th century also saw the demographic of Hoton change from working class to wealthy middle class.

Hoton Quirk Alert: Grade II Extraordinaire
Joining Wymeswold Road in Hoton from the A60, you are greeted by a most extraordinary unbroken run of Grade II listed buildings on your left-hand side. It starts with the medieval tower of St Leonard's church, which is immediately followed by 1 Wymeswold Road, the three-storyed, three-bayed Hoton House which dates from the 18th century. Next is number 3, another Grade II listed 18th century house, which is followed by four adjoined cottages, numbers 5, 7, 9 and 11, all Grade II listed and including Cobblers Cottage at No 5, and No 11 which demonstrates a beautiful cruck-framed exterior at the building's furthest end. No 11 is then separated from the next building by Hollytree Close, with Holly Tree Farmhouse then immediately continuing the trend, again Grade II listed and late 18th century. Next door to that is the barn to Holly Tree Farmhouse, and which is also Grade II listed but dates back to the early 17th century. And next to that is another Grade II listed property (No 23), that dates from the late 17th/early 18th century. Further outbuildings to Holts Farmhouse are also Grade II listed, while No 28 (over the road) is Grade II listed, too.

WYMESWOLD ROAD: GRADE II ROW

Hoton House, No 1 Wymeswold Road, Hoton, is Grade II listed and dates from the late 18th century.

Next door (No 3) is also a late 18th century, Grade II listed house.

This is the cruck-framed end cottage of numbers 5, 7, 9 and 11.

And this is the early 17th century barn to Holly Tree Farmhouse, and which is also Grade II listed.

NAME (STATUS):	**KEGWORTH** (Village)
POPULATION:	3601
DISTRICT:	North West Leicestershire
EARLIEST RECORD:	*Cacheworde*, 1086 (Domesday Book); *Caggworth*, c.1125
MEANING:	Possibly "enclosure of a man called Cægga or Kaggi",
DERIVATION:	From the Old English personal name, *Cægga* or the Old Scandinavian name, *Kaggi* (meaning red-beard) plus the Old English word *worth* (enclosure, enclosed farmstead or settlement). Alternatively, it might derive from the Old English word *caega* meaning "key" and could thus mean "locked enclosure".
FAMOUS RESIDENTS:	**Thomas Moore** (1779-1852), Poet; **John Kirk**, Social Reformer

Kegworth Pub: The Red Lion and "Friends"

When Ye Olde Flying Horse shut in November 2013, it was the fifth pub to close in Kegworth in around ten years, leaving just three in what is a very large village. Of the survivors, the Red Lion was founded in the 18th Century, although it was known as the Horse and Groom in those days. It also has its own collection of odd trivia, like the fact that it was the meeting place of Lodge 28 of the Nottingham Oddfellows Friendly Society for many years. Its garden also once played host to a real live lion from a visiting circus – although it was: a) in a cage, and b) not red. Finally, troops were actually billeted here during World War II.

The Red Lion, Kegworth, formerly known as the Horse and Groom.

The Anchor Inn can be found at the north-eastern entrance to the village.

Meanwhile the Cap and Stocking is currently in its second incarnation as the current building was built on the site of the original in 1910, while in the original's 19th century heyday, the road itself was called Cap and Stocking Lane and obviously lent its name to the pub. During the 1910 rebuild, the staff used a temporary hut in the garden as a bar while the Landlord, William Pegg Woolley, and his family were housed in a nearby cottage; Woolley's descendants went onto run the Cap and Stocking for another 70-plus years. As for today, the Cap and Stocking is one of very few pubs that still deliver beer out of a jug.

Kegworth Church: St Andrew

Kegworth St Andrew's church is unusual in that its tower, spire, nave, transepts and chancel are all original – each built in around 1370 when the two previous Kegworth manors were united under one Lord of the Manor. In fact, even the panelled font dates from this period, too. Of course, most other churches of this age have undergone a full or part-re-build at some stage in the last 700 years, but the only structural change to St Andrew's occurred in the 15th century when the nave walls were raised to accommodate a clerestory. That said, the 14th century nave roof is home to fourteen carvings of men and women playing a variety of different instruments, but only one of these figures is the original, the rest having been beautifully re-carved

St Andrew's 14th century church at Kegworth.

St Andrew's steeple and chancel rear up behind the Grade II listed Harrison House, once the old Grammar School and with the date 1575 displayed above the door – although the house underwent alterations in the 17th, 19th and 20th centuries.

during the restoration of 1860. Finally, the lower reaches of the tower pre-date everything else and are 12th or 13th century, and clearly part of the previous church.

Kegworth Historic Trivia: Stockings and the Kegworth Air Disaster

Nearby evidence of Anglo-Saxon burials, and a 7th century pin suggest that the Kegworth area was already established as a settlement some 1400 years ago. At the time of the Norman Conquest, the manor was owned by Harold Godwinson, but following his defeat and death at the Battle of Hastings, William I granted it to Earl Hugh of Chester. Kegworth was then granted its market charter in 1290, a somewhat kinder act than the 1555 Act of Parliament, which ordered every man in the parish to work unpaid for four and later six days a year maintaining the local roads!

Spinning forward to the late 18th century and early 19th century, Kegworth became a focal point for the hosiery and lace industries with the local hand frame stockingers becoming renowned for the quality of their silk stockings; indeed, customers included Queen Victoria, the Prince of Wales, the Danish Royal Family and the King of Spain. By the 1890s, a motorbike factory had opened in Kegworth and which was later destined to become Slack and Parr, a leading manufacturer and supplier of advanced engineering products. However,

hosiery didn't survive anywhere near as long with the last socks and stockings being made in the 1940s.

Alas, despite its previous history, the village is most famous for what became known as the "Kegworth Air Disaster". The disaster occurred on the 8th January 1989 when a Boeing 737-400 fell just short of the East Midlands Airport runway and crashed onto the embankment of the M1 motorway near Kegworth. Of the 126 people aboard, 47 died and 74 sustained serious injuries. The plane had taken off from Heathrow bound for Belfast and was at a height of 28,300 feet when a blade detached from the fan of the left engine. The pilots were immediately aware of a problem due to a pounding noise, severe vibrations, smoke in the cabin and a smell of burning, and so the flight was re-directed to East Midlands Airport for an emergency landing. They then made the disastrous decision to turn off the *right* engine, due to confusion over the air conditioning system which had always traditionally fed air into the flight deck from the left engine and into the cabin from the right engine. Unfortunately, the 737-400 operated in a different way to previous versions of the 737 (the 737-400 had only been flown by British Midland for a total of 520 hours at this time). Even worse, on final approach to East Midlands, more fuel was pumped into the left engine to maintain speed, which caused it to fail completely and then burst into flames. The crew desperately tried to restart the right engine, but they

The Hermitage, Kegworth, home to a doctor in the late 20th century who happily co-existed with the house's resident White Lady.

were now flying too slowly for this to work. Just before crossing the M1 motorway, and an agonising quarter of a mile short of the runway, the tail of the 737-400 struck the ground, bouncing it back into the air and over the motorway. It then crashed into the embankment on the western side of the M1 and broke into three sections, knocking down trees and lamp posts as it went. Staggeringly for such a busy section of the M1, no vehicles were taken out by the crashing aeroplane. However, there must have been people on both sides of the motorway who saw it happen and who, presumably, have been haunted by it ever since.

As an addendum to the Kegworth Air Disaster, Nat West Bank at that time used Kegworth as one of their two computer centres on the grounds that it was "low risk and anonymous". Given that the centre was home to some of the most powerful IBM mainframe systems in the UK, the disaster prompted a huge overhaul of banking IT disaster recovery, ultimately leading to a de-centralization of critical functions during the 1990s.

Finally, there is a memorial to the victims of the disaster in Kegworth's village cemetery, and which also includes those who took part in the rescue operation, and who are often unrecognised victims, too.

Kegworth Quirk Alert: Beer-Swilling Foxes, White Ladies and Foul-Mouthed Birds

So, no, this isn't a typical Saturday night out in Kegworth! These are stories from the last century that have become part of local folklore and we return firstly to the Horse and Groom (now known as the Red Lion), in the 1930s. At that time, the landlord owned a pet mynah bird that was renowned for its bad language, so whenever a lady customer came in, the bird had to be removed from the bar so as not to offend sensibilities! Chances are it might work the other way around today. But anyway, sticking with pubs, the former pub known as The Lantern was renowned for poltergeist activities while The Anchor is apparently still the venue for strange goings on, today, as is the aforementioned Red Lion which has its own ghost that is thought, perhaps, to be the White Lady from down the road at the Hermitage. Apparently, the doctor who lived at the Hermitage in the late 20th century co-existed quite happily with the White Lady, who mainly appeared on the landing, her approach signified by the rustle of her skirts. Finally, another former pub, the Fox and Hounds, was home to a pet fox in the 1920s that was free to roam wherever it pleased, but which also had a penchant for customers' beer. One such customer took exception to the beer-slurping fox, and returned later that evening with a large dog which proceeded to chase the fox. The story goes that the chase took both fox and hound up the bar room chimney and neither creature was ever seen again!

Finally, local legend has it that St Andrew's church spire was once fixed by a steeplejack called Wooton who, on completing his task, promptly took out a horn and played a tune whilst sitting at the top!

Memorial in Kegworth cemetery to those who died in the Kegworth Air Disaster.

NAME (STATUS):	**LEICESTER** (City)
POPULATION:	329,600 (City); 509,000 (Leicester Urban Area)
DISTRICT:	City of Leicester
EARLIEST RECORD:	*Ratae Corieltauvorum* AD 50; *Ligera ceastre*, early 10th century; *Ledecestre*, 1086 (Domesday Book)
MEANING:	Roman town of the Ligore people where Ligore is a tribal name, derived from the ancient River Legro (now the River Soar)
DERIVATION:	From the Ligore tribal name plus the Old English word *ceaster* (Roman station or walled town)
FAMOUS PEOPLE:	Too numerous to name here!

The Globe, Leicester.

Leicester Pub: The Globe

There are some great pub names in Leicester, including The Firebug, The Ale Wagon, The Last Plantagenet and The Dry Dock – which is actually a pub inside a boat! However, the pub featured here is The Globe, a very old building that has been serving as a pub since 1720 when quality ales were brewed here using spring water drawn from a well beneath the pub, and which still exists today. Prior to 1720, the building had served as a cattle merchants as well as the final accommodation for women awaiting execution in nearby Gallowtree Gate. And yes, such a history means that the pub has the inevitable haunting, this one a woman on the stairs … although there are also reputed to be two arguing

brothers and a young boy in the cellar who turns off the beer!

Leicester Church: Leicester Cathedral (St Martin's)

Leicester Cathedral has only been known as such since 1927, when the Diocese of Leicester was re-established. Before that it was known as St Martin's and, although most of the church dates from the 13th century to the 15th century, at least two predecessor churches graced this spot; a Norman church built in the 12th century and a Saxon church pre-dating that, also dedicated to St Martin, and which was recorded in Domesday Book (1086). The spire wasn't added until 1757 when it was built on top of the original Norman tower. The current church was then restored in the 1860s by the Victorian Architect, Raphael Brandon. He completely replaced the Norman tower and 18th century spire at this time, as both had become unsafe, and added a new 220ft spire, and a new west window. Today, the cathedral includes three separate chapels dedicated to St Katherine, St Dunstan and St George. The tower contains 13 bells including a peal of 12.

One other landmark of 1927 is that the re-classification of St Martin's as Leicester Cathedral meant that the city regained its own bishop for the first time in over 1000 years – as Leicester's first bishop dates all the way back to 680, when the Saxons installed Cuthwine. For two hundred years, a succession of bishops followed,

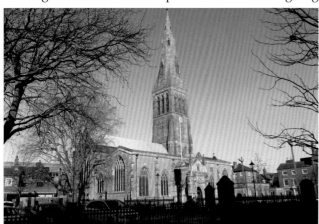

Leicester Cathedral, also known as St Martin's.

The Grade I listed St Margaret's church dates back to the 13th century, and is located at the northern edge of the City Centre.

but it all came to an end in the late 9th century when the invading Danes forced the last Saxon bishop to flee south. Thereafter, Leicester was ruled by the Bishops of Lincoln and later by the Bishops of Peterborough ... until 1927 and the restoration of their own bishop again.

Finally, from 1982 until 2015, the chancel floor of Leicester Cathedral was home to a cenotaph memorial stone to King Richard III. However, that was surpassed in March 2015, following the exhumation of Richard's body in 2012 from a site at nearby Greyfriars. The body was formally recognised as Richard in 2013, and was then reinterred in a new tomb in the chancel of Leicester Cathedral in March 2015.

Leicester Historic Trivia: Leicester Lite

Much of Leicester's history has already been covered in depth in the *Conventional Leicestershire and Rutland* section, therefore, only a couple of historic morsels are included here. So firstly, in the 12th century, Geoffrey of Monmouth wrote in his *Historia Regum Britanniae*, that the city of Kaerleir was founded by a mythical Brythonic king called Leir and, indeed, Leicester's name in Welsh is actually Caerlŷr. It is also thought that Shakespeare's King Lear is loosely based on this story,

Completed in 1800, this impressive Georgian building on Hotel Street was intended to be Leicester's first hotel – and hence the road name. However, the developer ran out of money and the building eventually became the Assembly Rooms, including a ballroom and a coffee room.

The King Power Stadium, home of Leicester City since 2002.

while there is a statue depicting a scene from King Lear on King Lear's Lake in Watermead Country Park on the northern outskirts of Leicester. According to Monmouth, his Leir was supposedly buried by Queen Cordelia in a chamber beneath the River Soar near the city which was dedicated to the Roman god Janus.

In the 19th century, tapping into the expanding railway network was Thomas Cook (1808-1892). By 1841, he had organised the first ever public excursion taking a group of 570 temperance campaigners from Leicester to a rally at Loughborough 12 miles away. Cook then arranged a succession of trips in the Midlands, but in 1845, he undertook his first commercial venture, organising a trip from Leicester to Liverpool, providing tickets at 15 shillings for first-class passengers and 10 shillings for second class. Thereafter, his business went rapidly global.

The railways also fuelled industry in Leicester, and a large proportion of its rapidly exploding population were employed in hosiery, textiles and footwear. During this period, local manufacturers such as N. Corah & Sons and the Cooperative Boot and Shoe Company were opening some of the largest manufacturing premises in Europe with the former the largest knitwear company in Europe. By the end of the 19th century, Corahs had diversified into other lines including the production of football and rugby jerseys and uniforms for the British army, while Corahs' usage of St Margaret as a label for its clothing was courtesy of its proximity to the nearby parish church. By the 1960s, Corahs employed over 6000 workers in its Leicester factories but the subsequent decline of the hosiery industries due to foreign competition eventually saw Corahs closed in the 1990s.

Leicester Quirk Alert: Diversity

When Arthur Mee wrote the *King's England* series of books in the 1930s, his opening sentence for Leicester was: "It stands in the middle of our great Midland county and it would be hard to think of a city more truly English." It is likely, therefore, that Arthur would raise an eyebrow at some of today's statistics. For starters, around 70 different languages or dialects are spoken in the city, while English is not the "preferred" language of 45% of primary school pupils. This is largely because following World War II, Leicester has continually experienced large scale immigration, and today, immigrant groups make up around 50% of Leicester's population, making Leicester probably the most ethnically diverse city in the United Kingdom and the first to not have a white British majority. Many of the resident Asian population can trace their immigration back to the early 1970s, following Idi Amin's announcement in 1972 that the entire Asian community in Uganda had 90 days to leave the country. Around a quarter of these refugees – between 5000 and 6000 people – settled in Leicester, and by the end of the 1970s a similar number moved from their original locations to Leicester, too.

NAME (STATUS):	**MOIRA** (Village)
POPULATION:	2458
DISTRICT:	North West Leicestershire
EARLIEST RECORD:	*Moira*, 1816 (a relatively modern former mining village)

DERIVATION AND MEANING: Derived from the Irish earldom of Moira, from the County of Down. This is because the 2nd Earl of Moira, Francis Rawdon-Hastings, was also titled as the Marques of Hastings on 6 December 1816, and the Hastings family owned the castle in nearby Ashby-de-la-Zouch. Conversely, the Moira in County Down is very old, dating back to 634 when it was known as *Maighe Rath,* meaning "plain of wheels", and perhaps referring to a meeting of routes.

Moira Church: Methodist Churches

Given that Moira was only founded in the early 19th century, it doesn't have an old church. It did, however, have what are described as "two small Methodist chapels" in 1863 – possibly one Wesleyan and one Primitive. It is thought that the Wesleyan chapel is probably the current Moira Centenary Methodist church on Measham Road. This is because a "Wesleyan Reform chapel" is also mentioned in 1881, and can be seen on the Ordnance Survey map of 1884, while the Ordnance Survey map of 1961 shows that the 1884 version has been replaced by a larger building which eventually became the Centenary Methodist church. As for 1863's other "small Methodist chapel", it is thought that this might have been the Primitive Methodist chapel on the edge of Overseal, although there is also another Wesleyan Reform church on Donisthorpe Road, too.

Moira History: Earldoms and Coal

Moira derives its name from the Irish earldom of Moira from County Down, this being one of the titles held by the Hastings family of Ashby-de-la-Zouch. This all came about when, following the death of the 10th Earl of Huntington in 1787, the Earldom lay dormant for around 30 years. During this time, the Baronies of Hastings and Hungerford passed to the 10th Earl's sister, Elizabeth, who was married to Lord Rawdon, and this was the chap who was created the first Earl of Moira in Ireland. Their son, Francis Rawdon, assumed the name of Rawdon-Hastings, and succeeded his father as Earl Moira. Already *Baron* Rawdon of Rawdon in Yorkshire, Francis also gained the titles of *Earl* of Rawdon and Marquis of Hastings in 1816.

However, it was the titled name of Moira that was chosen for the rapidly developing coal-mining village of "Moira Town" in around 1811. As for Francis Rawdon-Hastings, he was an outstanding military commander who was appointed Governor-General of India in 1812, and latterly, due to ailing health, Governor-General of Malta in 1824, where he eventually passed away in November, 1826. One final addendum to this part of Moira's story: for in taking that name in the early nineteenth century, it became one of

The Railway Inn at Moira is also one of the venues for the Moira Furnace Folk Festival.

The Rawdon Arms at Moira is named after the 19th century Lords of the Manor.

Wesleyan Reform Church, on Donisthorpe Road, Moira.

just a handful of places in England ending with the letter "a".

It was also Francis Rawdon-Hastings who lent the first half of his surname to the nearby local colliery, initially sunk in 1821. Rawdon Colliery went on to be worked until the 1990s when it finally ran out of viable coal seams, having survived the extensive pit culls of the 1980s. Historically, although a plan of the district from the 1770s shows seven pits in the Moira area, coal had been mined here for many centuries before then; indeed in the 13th century, tithes of coal had been granted by Isabella de Hastings to the Convent of Breedon. However, it was the construction of the Ashby Canal between 1794 and 1804 that provided the biggest boost to Moira's coalfields. Built to link the collieries of north-west Leicestershire with the Coventry Canal at Bedworth, it thus linked what was to become Rawdon Colliery with the expanding country-

Memorial in Moira to the miners of Rawdon Colliery.

Moira's memorial to those local miners who were killed in action during World War I.

wide canal network. This included links to the ports of Liverpool and Hull via the Coventry Canal link to the Trent and Mersey Canal at Fradley Junction, and ultimately to London via the Coventry Canal, Oxford Canal and the Grand Union Canal. 1804 was also the year that the Double Pits were sunk at Moira and which were followed shortly afterwards by the Furnace Pits, the latter forming the deepest mines at a depth of 603 feet. By 1815, "Moira Coal" was introduced to the London market via an article in *The Times* and which commenced with: *"Those who are curious in the truly English blessing of Coals, and give attention to domestic comfort and economy, would do well at this season*

Moira Furnace, a restored 19th century blast furnace that was originally built by the Earl of Moira in 1804, and which is located alongside the Ashby Canal. One of the best-preserved examples in Britain, the site also includes a museum featuring lime kilns and craft workshops.

to attend to a new quality of coal found in Leicestershire at Ashby-de-la-Zouch and called Moira Coal, being found on the estate of the Nobleman of that Title". It also goes on to state that: *"It will be found a most agreeable and desirable fuel for the Public Office, the study, bedroom, apartment of the sick, hospital, parlour, and drawing room"*, and that it *"requires no attention to keep alight through a long night"*.

In 1846, the Ashby Canal was sold to the Midland Railway Company for £110,000, while 1849 saw the opening of the Leicester, Ashby and Burton Railway, thus connecting the Moira pits with the national rail network via private sidings. By the end of the 1930s, the Moira Colliery Company Ltd included pits at Church Gresley, Reservoir, Rawdon, Netherseal and Donisthorpe, while the Second World War saw them collectively increase their output from 800,000 tons of coal in September 1939 to 1,680,933 tons in September 1944.

Finally, one other benefit delivered by coal mining was the discovery in 1832 of large quantities of salt water around 300 feet from the surface and which were found to contain valuable medicinal properties. This gave rise to the nearby Bath Hotel in Moira which used the salt water to treat sufferers from rheumatic and scorbutic complaints, and which was later extended to the Royal Hotel in Ashby.

Moira Quirk Alert: Moira the Squirrel!

The site of the former Rawdon Colliery is now the

The Marquis Bridge, Conkers Waterside.

home to a family-oriented discovery centre called Conkers, which includes 120 acres of maturing woodlands (part of the National Forest), lakes, ponds and play areas. It is also home to over 100 interactive exhibits, an 18 stage assault course challenge for older children and adults who ought to know better, while children's parties are attended to by Ernest the Badger, Gabriel the Fox, Ashby the Rabbit and Moira the Squirrel, the latter around 5ft 5in tall and with fur that looks suspiciously synthetic!

Conkers Waterside in autumn.

Threes-Up!

	NORTH END	**SCOTLAND**	**SKETCHLEY**
STATUS:	Housing Estate	Hamlet and Village Extension	Former Village, now a Suburb
POPULATION:	North End: c.1000; Mountsorrel: 8223	c.10 and c.60	Sketchley: c.2000; Burbage: 14,568
DISTRICT:	Charnwood	North West Leicestershire and Harborough	Hinckley and Bosworth
EARLIEST RECORD:	20th century	20th century	Sketchley (1564)
MEANING:	Place at the north end (of Mountsorrel)	Named after a farm (NW Leics.) and Scotland Lane (Harborough)	Probably woodland clear ing of an unknown Anglo-Scandinavian chieftain
DERIVATION:	As above	As above	From the chieftain's personal name plus the Old English word *lēah* (woodland clearing).

Three's Up Trivia!

North End is a housing estate at the northern end of the large village of Mountsorrel. In fact, it is wedged in between the large villages of Mountsorrel and Quorn, while a wide arc of the River Soar passes the housing estate to the east. To the west of North End is a granite quarry known as Buddon Wood Quarry, which at 785,400 m², is one of the largest granite quarries in Europe and which produces three million tons per annum; indeed, one of North End's main streets is called Granite Way, and which therefore feels the force of the daily blast which occurs at 12:30 pm on most weekdays!

Meanwhile, the short journey south into adjoining Mountsorrel by way of Loughborough Road and Market Place, offers first a sculpture of a swan, then the

The elegant Grade II-listed Buttercross Market, just south of the point where North End merges with Mountsorrel. It was built in 1793 by Sir John Danvers to replace the 15th century market cross that he had sequestered to his own estate at Swithland 2 miles to the west, and where it still survives today.

Formerly known as the Duke of York, the Waterside Inn at the "North End" of Mountsorrel was built in 1795 after the majority of the River Soar was made navigable. It initially had stabling for 12 horses and a piggery; the stables were converted into a restaurant in the 1960s.

This house in North End, Mountsorrel, was built in 1783 for Ralph Tebbutt, and also provided the model for the Liverpool birthplace and home of William Gladstone. Originally known as Mountsorrel Hall, it was a vicarage until 1983.

Timber-framed house, Burton Overy.

The Bell Inn, Burton Overy.

Swan Inn (*top left, opposite*), then the Grade II-listed St Peter's church and finally the elegant Grade II-listed Buttercross Market. Mountsorrel was also the site of a Rolls-Royce factory from 1945, but when the site closed in 1994, the buildings were demolished and a new housing estate built in its place. Finally, Bond Lane in North End is home to the Stonehouse Family Farm and Motor Museum, with the latter including a collection of 1960s' sports cars.

Meanwhile, the **Scotland** in the Shire-Ode refers to two tiny and separate hamlets in Leicestershire. The

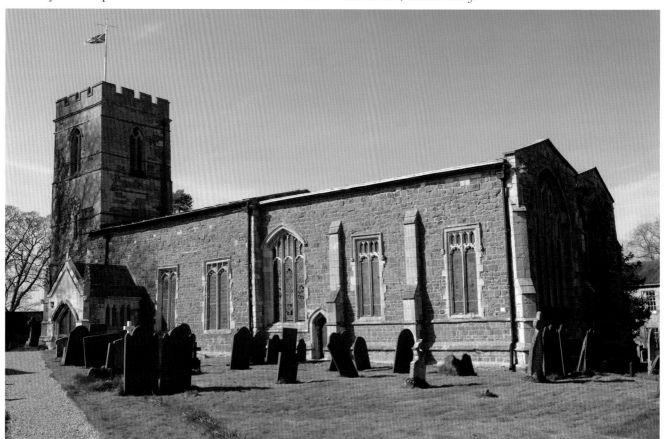

St Andrew's church, Burton Overy, is located next to the southern end of Scotland Lane. The tower is the oldest part of the church and dates from the late 13th century.

first is situated in the North West Leicestershire parish of Staunton Harold, close to the border with Derbyshire and is sited in between Calke Abbey to the west and Breedon on the Hill to the east. This particular Scotland is comprised of two farms on Burney Lane, the first called "Scotland's Farm" and the second a bit further up the road called "Little Scotland Farm". The other **Scotland** is down in the south of the county in the Harborough district. Rather appropriately, it is located a mile or so to the east of Great Glen in the valley of the River Sence. The place is really a northern extension of the pretty village of Burton Overy along Scotland Lane and round Elms Lane, both of which are located just north of St Andrew's church – appropriately named after the patron saint of Scotland! And who knows, perhaps the naming of this area as "Scotland" is the place's first pitch at independence from Burton Overy!

Finally, **Sketchley** is nothing to do with the brand of dry cleaners owned by Johnsons Cleaners UK Ltd., and which dates back to Liverpool in 1817, but is a small south-western suburb of the Leicestershire town of Hinckley, and which is adjoined to the east by Sketchley Hill. Back in the days when Sketchley was a village, it was the birth-place of Edward Taylor (1642-1729), son of a non-conformist yeoman farmer, and who became one of the early American colonists. He emigrated to Massachusetts Bay Colony in 1668 following the Act of Uniformity which had cost Taylor his teaching post. On crossing to America, he began to keep a diary which he also carried forward into his first three years in America, and which was later published. During that period he was admitted to Harvard College as a second year student and, following his graduation in 1671, he became pastor and physician at Westfield, on the remote western frontier of Massachusetts, where he lived until his death in 1729. However, during his time there, he was a prodigious writer, but left explicit instructions to his children that they should "never publish any of his writings". His poetry therefore remained unpublished for more than 200 years, until discovered by Thomas H. Johnson in 1937 (no connection to Johnsons Cleaners, though), who brought to light a 7000-page manuscript of Taylor's poetry in the library of Yale University and published a selection from it in *The New England Quarterly*. Thereafter, the man originally from Sketchley became widely recognised as America's finest colonial poet.

Scotland Lane, "Scotland", Burton Overy. **Inset:** *The top of Burton Overy, looking towards Scotland!*

NAME (STATUS):	**PICKWELL** (Village)
POPULATION:	c.300
DISTRICT:	Melton
EARLIEST RECORD:	*Pichewelle*, 1086 (Domesday Book)
MEANING:	Spring or stream by the pointed hill(s)
DERIVATION:	From the Old English words *pīc* (pointed hill) and *wella* (spring or stream).

Pickwell Geographic and Etymological Trivia

As its etymological name suggests, the village of Pickwell is indeed perched on top of a hill and is also the site of a spring which rises here as the source of a small stream. Located around 5 miles south-east of Melton Mowbray, the village used to have its own ecclesiastical parish, but since the early 20th century it has belonged to the parish of Somerby, a slightly larger village around half a mile to the south-west. Meanwhile, the only pub in the two villages is the Stilton Cheese Inn at Somerby.

Pickwell Church: All Saints

All Saints' church is Grade I listed, and still retains some of its original Norman arches in the nave, with the rest of the arches dating from the 13th century. The clerestory

The Stilton Cheese Inn, Somerby, half a mile south-west of Pickwell.

and one of the chancel windows date from the 14th century while the tower dates from the 15th century.

Pickwell Historic Trivia: Mowbray's and Caves

Pickwell was owned by an Anglo-Saxon called Ordmar during the reign of Edward the Confessor, but by the time Domesday Book was compiled in 1086, the land was owned by a Norman, Geoffrey de Wirce. However, by the early 12th century, the manor had passed to the de Mowbray family and they continued to hold it until the late 15th century. The manor then appears to have been held by the Cave family from around 1532 to 1638, when William Cave sold the manor to Elizabeth Hicks. However, the Caves still lived in Pickwell, as the rector during the English Civil War of the following decade was a certain John Cave, and who also happened to be a staunch Royalist. His reward for that was to be fired at by Roundhead troops while on another occasion they are said to have "dragged him from his pulpit". Such victimisation probably only served to strengthen the Caves' Royalist loyalty, as John's son, William, eventually became chaplain to Charles II.

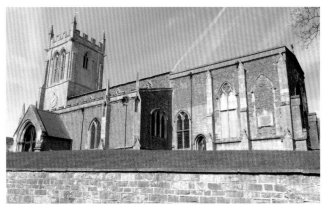

All Saints' church, Pickwell.

View down Main Street towards All Saints' church.

The war memorial in the centre of Pickwell.

NAME (STATUS):	**PRESTON** (Village)
POPULATION:	173
DISTRICT:	Rutland
EARLIEST RECORD:	*Prestone*, 12th century
MEANING:	Farmstead of the priests
DERIVATION:	From the Old English words *prēost* (priest) and *tūn* (farmstead).

Preston Church: St Peter and St Paul

Parts of St Peter and St Paul such as the north arcade of the nave date back to Norman times – around 1150 – while the south arcade is a little later from around 1200. The tower followed in the 13th century which was also when the original chancel was rebuilt; the font also dates from the same century. The clerestory dates from the 15th century. However, all are pre-dated by a carved Roman stone in the south wall!

Preston Historic Trivia: Berewicks and Advowsons

Originally recorded as a bere-wick (an outlying manor, farmstead or hamlet) of Ridlington in Domesday Book (1086), the manor was later held by various members of the de Montfort family, while July 1208 saw a two day visit from King John. Meanwhile, after 1471 the advowson – the right to appoint a nominee to a vacant ecclesiastical post – passed through various families connected to the manor with the Belgrave family the last to appoint a rector.

St Peter and St Paul's church, Preston.

Preston Quirk Alert: Eastern Treasures

The church of St Peter and St Paul is also home to an interesting collection of objects from the Middle East, donated by Lt. Col. J.A. Codrington in 1923. The objects include hanging lamps and some candlesticks from Damascus and a Turkish almsbox with a painting of St George and the Dragon on it. Also present are two pieces of a Turkish marble floor mosaic that originated from the long-since destroyed 5th century St John the Baptist church in Istanbul that was sacked by the Turks when they took what was then known as Constantinople in 1453 as part of the consolidation of the Ottoman Empire. Similarly, there is a piece of Verde Antique that once belonged in the ancient church of St Sophia in Nicaea, from what is also today part of north-western Turkey. Finally, the cypress trees in the churchyard also originate from the Middle East, having been sourced from the Garden of Gethsemane.

Some of the beautiful ironstone houses and cottages in Preston.

NAME (STATUS):	**QUORN or QUORNDON** (Village)
POPULATION:	5177
DISTRICT:	Charnwood
EARLIEST RECORD:	*Querendon*, 1153-89; *Quernendon*, 1209
MEANING:	Hill where mill-stones are obtained
DERIVATION:	From the Old English words *cweorn* (quern or hand-mill) and *dūn* (hill).
FAMOUS RESIDENTS:	**Gordon Banks** (b.1937), legendary England goalkeeper and 1966 World Cup winner; **David Gower** (b.1957), legendary England cricketer; **Hugo Meynell** (1735-1808), legendary father of fox hunting.

Quorn Etymological and Geographical Trivia

As indicated above, this Charnwood village used to go by the name of Quorndon until 1889 when it was shortened to Quorn to avoid postal clashes with the Derbyshire village of Quarndon. As also stated above,

the name means "hill where millstones are obtained", and indeed, granite millstones were quarried here as long ago as the early Iron Age; some of the larger millstones can still be seen in the area today.

Quorn Pub: The Quorndon Fox

The Quorndon Fox is an 18th century inn and restaurant which

The Quorndon Fox dates back to 1740.

The White Horse, established 1769.

dates back to 1740 when it was called The Double Necked Swan. Its name change occurred after Hugo Meynell brought fox hunting to the village later that century, and also reflects the village name prior to 1889. Today, the garden of the pub still contains a square tower, rumoured to be a lookout post so that food could be prepared for approaching guests.

Quorn Church: St Bartholomew's

The Grade I listed St Bartholomew's dates back to the early 12th century when just a chapel stood on the site of today's church and, indeed, elements of the Norman chapel still survive. The most striking survivor is the Norman south doorway with its arch including a double row of chevrons, while some of the stones of Mountsorrel granite in the nave and chancel walls also date back to Norman times, too. The porch that houses the Norman doorway is 13th century while the tower is 14th century. However, the focal point of the church has to be its sublime 14th century Farnham Chapel, built on the south side of the church in 1392 by John Farnham. It is here where you will find numerous impressive monuments to the landowning Farnham family – and who have lived in Quorn for nearly eight centuries; indeed, the chapel is one of very few surviving family chapels housed within a parish church in the country. The chapel is also still owned by the Farnham family today and can only be accessed with the permission of its trustees, access being only through an external door – although you can still see it from inside the church through a partition of railings, while 16th century plaster screens between the arches separate the rest of the chapel from the church. The chapel's most impressive monument is the altar tomb dedicated to John Farnham who died in 1587 and upon which rest the striking effigies of John and his wife Dorothy Walwyn. John Farnham had been one of Elizabeth I's courtiers, but a panel on one wall shows him in armour conducting a siege of musketeers, suggesting that he was a soldier before retiring to Elizabeth's court.

Remarkably, a similarly sized chapel was also built on the north side of the church by the Nether Hall branch of the family, a branch created when Thomas

Farnham broke away from the "old" family. He built his hall on the eastern side of Quorndon and it became known as the Nether Hall, distinguishing it from the seat of the "older" branch of the family who owned what became known as Over Hall. However, when the Nether Hall branch died out in the late 17th century, the north aisle of the church was assimilated into the general church. Then in the late 19th century, the monuments of Nether Hall were moved from the north chapel to the Farnham Chapel – including the afore-mentioned tomb of John Farnham.

Other relics of the church include a 13th century oak chest which was used to store parish records until an 1812 Act was passed imposing the use of iron chests. Finally, in the early 1980s, St Bartholomew's merged with Quorn Methodist church to become St Bartholomew's united church.

Quorn Historic Trivia:
Farnham's and Meynell's

At the edge of the Quorn parish is Buddon Wood, and the quarrying of stone here dates back to the Iron Age, while the Romans continued the quarrying, using the stone for buildings in Leicester.

The first written reference to Quorn is post-Domesday Book when it appeared in the will of Ranulph, fourth Earl of Chester in 1153 in which he donated the "chapel at Quorn" to the Abbey of St Mary in Leicester. And indeed, Quorn was not a parish in its own right until 1868 when Quorndon (as it was then known) became an ecclesiastical parish; prior to then it had belonged to its mother church at Barrow upon Soar.

The Farnham family were first granted land at Quorn in 1243. However, the family effectively split into two in the mid-15th century, with the breakaway faction led by Thomas Farnham going on to inhabit Nether Hall to the east of the parish and the older faction inhabiting Over Hall to the west. A successful lawyer, Justice of the Peace and a King's Commissioner, Thomas Farnham built up a considerable estate, all of which was put at risk by his frivolous son, John, who racked up large debts and ended up having to sell off parts of the estate. Two generations on, and another John Farnham, an ex-

soldier, became a courtier of Elizabeth I. The estate recovered under his tenure with Elizabeth granting him large tracts of land in numerous counties and which had been formerly owned by religious institutions. The recovery was extended by Thomas Farnham, John's younger brother, who had been appointed to the honourable and lucrative position of Teller of the Exchequer, an office that he held under both Edward VI and Mary I. However, Thomas died fairly young, and the estate eventually passed to his brother, Matthew. In 1588 Matthew Farnham gifted Nether Hall and certain lands in Quorndon to his son, Humphrey, but retained for himself the New Hall in Quorndon (later called The Hall on the Green), as well as some lands for his own use. Matthew died in 1594, and when his two Farnham successors died in quick succession, the imposed death duties took their toll and it became necessary to sell parts of the estate in order to stay solvent. By the end of the 17th century, a certain Henry Farnham was in charge of Nether Hall, but his redevelopment of the hall incurred such enormous debts that on his death in 1684 the Nether Hall was left to trustees to sell in order to pay his debts and provide something for his family. The buyer of Nether Hall was George Morton of Sileby, the first of a rapid succession of owners, culminating in Justinian Raynesford who sold it to a certain Hugo Meynell. Of course, Hugo went on to become Quorndon's most famous resident and is commonly known as "the father of fox hunting". He already possessed a pack of fox hounds even before he bought the Nether Hall in 1753 and which by this stage had become known as Quorn Hall. He immediately started fox hunting in the Quorn area, founding the world-famous Quorn Hunt; his hunting country extended from Nottingham to Market Harborough. That said, some sources suggest that the Quorn Hunt had been established as early as 1696, and Hugo Meynell was actually its second Master (from 1753 to 1800).

Anyway, by 1755, Hugo Meynell had completed the build of the necessary stables and kennels for horse and hound, after which he went on to become an exception-ally successful breeder of both. He also pioneered an extended chase at high speeds through open grassland.

Threeways and the White Hart on High Street. Parts of the White Hart actually date back to the 15th century.

St Bartholomew's church, Quorn, with the Farnham Chapel near-side.

Quorn Hall was built by the Farnhams in around 1680, and was home to the famous Hugo Meynell in the late 18th century and, more recently, an international residential education centre run by Leicestershire County Council. However, you can't get anywhere near it for security now, so these former outlying stables are the best I could do!

Quorn and Woodhouse Station, one of four stations on the preserved Great Central Railway which runs between Loughborough and Leicester North.

Borrowing the pioneering breeding techniques of his Dishley neighbour, the sheep farmer Robert Bakewell, Meynell bred a new form of hound that possessed greater pace and stamina and a better sense of scent. He also considerably enhanced the hall around 1790, adding an additional storey and laying large pleasure grounds near the river.

By the time that Hugo Meynell gave up the management of the Quorn Hunt, it had acquired such a national reputation that many sportsmen aspired to become Masters of the Quorn Hunt. Consequently the long list of Masters includes only four Leicestershire men. As for Hugo Meynell, he sold Quorn Hall and his hounds to Lord Sefton in 1800 after his son was killed in a riding accident. Sefton also became Master of the Hunt, as did most of his successors who bought both hall and hunt, until Lord Southampton became Master of the Hunt. When he moved to Belgrave Hall in 1830, though, his successors had no connection with the Hunt, and ran the hall as a girl's school. Therefore when Sir Richard Sutton first became Master of the Hunt in 1847, he rented only the stables and kennels, but after a year or two he bought Quorn Hall and estate and spent considerable sums of money restoring the building. Nevertheless, on Sir Richard's death in 1855, the hall and estate was sold to the firm of Cartwright and Warner. Edward Warner lived at Quorn Hall himself and rented the stables and kennels to Lord Stamford who resided at Bradgate Park and was Sir Richard Sutton's successor as Quorn Hunt Master. When Lord Stamford retired from the Hunt he sold his stud and hounds by auction. It is thought that between 6000 and 7000 people were present, including most of the leading sportsmen in the country and a large number of the nobility, including representatives of the Prince of Wales and the French Emperor, Napoleon III. Thereafter, the Quorn Hunt Masters kept their hounds and horses either in Melton Mowbray or on their private estates, or in the rented quarters at Quorn Hall.

The last Master resident at Quorn Hall was Captain W. P. Warner, and he brought the hounds back to Quorn Hall in 1886. He also made a number of significant improvements to both the hall and the gardens. Then in 1906, new and more modern quarters for the horses and hounds were built at Barrow and this time the Hunt left Quorn Hall for good. With superior facilities for breeding and rearing hounds, the new kennels covered 10 acres, compared with just the 1 acre at pre-1906 Quorn Hall.

When Captain Warner passed away in 1929, the hall was leased to the Quorn Country Club Ltd, and it was soon fully licensed, with full catering facilities and holding dinner dances. Squash and tennis courts were added, as was a billiards and table tennis room but, alas, by 1931 the club had moved to smaller quarters due to economic pressures. Quorn Hall was next purchased by Loughborough College, the intention being to use the hall as a hostel for students, and to rent out the farm, grounds and cottages. However, the Second World War somewhat intervened and the hall became home to the Navy, with an extra storey added to the old wing along with considerable other extensions in 1941. Also established in the grounds of Quorn Hall during Second World War was Quorn Camp, used as a Prisoner of War camp, and which also hosted a number of the US Army 82nd Airborne Division's 505th Parachute Infantry Regiment. These were the paratroopers who helped liberate the town of Sainte-Mère-Église, in Normandy, on the morning of D-Day and included Private John Marvin Steele who famously became caught on the town's church spire.

As for the Farnham family, they continued to live in Quorndon House on Meeting Street right up until 1993, thus having been incumbent as Quorn's local squires for 750 years, while later, Quorn Hall became an international education centre run by Leicestershire County Council. Meanwhile, the Quorn Hunt still claims to be the United Kingdom's most famous hunt and despite the restriction of fox hunting as a result of the Hunting Act 2004, the Quorn continues to go out on four days of the week during the autumn and winter months, covering a wide area of Leicestershire, plus parts of southern Derbyshire and Nottinghamshire, too. There are usually between one hundred and one hundred and fifty mounted followers, plus about twice as many who follow the hounds on foot, plus others with cars and bicycles, while over eight hundred farmers in the area allow the hunt to use their land. With other hunts also established in Leicestershire it is therefore no surprise that the fox is the symbol of Leicestershire County Council, Leicestershire County Cricket Club and Leicester City FC.

Finally, today, Quorn and Woodhouse Station is on the preserved Great Central Steam Railway, a heritage railway running from Leicester North Station to Loughborough Central, and which is currently the only double track mainline heritage railway in Britain. The station was given a makeover so that it reflected World War II and the 1940s, thus allowing for a number of period re-enactments in recent years. When the line was in its original heyday, a number of royal visitors, including the Prince of Wales (later Edward VIII), disembarked there – usually to take part in the Quorn Hunt!

Quorn Quirk Alert:
Q, a Squint, and the 1986 Connection
The area of Quorn known as "The Banks" comprises an ornate paved area with seating, designed to resemble

the letter "Q" when seen from the air. Meanwhile, in one corner of the chancel of St Bartholomew's there is a small slot shaped window known as a "squint", and which looks into the Farnham Chapel. Once part of the exterior church wall, it allowed lepers and other "undesirables" to see the main altar, without entering the building. Finally, the Farnham Chapel was built in 1392 by John Farnham. One wonders if he was "The Voice" of the 14th century. Certainly, he was someone's son ... but did he ever look down the barrel of a gun?

A Stanier LMS 8F Class 2-8-0 steam train alongside Quorn and Woodhouse Station on the Great Central Railway.

A chance encounter with a steam roller ralley at Quorn, with the village green and church providing the perfect backdrop.

NAME (STATUS):	**SEATON** (Village)
POPULATION:	250
DISTRICT:	Rutland
EARLIEST RECORD:	*Segentone, Seieton*, 1086 (Domesday Book)
MEANING:	Probably farmstead of a man called Sǽga, but alternatively, it may refer to an unrecorded stream name called the *Sǽġe*, meaning "slow-moving"
DERIVATION:	Most likely from the Old English personal name, *Sǽġa*, plus the Old English word *tūn* (farmstead).
FAMOUS RESIDENTS:	**Thomas Minot** (d.1375), Bishop of Durham, 1363 to 1375 (he was also parson at Seaton from 1351 to 1354)

The George & Dragon, Seaton.

Seaton Pub and Church:
The George & Dragon and All Hallows

In keeping with the rest of the beautiful village of Seaton, the George & Dragon Country Inn is an attractive 17th century stone-built pub. Meanwhile, the tower of All Hallows church dates back to the late 13th century and the spire the 14th, but the south doorway with its moulded arch along with the chancel arch are both Norman, with the latter boasting particularly fine Norman capitals. There is also some Norman work at the eastern end of the south arcade, while the rest of the north and south arcades were re-built in the 12th

All Hallows church, Seaton.

century. Even older are the ancient tombstones that have been built into the outer walls while inside is a large ironbound chest that dates back to the time of Richard I.

The church – which is fairly long at 122ft – was restored between 1874 and 1876 by the Victorian architect N.M. Fawcett of Cambridge. He replaced the roofs and renewed many of the windows, also inserting new, small windows into the clerestory. As for the original font, for some reason this was sawn up at the restoration, and its eight sides, stem, and four legs now form the back and supports of a stone seat at the west end of the south aisle.

Seaton Historic Trivia: The Seaton Viaduct, Junctions and a Seat at Seaton

Easily the most striking feature in Seaton's part of the Welland Valley is the Harringworth Viaduct – and which also goes by alternative names of the Seaton Viaduct and the Welland Viaduct. The viaduct is three quarters of a mile long, and took four years to build between 1874 and 1878. It has 82 arches, each of which has a 40 foot span and some of which are up to 72 feet high all of which collectively make up the longest masonry viaduct across a valley in Britain. However, today the railway is now generally only used for freight traffic, although in early 2009 a single daily passenger service was introduced by East Midlands Trains between Melton Mowbray and St. Pancras via Oakham and Corby, the stations either side of the viaduct. This is the first regular daily passenger service to operate across the viaduct since the 1960s.

For railway completeness, Seaton once had its own station too, although this was on a different line, this being the London and North Western Railway, a single track line which ran from Rugby to Stamford Railway and which opened in 1850. Then in 1873 it actually became a junction station when the LNWR double tracked the line from Rugby to Seaton and opened a new double track line from Seaton to Wansford, a few miles west of Peterborough. Rugby to Peterborough was then operated as the main line and Seaton to Stamford as a branch line while in 1894, another branch line was laid to run from Seaton to Uppingham.

However, none of these lines linked to the Midland Railway line that passed over the Harringworth Viaduct, and the nearest station on this line to Seaton was actually at Harringworth. The Uppingham branch eventually closed to passengers in 1960, and the Rugby to Peterborough line and Stamford branch line both closed in 1966.

Finally, when Henry Royce (co-founder of Rolls Royce) was created a baronet in 1930 for his services to British Aviation, he took Seaton as his ... well ... his seat! This was because his family had once worked in the village as millers.

Seaton Quirk Alert:
The George & Bearded Dragon

In September 2011, a family from Seaton Road at nearby Harringworth were mourning the loss of Giz, a type of lizard known as a pogona. They had owned Giz for five years, keeping him in a pen in their garden during summer time – although he had already picked up a reputation for escaping, but usually only to the nearby gardens of the family's neighbours, who had become quite used to taking him back home again. However, this time around he had made a proper escape bid, almost certainly striking out north-west, under the famous Harringworth (or Seaton) Viaduct and then uphill through the Welland Valley and into the village of Seaton, around 2 miles from his home. And it was here that he was found at lunchtime one day, having somewhat inevitably been drawn to the George & Dragon; inevitable because a pogona is more commonly known as ... the bearded dragon! The pub owner was quoted as saying: "I went outside to get a delivery from the wine merchant and Giz was just sitting on the step. He then walked into the pub. He was as cool as a cucumber." Happily, Giz was reunited with his owners after they read an article on him in the local newspaper. With winter just around the corner, they had been resigned to never seeing him again ... although they did notice that he'd put on a few pounds during his adventure and no longer welcomed his old food from the pet shop!

ANCIENT TREASURES

Left: *The Norman (south) doorway.*
Above: *This ironbound chest dates back to the late 12th century.*

Some of the 82 arches of the amazing Harringworth (Seaton) Viaduct.

NAME (STATUS):	**SOAR** (River)
DISTRICT:	Harborough, Blaby, City of Leicester, Charnwood
EARLIEST RECORD:	The River Soar was known as the River Legro in Roman times
MEANING:	A Celtic or pre-Celtic river-name probably meaning "flowing one"
LENGTH:	59 miles (95 km)
SOURCE (ELEVATION):	Wibtoft, Warwickshire (440ft [134m])
MOUTH (ELEVATION):	Trent Lock, Leicestershire (98ft [30m])

Left: *The River Soar by the Otter Inn, just south of Kegworth.*

River Soar Geographic Trivia:
From Wibtoft (Warwickshire) to Trent Lock (Leicestershire side)

The River Soar rises in Warwickshire close to the village of Wibtoft and a mere mile or so from the Leicestershire border. From here it flows eastwards to the border and under the A5 before heading largely northwards for around 4 miles and reaching the village of Sharnford, named after a *scearn* or muddy ford across the Soar. The river is also joined by the Soar Brook at Sharnford, after which it heads off north-eastwards to first Croft, passes between Narborough and Littlethorpe and is then joined by the River Sence just east of Enderby. It then continues on its north-eastward journey to Aylestone on the outskirts of Leicester where it is joined by both the River Biam and the Grand Union Canal. The river then heads into Leicester City Centre, passing Leicester City's King Power Stadium on the way and also the stretch known as the Mile Straight which is home to Leicester Rowing Club, formed in 1882.

Now heading north-north-east, the River Soar passes over Freemens Weir before splitting and recombining with the canal, creating an area of Leicester called Bede Island. The river then splits again, forming Frog Island

and Abbey Park, before reuniting again at Belgrave where it passes beside the National Space Centre. The River Soar exits Leicester still heading largely north-north-east and passes first Birstall to the west, flows through the attractive Watermead Country Park and then past Wanlip to the east. After this point, the river turns to the north-west where it is joined by the River Wreake and then by another tributary the Rothley Brook. Still continuing in a north-westerly direction, the River Soar passes the villages of first Mountsorrel, then Quorn and then Barrow-on-Soar, at which point an arm of the Grand Union Canal splits away and runs parallel with the Soar for several miles. The Soar then passes to the east of Loughborough and under Cotes Bridge before reaching Stanford on Soar where it begins a stretch marking the boundary between Leicestershire and Nottinghamshire. Heading due west from Stanford, the river is re-joined by the canal before they both reach Zouch. Still marking the county boundary, the river now turns north, passing the Devil's Elbow and then flowing to the east of Kegworth. It then travels its final 2 miles in a northerly direction, joined first by the Kingston Brook, then passing Ratcliffe on Soar power station, and then Red Hill Marina, before finally flowing into the River Trent at Trent Lock.

Part of the Soar Navigation known as the Mile Straight in Leicester. **Inset:** *Locks on the Soar Navigation at Birstall.*

At Mountsorrel, river and canal briefly divide where the river performs a wide semi-circular meander, and the canal (inset) passes straight on through a lock.

River Soar Historic Trivia: Navigation

Although large parts of the River Soar were canalised in the 18th century, the first attempted usage of the river for barges was actually secured in 1634 when Thomas Skipworth of Cotes obtained a grant from Charles I – although the scheme never reached fruition. It was more than 150 years later before the Leicester Canal (a branch of the Grand Union Canal) was opened in 1794, making the Soar navigable for 40 miles (64 km) from where the Grand Union Canal joins it at Aylestone to the mouth of the Soar at Trent Lock. Canal branch lines were then opened over the next twenty years, starting with a branch to Melton Mowbray in 1795 which ran from the Leicester Canal between Cossington and Syston. However, one line that was proposed in 1797 – the Leicestershire & Northamptonshire Union Canal, which would have linked the River Soar to the River Nene – was never completed, with only 17 miles of the 44 miles built before the money ran out – although it was eventually extended to Market Harborough in 1809. Nevertheless, in 1814, the Leicester Navigation and the Grand Junction Canal were linked and named the (old) Grand Union Canal – not to be confused with the later and more famous 20th century canal of the

same name. By 1832, the River Soar at Leicester was also linked to the Leicester and Swannington Railway, thus enabling the Soar to transport coal from the pits in the north-west of the county. However, as railways became more popular, usage of the canals began to fall away. The first victim was the Melton Mowbray branch which closed in 1877, while 1894 saw the Grand Union and the Leicestershire & Northamptonshire Union canals purchased by the Grand Junction Canal Company. Eventually, the whole stretch of waterway from Norton Junction in Northamptonshire through to Leicester (35 miles) and on to the River Soar's connection with the Trent and Mersey Canal at Trent Lock was merged with the Grand Junction Canal in 1931 to form the (new) Grand Union Canal.

Today, it is still possible to navigate the River Soar to the Trent and Mersey Canal, then to the Coventry Canal and then to the North Oxford Canal, thus completing a circuit known as the Leicester Ring.

Despite the reduced importance of canals in the late 19th century, there were still 231 listed hosiery manufacturers in Leicestershire in 1895, and many of these were still located along the banks of the Soar, and still used the canal network for transportation of goods. By the 1960s, though, many of these companies had become defunct, and waterside warehouses and factories became derelict. However, over the last twenty years, Leicester City Council has been developing the Soar waterfronts, while the Leicester Regeneration Company began building luxury waterside apartments. Most striking of all was the construction in 2002 alongside the canal of what was originally called The Walkers Stadium, the new home of Leicester City, but which has more recently been re-badged as The King Power Stadium, while old warehouses have also been converted into student accommodation for De Montfort University. Also purchased by Leicester City Council in 2012 was Donisthorpe Mill, a historic mill that was manufacturing textiles as far back as the 1730s, and which was awarded listed status in 1975. Alas it became derelict towards the end of the 20th century and suffered from a disastrous fire in July 2012 which destroyed its roof, clock-tower and most of the interior; the council, however, plan to restore it.

Exactly the same configuration applies at Kegworth, with the river performing another semi-circular meander (left) and the canal heading straight on (right).

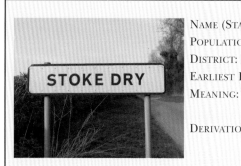

NAME (STATUS):	**STOKE DRY** (Village)
POPULATION:	35
DISTRICT:	Rutland
EARLIEST RECORD:	*Stok*, 11th century; *Stokedreye*, 13th century
MEANING:	Probably "outlying farmstead or hamlet near a brook or stream that has dried up"
DERIVATION:	From the Old English words *stoc* (place, outlying farmstead or hamlet, secondary or dependent settlement) and *dryge* (dry).

Stoke Dry Church: St Andrew's

Although much of St Andrew's was rebuilt in the 13th and 14th century, the nave still dates from the 12th century with one of its arcades including clustered columns, while the church also retains its original Norman chancel arch shafts which date from around 1120; the rest of the chancel was re-built in the 14th century. Recognisable carvings on the Norman columns and capitals include the eagle of St John, a figure holding a book, the devil trying to shut off the sound and run away from the Sanctus bell, and a man at a bell rope – one of the earliest representations of bell ringing in England. A number of medieval wall paintings also survive such as one of St Andrew, plus others showing the martyrdom of King Edmund, what could be the murder of Thomas Becket, and a stunning 13th century mural on the south wall depicting St Christopher carrying Jesus on his shoulders. The south aisle was added in the 13th century and the tower in the 14th century, although its lower courses date to its 13th century predecessor. The north aisle and clerestory were then added in the 15th century and the tower was topped by a 17th century belfry; the south porch also dates from the 17th century, too. Inside, the church, the Digby Chapel contains numerous monuments to the Digby family.

Nevertheless, despite the church's standard features of tower, nave, chancel, north and south aisles and north and south porches, it has a rather unusual look. This is due to the slim west tower and the fact that the north porch includes a second-floor room complete with its 16th century oriel window – plus the fact that the north porch also remains the main entrance to the church.

View from the north of St Andrew's church, revealing its two-tier porch, the first floor of which is rumoured to have housed the Gunpowder Plot conspirators.

Looking up the main road through Stoke Dry, a tiny village of only 14 houses. The population doubles every summer when the village is visited by the 16-strong Rutland Morris Men!

St Andrew's church, Stoke Dry.

Alabaster monument of Kenelme Digby (d.1590) and his wife (d.1602). They were the grandparents of Sir Everard Digby who was executed in 1605 for his part in the Gunpowder Plot.

View from St Andrew's churchyard towards Eyebrook Reservoir, and which once hosted Lancaster Bombers flying from RAF Scampton as 617 Squadron's final practice run prior to their Dambusters attack on the Ruhr valley dams in May 1943. I guess this was their Dry run! Alas, it is no laughing matter that 53 of these heroes did not return.

Stoke Dry Historic Trivia:
Gunpowder and Dambusters

It is claimed that St Andrew's church is where the Gunpowder Plot conspirators met – in that small room above the north porch – although the only basis for this is that the manor was part of the estate of Sir Everard Digby, one of the 1605 plotters. Born in 1578, Sir Everard had been brought up a Protestant, but became a Catholic after being converted by John Gerard, a famous Jesuit priest of that time. Thus it was that when James I ascended to the throne in 1603 Digby, along with his co-conspirators led by Robert Catesby, sought to wipe out the King, the Lords and the Commons in one fell swoop. And it was Digby who put up most of the money required for the plot, while it was also his job after the event to organise the required Revolution, initially via a planned hunt on Dunsmoor Heath near Rugby, arranged for November 5th 1605, and to be attended by numerous Roman Catholic gentry. Of course, Guy Fawkes was caught hiding beneath the House of Lords on the evening of the 4th, and was tortured until he revealed the names of his co-conspir-

ators. Catesby, realising that something had gone wrong, galloped the 80 miles to Dunsmoor Heath, where they found Digby and considerably fewer sympathisers than they'd hoped for. They were soon captured, and although Catesby was killed fighting, Digby was captured and later executed.

Stoke Dry Quirk Alert:
A Mind-Blowing Revelation

Earlier, we mentioned medieval murals in St Andrew's church, including the martyrdom of King Edmund. Well here it is, below, with experts dating it to between 1280 and 1284. It depicts St Edmund being shot full of arrows, but do you notice anything anachronistic? "No", say you. Well look again. Those bowmen look suspiciously like North American Red Indians ... except Columbus didn't discover America until 1492! This surely therefore adds great weight to the theory that the Vikings ventured Stateside considerably earlier than Mr Columbus ...

How is it that a 13th century wall painting in Stoke Dry depicts North American Red Indians over 200 years before Columbus discovered America? Discuss...

LEICESTERSHIRE AND RUTLAND: UNUSUAL & QUIRKY

NAME (STATUS):	**STOUGHTON** (Village)
POPULATION:	351
DISTRICT:	Harborough
EARLIEST RECORD:	*Stoctone*, 1086 (Domesday Book)
MEANING:	Farmstead at an outlying hamlet
DERIVATION:	From the Old English words *stoc* (outlying farmstead or hamlet, or secondary or dependent settlement), and *tūn* (farmstead).

Stoughton Church: St Mary and All Saints

St Mary and All Saints' church dates from the 14th century, although much of it was restored in the 19th century. It is also home to a number of monuments which are dedicated to members of the Farnham and Beaumont families. These include a tomb of Thomas Farnham, Teller of the Exchequer to Mary I, along with his wife and five children, while one of those daughters has a wall monument of her own, kneeling with her husband, Sir Thomas Beaumont and ten children … one of whom became the wife of Sir Thomas Richardson, Speaker of the Commons in Charles I's time. Other famous Beaumont memorials are to

Admiral Basil Beaumont (1669-1703) and Sir George Beaumont, MP for Leicester in nine parliaments. The churchyard is also home to a 14th century cross, reputed to be the county's most beautiful.

Stoughton Historic Trivia: Stoughton Grange

Although Stoughton Grange was demolished in 1926, the name was significant for several hundred years by virtue of two distinct incarnations. The first incarnation was as the principal grange or farm of Leicester Abbey – or as it was also known, the Abbey of Saint Mary de Pratis. The abbey was a house of the Augustinian order

St Mary and All Saints' church, Stoughton.

The medieval cross in the churchyard of St Mary and All Saints.

Approach to Stoughton from the west.

founded in medieval Leicester in the 12th century by Robert de Beaumont, the 2nd Earl of Leicester, and it grew to become the wealthiest religious establishment within Leicestershire. The 2nd Earl then granted *Stoctone* to the abbey in 1157, and the land of Stoughton became a great source of income for its mother house. The 13th century then saw the church of St Mary and All Saints added to the Stoughton estate and which was followed in the 15th century by the first Stoughton Grange, a farmhouse constructed by Abbot John Penny. However, a century later in 1538, the abbey and estates were surrendered to the Crown following the Dissolution, only for Queen Elizabeth I to grant Stoughton to John Harington in 1560, after which it was purchased by Elizabeth's Chancellor, Thomas Farnham. This triggered a three hundred year ownership of the estate by the Farnham family and its descendants, although the family name did change through the marriage of a Farnham to a Beaumont, thus bringing the estate back full circle to its 12th century owners! But when Catherine Beaumont married William Busby, and their daughter, Anne Busby, married Anthony Keck, the house and estate passed to the Keck family. Their son, Anthony James Keck, re-fashioned the house in a Gothic style. He also married Elizabeth Legh, and although they had six children, the only son to survive was George Anthony Legh Keck who lived at the house until he married his cousin Elizabeth Atherton in 1802. At this point, he moved in at the Atherton family's Bank Hall in Lancashire, and Stoughton became merely a second home, although he remained a member of parliament for Leicestershire at various times between 1797 and 1831, and frequently travelled between the

estates; three Gothic lodges were added during his tenure, too. The last incumbent of Stoughton Grange was Harry Leycester Powys Keck, who inherited it in 1871, the same year that he was High Sheriff of Leicestershire. However, the house was put up for sale in 1913, but was never sold and thus remained unoccupied until it was eventually demolished in 1926. The three Grade II-listed gothic lodges do survive, though, and still bear the Keck family arms. As for the estate, that was bought by the Co-operative Wholesale Society Ltd. in 1919 and the site of the mansion became the centre of the society's dairy-farming in Leicestershire and became known as Grange Farm. Many years later, what was known as Stoughton Farm Park (formerly Stoughton Grange Farm), was closed following the foot-and-mouth crisis and is now home to a number of small businesses.

A portrait of George Anthony Legh Keck, painted by Thomas Phillips in 1830, can be found in the Leicester Arts and Museums Service Collection.

Stoughton Quirk Alert: Pennbury

Close to the village of Stoughton is Leicester Airport, previously known as Stoughton Aerodrome. This small aerodrome was built in 1942 and was originally known as RAF Leicester East. Anyway, in 2008, the airport site along with adjacent land became the subject of a proposal to build an eco-town of between 15,000 and 20,000 new homes, and the provisional name for the eco-town was Pennbury. However, the proposal received fierce local opposition due to the inevitable increased traffic and destruction of the countryside, and a year later, the proposal was canned by the government.

NAME (STATUS):	**TEIGH** (Village)
POPULATION:	48
DISTRICT:	Rutland
EARLIEST RECORD:	*Tie*, 1086 (Domesday Book)
MEANING:	A small enclosure
DERIVATION:	From the Old English word *tēag*.

Teigh Church: Holy Trinity

The earliest reference to a church at Teigh dates back to 1100. However, the majority of Holy Trinity church was rebuilt in 1782 for the fourth Earl of Harborough by the architect George Richardson. The only surviving elements from the medieval church are the lowest stage of the tower which dates from the 13th century, with some later 14th century work immediately above it; the medieval frieze around the battlements was created in the 18th century. Internally, one notable quirk is that the pews on either side of the nave don't face the altar, but actually face each other, on three-tiered rows, while another quirk is the triple pulpit that frames the entrance to the nave from the west. This arrangement includes the Gothic pulpit, prayer desk and lectern, designed so that the rector and readers would be in different positions and at different heights during the service. As for the good-sized window frames, these are still the 1782 originals, but the tracery and stained glass was added in 1893, while the plastered and slightly coved ceiling is attractively decorated with a number of crests and arms. Finally, above the altar is a Flemish painting of the Last Supper, and which dates from around 1600.

Teigh Historic Trivia: An Honorary Muscovite

In 1611, Anthony Jenkinson was buried in Teigh churchyard. Born at Market Harborough in 1529, Jenkinson was one of the first Britons to explore the Grand Duchy of Moscow, or Muscovy as it was also known, and is also widely acknowledged to be the first Englishman to enter Central Asia. A traveller and an explorer, he was also the main trader of the Muscovy Company, a trading company set up in 1555 and which monopolised trade between England and Muscovy until 1698, and indeed survived as a trading company until the Russian Revolution of 1917. Much of Jenkinson's trading was also carried out on behalf of the English Crown, and during his travels, he met Ivan the Terrible several times. He also detailed the accounts of his travel through several written works, including his forays further east, having reached Khiva and

Holy Trinity church, Teigh which was largely rebuilt in 1782.

Holy Trinity church seen from the south-east.

Bukhara when trying to reach Cathay overland from Moscow. His establishment of overland trade routes through Russia to Persia certainly expanded the influence of Elizabethan England.

Teigh Quirk Alert: Folville, Coalville and the Lucky Thirteen

Between 1321 and 1340, the village rector of Teigh was a particularly infamous character called Richard Folville, member of a notorious robber band captained by his older brother Eustace; in fact, most of his relations, who included the Folvilles of Ashby Folville in Leicestershire and Newbold Folville in Huntingdonshire, were lawless and outlawed. Unfortunately, Richard Folville's vocation did not deter him from indulging in serious organised crime. It is thought that Richard masterminded the gang's most daring plot in 1332, the abduction and ransom of the justice Sir Richard Willoughby, later Chief Justice of the King's Bench. However, Folville managed to stay one step ahead of the law until 1341, when he and some of his retinue were cornered

in Holy Trinity church at Teigh by Sir Robert Coalville, a keeper of the King's peace. After a prolonged struggle, which resulted in at least one fatality as Richard fired arrows from the church, Sir Robert succeeded in drawing Richard from the building. Once in custody Folville was promptly beheaded, in his own churchyard! However, the story doesn't end there, because after the event Pope Clement VI graciously instructed Thomas Bek, Bishop of Lincoln, to absolve Sir Robert Coalville and his men for killing a priest (i.e. Richard Folville)...but only on the condition that they were whipped at each of the main churches in the area, by way of penance!

Finally, Teigh was one of the First World War's few Thankful Villages, and the only one in Rutland to have not lost any of its own, with all thirteen who served (eleven men and two women) returning safely.

Centenary memorial in Teigh listing the 13 villagers who went to fight in World War I and who all came back – making Teigh one of very few Thankful Villages.

The Old Rectory at Teigh. This Grade II listed building dates from 1740, and also doubled up as Hunsford parsonage in the BBC's 1995 adaptation of Pride and Prejudice.

NAME (STATUS):	**TINWELL** (Village)
POPULATION:	234
DISTRICT:	Rutland
EARLIEST RECORD:	*Tedinwelle*, 1086 (Domesday Book); *Tiningewelle*, mid-13th century
MEANING:	Possibly "spring or stream of the family or followers of a man called Tyni"
DERIVATION:	From the Old English personal name, *Tyni*, plus the Old English words *inga* (of) and *wella* (spring or stream).

Tinwell Church: All Saints

Boasting the only saddleback church roof in Rutland, All Saints' church also owns a tower that dates back to Norman times, while the nave arcade and the chancel arch are 13th century; the chancel itself is 15th century, as is the clerestory. It is also in the chancel where you will find the tomb of Elizabeth Cecil, sister to Lord Burleigh who was one of Queen Elizabeth I's most trusted counsellors.

Tinwell Historic Trivia: A Shrunken Village and an Air Disaster

Today, the village of Tinwell is close to the site of the shrunken medieval village of Ingthorpe, which was located at the northern edge of the parish, close to the River Gwash. Meanwhile, on 8th July 1944, two C47s collided after taking-off from nearby RAF Spanhoe for an exercise. One crew member managed to parachute safely but eight others and 26 Polish paratroopers of the Polish 1st Independent Parachute Brigade perished in the crash. The American casualties from 315th Troop Carrier Group were taken to the Cambridge American Cemetery for burial and the Polish casualties were taken to the Polish Cemetery at Newark. All those killed are commemorated in the church.

Tinwell Quirk Alert: Gulliver's Place

Tinwell is the location of Tinwell Forge, a beautiful building dating from 1848 and which still has a Victorian post box built into one wall. However, Tinwell Forge is also the member of a very exclusive group of British buildings, as it was also one of the original ornaments made as part of the 1980s' Lilliput Lane series!

Tinwell Forge – the real one, and not a 1980s ornament!

This village sign was made to commemorate the year 2000.

All Saints' church, Tinwell.

NAME (STATUS):	**TIXOVER** (Village)
POPULATION:	163
DISTRICT:	Rutland
EARLIEST RECORD:	*Tichesovre*, 1086 (Domesday Book)
MEANING:	Promontory where young goats are pastured
DERIVATION:	From the Old English words *ticcen* (kid or young goat) and *ofer* (flat-topped ridge, hill or promontory).

St Luke's church, Tixover.

Tixover Church: St Luke's

St Luke's church is located around three quarters of a mile from the village of Tixover, alongside the River Welland and down a lengthy track; in fact, the church cannot even be seen from the village. However, in medieval times, the main part of the village lay to the north of the church, meaning that it is probably one of those classic medieval villages that moved during the 14th century due to the devastation wrought by the plague. Furthermore, it was also once known as the church of St Mary Magdalene, but whether it changed its name at this time, too, is not known.

Regardless of its name, though, the large church tower dates back to Norman times, probably the early 12th century. It has some impressive arched bell-openings on the top stage with the south set decorated by zigzag carvings inside the shafts and arches, while the bell tower is home to a medieval bell inscribed with the words: *Sancta Fides Ora Pro Nobis*. The battlements were added to the tower at a later date, while the chancel and nave date to the early 13th century and, unusually, the chancel is longer than the nave; the font is 13th century, too. The south porch dates from the 15th century, but the date of the windows is disputed, with Pevsner dating them to the Tudor period, but later scholars suggesting that they, too, may be 13th century. As for the pews, these are Jacobean and the stone pulpit dates to 1859. Finally, the, church is home to numerous monuments to the Dale family who owned the manor during the 16th and 17th centuries. These include an impressive monument to Roger Dale who died in 1623, and which was erected by Margaret Dale, his third wife. The monument depicts Roger and Margaret kneeling on either side of a prayer desk, while the kneeling figures of their two daughters are portrayed on the base.

Tixover Historic Trivia: Tixover Manor

When Tixover was recorded as *Tichesovre* in the Domesday Book (1086), it belonged to the Kings Manor at nearby Ketton. The manor was then acquired by the Bishops of Lincoln in

The nave of St Luke's church looking towards the chancel.

The 13th century font at St Luke's church.

Looking down the nave of St Luke's towards the Norman tower arch.

Tixover village.

1104 but by 1130, they had passed it on to the Abbey de Cluny. By the early 16th century, though, the manor of Tixover belonged to the Dale family, while centuries later it passed to first the Stafford family and, finally, the O'Brien family who sold all their holdings in the 1970s. Meanwhile, Tixover Quarry is a popular off-road driving centre, which is used by *Land Rover Owner* magazine for vehicle tests and photo shoots.

Tixover Quirk Alert: Sequestered

Many of the monuments in St Luke's church were vandalised during the English Civil War. However, it is also thought that a number of alabaster monuments were sequestered so that they could be ground down and used as a cure for sheep murrain – where the latter is a medieval term used to describe various infectious diseases that resulted in sheep death, almost certainly inclusive of foot-and-mouth disease.

Tixover's Victorian post-box.

NAME (STATUS):	**TONGE** (Village)
POPULATION:	c.100
DISTRICT:	North West Leicestershire
EARLIEST RECORD:	*Tunge*, 1086 (Domesday Book)
MEANING:	The tongue of land
DERIVATION:	From the Old Scandinavian word *tunga* (tongue of land).

Tonge General Trivia: Railways – Old and New

Tonge is a tiny village in North West Leicestershire in the parish of Breedon on the Hill, and this quintessentially English, chocolate-box ideal has two railway stories to tell … and there is little doubt as to which one fits the village ambiance best. The railways first came to Tonge in 1874, when the Midland Railway built a station here known as Tonge and Breedon Railway Station. It was on the line that ran from Leicester to Burton upon Trent, although passenger services were withdrawn in 1930 and thereafter it was used only for freight by the London, Midland and Scottish Railway company – although there was an intervening period during World War II when it became known as the Melbourne Military Railway. However, in 1945, the War Department returned the line and station to the LMS, and it continued to be used for freight until British Railways closed it in 1980. The track was then dismantled, but now forms part of National Cycle Route 6.

So, that's the old railway story. More recently, though, HS2 Ltd (the company who will be delivering the forthcoming High Speed Link from London to the North) names Tonge as one of the Leicestershire villages that will be most affected by intrusive noise levels if the project goes ahead. The plans for Tonge and Breedon would also see a huge embankment built of around 33-50ft (10-15m) in height on which trains will hurtle by at speeds of up to 250mph. So as well as the sickening noise pollution, this beautiful village will also be subjected to a massive eyesore, which will be accompanied by an electricity supply cable that will run an additional 5 metres up in the air. As the local action group's website states: "No trains anywhere in the world run as fast as HS2 is planned to run but engineers agree that wheel noise, wind noise and overhead pick-up noise all increase sharply at higher speeds. That is why HS2 can only guess at what the actual noise levels will be."

TONGE: CHOCOLATE BOX VILLAGE

The River Welland at Barrowden.

NAME (STATUS):	**WELLAND** (River)
DISTRICTS:	Northants -> Harborough, Rutland -> Lincolnshire
LENGTH:	65 miles (105 km)
SOURCE:	Sibbertoft, Northamptonshire
SOURCE ELEVATION:	515ft (157m)
MOUTH:	Fosdyke Wash
MOUTH ELEVATION:	3ft (1m)
EARLIEST RECORD:	*Weolud*, 921 (Anglo-Saxon Chronicle)
MEANING AND DERIVATION:	Uncertain, but like most rivers is Celtic in origin. The name could mean "good or well river", with the later name influenced by the fertile or "well land" around it.

River Welland Geographic Trivia: From Sibbertoft to The Wash

The River Welland rises in the Hothorpe Hills in Northamptonshire, close to the village of Sibbertoft, before flowing around 2 miles in a north-westerly direction to the border with Leicestershire a mile or so south-west of Husbands Bosworth. From here, it turns in a north-easterly direction, forming the border between Leicestershire and Northamptonshire, and passing just to the south of the Harborough District villages of Theddingworth and Lubenham, before briefly entering Leicestershire in full as it meanders through Market Harborough – and where it is joined by

An infant River Welland at Theddingworth.

The River Welland is still little more than a stream at Lubenham.

no less than the River Jordan – albeit the version that rises just 3.5 miles away in Northamptonshire! But anyway, emerging to the east of Market Harborough, the Welland then resumes its boundary-marking duties, first heading north for around 3 miles, and then turning eastwards again at Welham where it flows under a fine three-arched bridge on the Welham to Weston by Welland road, and which was built in 1881. A little further on and the river flows under an early 19th century four-arched bridge on the Medbourne to Ashley road. Thereafter, this eastward stretch sees the Welland pass to the south of the Leicestershire villages of Medbourne, Drayton, Bringhurst and Great Easton, before the border-marking baton is passed onto Rutland just south of Caldecott. Here, the course of the river begins heading north-eastwards again, now marking the boundary between Rutland and Northamptonshire and passing to the south of the Rutland villages of Thorpe by Water and Seaton. It is also just south of Seaton where the river forms two channels, with the county border following the smaller, northern channel. The river is also crossed here by the spectacular 82 brick-arched Harringworth Viaduct (also known as the Welland Viaduct), which was completed in 1879 and carries the Oakham to Kettering railway line over the valley. The Welland then heads on towards Barrowden where we find a medieval bridge with five pointed arches taking the road between Barrowden and Wakerley over the river. It then flows on to Tixover, before meandering right around Duddington, and it is also here that we find a mill dating from at least 1664, while the four-arched limestone ashlar bridge over the Welland at Duddington dates from the 15th century. From here, we then head north for Tinwell and the Rutland border with Lincolnshire; indeed, just over the Lincolnshire border at Stamford, the Welland marks the borders of Rutland, Northamptonshire, Lincolnshire and Cambridgeshire. From Stamford, the Welland heads off generally north-eastwards for its rendezvous with The Wash just north-east of Fosdyke.

River Welland (Upper) Historic Trivia: Bridges and Battles

A number of medieval bridges over the River Welland

are referred to in the previous section, but one bridge that isn't mentioned is the 19th century Grade II listed bridge which takes the driveway to Thorpe Lubenham Hall over the river. To the east of Lubenham, the river passes Old Lubenham Hall, a late 16th century house built in the shape of the letter H, and which was later modified in the early 18th century. However, Charles I was believed to have stayed at Old Lubenham Hall just before the Battle of Naseby, which was fought nearby in Northamptonshire on the 14th June 1645. The battle famously resulted in a crushing defeat for Charles at the hands of the New Model Army and brought an end to the first phase of the Civil War. Today, Old Lubenham Hall is a scheduled ancient monument.

The River Welland as it flows through Welland Park in Market Harborough.

Above: *The medieval bridge over the Welland between Barrowden and Wakerley.*

Above right: *The 15th century bridge over the River Welland at Duddington.*

Right: *The Welland at the bridge just south-east of Ketton.*

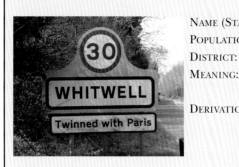

NAME (STATUS):	**WHITWELL** (Village)
POPULATION:	41
DISTRICT:	Rutland
MEANING:	Whitwell is named after the white spring which flows beneath the church
DERIVATION:	From the Old English words *hwīt* (white) and *wella* (spring or stream).

Whitwell Church: St Michael and All Angels

Although mentioned in the Domesday Book of 1086, the oldest part of the current church of St Michael and All Angels dates from the 12th century, this being the nave. Originally, it was almost certainly an aisle-less church, but in the 13th century, a south arcade of three bays and a south aisle was added, along with the bell-cote; the chancel may also date from this period, too. The church was then further altered in the 14th century when new windows were inserted and a new roof erected. The north wall of the nave was also increased in height and received new windows along with a doorway and buttresses.

The church was also subject to general restoration in both 1881 and in 1930, with the former occurring a year after the death of Charles Spencer Ellicott, who was rector here for sixty years; he was replaced by his son, who also happened to be the Bishop of Gloucester and Bristol. Other church relics include the font, which dates to around 1200, 14th century glass in a chancel window depicting the Crucifixion, a paten (the plate used to hold the Eucharistic bread) which is date-marked 1570-71, and a bread holder dating to 1718-19.

Whitwell Historic Trivia: Whitwell Harbour

Whitwell sits on the northern shore of Rutland Water. Constructed in 1976, Rutland Water is one of the largest artificial lakes in Europe and, by surface area it is the largest reservoir in the UK; it also provides a reserve supply of water to the south-east, the driest and most

St Michael and All Angels church, Whitwell.

Springtime on Exton Road, Whitwell.

populated quarter of the UK. On its north shore along-side Whitwell is what is known locally as Whitwell Harbour. The area is the location of the Rutland Water-sports Centre, which is owned by Anglian Water and caters for sailing, canoeing and windsurfing, whilst a pleasure boat known as the *Rutland Belle* also operates from here, putting into port at Whitwell North Shore and Normanton Church South Shore.

Whitwell Quirk Alert: Paris Match

Despite its charming pub, church and village buildings, Whitwell's main claim to fame is the fact that its village welcome sign announces it as being "twinned with Paris". Apparently, in an attempt to raise the profile of the village, the chairman of the parish council wrote to the Mayor of Paris in 1980 to suggest the twinning,

The Noel, Whitwell, a traditional pub with flagstones and an open fire.

explaining that Whitwell lay at the heart of England and wished to twin with an important capital on the European mainland. How could they possibly refuse? Anyway, the Parisian mayor at that time was none other than Jacques Chirac, and in his letter to the mayor, the chairman of Whitwell Parish Council rather cannily acknowledged that Monsieur Chirac was a busy man and so if they did not receive an answer within fifteen days, they would assume that the request had been approved. Presumably Monsieur Chirac took advantage of this thoughtful consideration, as no reply ever arrived, and thus the signboards were ordered and erected! These were initially wooden signs, but which were later replaced by metal ones created by Rutland County Council – and thus the twinning became fully endorsed locally as well as internationally!

WHITWELL VILLAGE

NAME (STATUS):	**WING** (Village)
POPULATION:	314
DISTRICT:	Rutland
EARLIEST RECORD:	Wenge, 12th century
MEANING:	The field
DERIVATION:	From the Old Scandinavian word vengi (field).
FAMOUS RESIDENTS:	**Francis Meres** (1565-1647), Wing rector and author; **Amelia Woodcock**, 19th century herbalist; **Sir Charles Vernon Boys** (1855-1944), physicist; **A. S. Brocklebank**, 20th century champion horsewoman

The King's Arms, Wing.

Wing Pub: The King's Arms and The Cuckoo Inn

The King's Arms on Top Street is yet another beautiful Rutland country pub, and this one dates back as far as 1649 – so presumably the king in question was Charles I, who lost his head in the January of that year. Until recently, though, Wing had another pub, The Cuckoo Inn, parts of which date back to the mid-17th century. Now a private home, the *Wing Quirk Alert* supplies insight into the naming of the former pub!

Wing Church: St Peter and St Paul

The earliest parts of St Peter and St Paul's church at Wing are the south aisle arcades, which are Norman and date from around 1140. The north aisle arcades are slightly later and date from the 12th century, while the

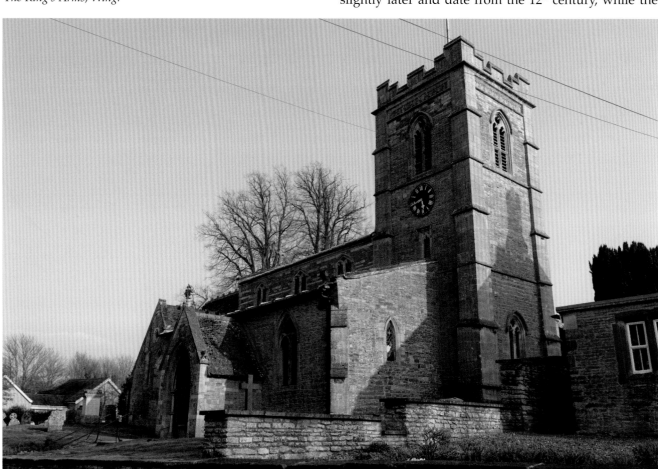

The church of St Peter and St Paul, Wing.

Wing village.

The turf maze at Wing.

tower and clerestory date to the early 15th century; the spire was dismantled in 1841 as it was deemed to be unsafe. The chancel was then rebuilt in 1875, with the south aisle rebuild following ten years later.

Wing Historic Trivia: Wing Manor

Wing isn't mentioned in the Domesday Book, although its Norse name-derivation suggests that there was a settlement here at that time, so it is likely to have been an outlying berewick of nearby Ridlington. The manor was certainly owned by the Earl of Warwick in the 12th century, although he then passed it on to the de Montfort family. However, in 1165 Robert de Montfort died and his brother passed one half of the estate to the Abbey of Thorney in Cambridgeshire and the other half to the Priory of St Neots. After the Dissolution in the late 1530s, both halves were leased to Sir Everard Digby of Stoke Dry, after which, the manor passed to Sir Thomas Smith (1556-1609), an MP who became the English master of requests in 1608, a year before his death.

In 1602, the author Francis Meres became rector of Wing. However, he had already written his most famous work by then, this being *Palladis Tamia, Wits Treasury* (1598), and which provides an important insight into Elizabethan poets, plus delivers the first critical account of the poems and early plays of William Shakespeare as well as listing their chronology. Meres also wrote a sermon entitled *Gods Arithmeticke* (1597), and two translations from the Spanish works of Luís de Granada entitled *Granada's Devotion* and the *Sinners' Guide* (1598). Sticking with rectors, Sir Charles Vernon Boys was born the eighth child of the Reverend Charles Boys at Wing in 1855, and went on to become a leading British physicist.

As for the 17th-century houses in Wing, many were built from limestone quarried at nearby Barnack and Clipsham, and roofed with either local Collyweston slate or thatch. A little later, Wing Hall was built between 1885 and 1891 by Edward Worrall, whose family had made their fortune developing a technique for dyeing velvet.

One of Wing's most renowned inhabitants was a 19th century woman called Amelia Woodcock. The wife of a labourer, she was known as the 'wise woman of Wing' and was so-called as she had a reputation for curing many people of disease, many of them chronic. When she first began practising, she used herbs gathered from the surrounding fields and woods, but later she made up her medicines after buying drugs from a chemist. In time, not only was she regularly visited by the wealthy of the day, but she even found herself consulted by members of the medical profession. Eventually, her fame spread so wide and far that visitors had to take lodgings in the neighbourhood until she was ready to attend to them. Even more remarkable, is that although she died in around 1850, her remedies were still on sale at Uppingham's Boots the Chemist store in the 1950s.

However, perhaps Wing's most famous inhabitant was A. S. Brocklebank, who lived at Wing Grange. A famous horsewoman from the early 20th century, she won the Championship at the Dublin Horse Show in 1912, 1913 and 1919 driving her tandem pair Optimist and Illumination. She was also four-times Champion at the Royal Show, while agriculturally she also established a noted herd of beef shorthorns called the Wing Herd.

Wing Quirk Alert: Amazingly Cuckoo

The village of Wing is home to a 40ft-wide circular turf maze, which was cut from the turf of the village green and which is also thought to date back to early medieval times, on the grounds that its design is similar to the pavement maze in Chartres Cathedral. One of only eight remaining in England today, its origin is unknown, although there are many myths, including references to the classical Cretan labyrinth. One other legend is that penitents were made to follow the course of the maze on their knees in atonement for their sins, while another suggests that the maze is connected to fertility rights. Yet another legend suggests that it warded off evil spirits. The Victorians were a little more practical though, as the Leicester and Rutland Directory of 1846 describes it as "an ancient maze in which the rustics of the parish run on feast days!"

An even more quirky legend lent its name to the former Cuckoo Inn. Apparently, the people of Wing once tried to keep spring in the village forever by erecting a fence around a cuckoo to stop it from leaving. Of course, the cuckoo flew over the fence and away, and as a result, people from the village were known as "Wing Fools".

NAME (STATUS):	**WORTHINGTON** (Village)
POPULATION:	1461
DISTRICT:	North West Leicestershire
EARLIEST RECORD:	*Werditone*, 1086 (Domesday Book); *Wrthington*, c.1130
MEANING:	Farmstead or estate associated with a man called Weorth
DERIVATION:	From the Old English personal name *Weorth*, plus the Old English words *ing* (associated with) and *tūn* (farmstead). However, another more recent theory suggests that it might derive its name from the family name of "Werden".

Worthington Pub: The Malt Shovel

The picturesque Malt Shovel is located on Main Street, and is one of the many venues throughout the summer where the Leicester Morrismen dance. The Morris side perform Cotswold Morris during the summer – white clothes with flowers in round straw hats. However, in winter they become Red Leicester, wear tatter coats with feathers in top hats, paint their faces red and perform Border Morris.

The Malt Shovel at Worthington...

...a splendid building when viewed from both directions!

Worthington Church: St Matthew's

The unusual-looking St Matthew's church at Worthington dates back to late Norman times. Even the windows of the church aren't much younger with most dating from the 13th century and the remainder added around 1300. There are also surviving fragments of a Perpendicular Gothic screen that was added later in the medieval period, while the octagonal sandstone font is

from the 14th century; a silver chalice also survives from 1569. The church also used to possess a steeple during these times – probably wooden – while the deep score marks at the side of the south door are thought to have been made by archers sharpening their arrows.

When the church was built in the 12th century, it was a chapel of the mother church at Breedon on the Hill, and is believed to have been built at Worthington for the benefit of the local medieval coal miners. The oldest part of the church is the nave which dates from the church-build time of the late 12th century, while the chancel is probably 14th century and may well have been modernised then to cater for the growing congregation, this courtesy of coal mining taking off at nearby Gelsmoor – and with perhaps both the area and the church seeing increased prosperity due to the industrial boom. Conversely, the church may not only have been disused by the early 18th century, but possibly derelict. However, the Wesleyan Revival of the mid-18th century saw the church re-roofed and restored, and by 1755, we see the record of incumbent ministers begin with the Rev. John Dalby – although it was the third in this succession, a certain James Dean, who was the first to be called Vicar when he took over in August 1819. Following fire damage to the roof in 1890, the church then underwent Victorian restoration, carried out by Temple Moore. Finally, in 1978 Worthington was re-united with Breedon when the vicar there also became the vicar of Worthington and so St Matthew's is now part of the United Benefice of Breedon and Worthington.

Worthington Historic Trivia: Octagonally Round

Following the Norman Conquest, the manor of *Werditone* was given to Henry de Ferrers. Jumping forwards by four hundred years, and by the end of the 15th century, the manor belonged to the Wynters family. Their family memorials can be found in Breedon church, but they also owned a cottage and croft close to what they called "the Chapel of Worthington", and to which they graciously donated a pound of pepper every Michaelmas!

Half way up Church Street in Worthington is the Round House, a late 18th century building that was used by the Parish Constable for locking up suspected crim-

St Matthew's church, Worthington.

Worthington at the crossroads of Breedon Lane, Church Street, Newbold Lane and Long Hedge Lane.

inals – and which is actually octagonal rather than round! But anyway, the idea was that the Parish Constable would detain suspected criminals here before he could bring them before the local Justices – for these were the days before a police force was established, the force not being formed until the mid-19th century. Today, the Round House is a listed building and a Scheduled Ancient Monument, while the local primary school uses an image of the Round House as their logo.

In 1820, Worthington Methodist Chapel was built, while 1874 saw the arrival of the railways in the village, with a station being built at Worthington on the Midland Railway's branch line from Melbourne to Ashby-de-la-Zouch.

The 20th century saw the village population expand rapidly, this in order to house coal miners and their families who worked at the nearby collieries. Alas, by the 1990s, the majority of local collieries had closed.

Worthington Quirk Alert:
Footy Connections and Old Yawny Box

For anyone who knows their 1970s football, they will know that the Shire-Ode in this book is riddled with references to some Leicester City all-time greats. Prime amongst them is Earl Shilton, the manager in the Shire-Ode, but a nod to Leicester City and England's greatest ever goalkeeper, Peter Shilton. Shilts remains England's most capped player with 125 caps, and also holds the world record for most competitive appearances, this over a thirty-year career including 342 appearances for Leicester City between 1966 and 1974. Also, talk of Earls will recall to some City fans' minds former striker Steve Earle – who happened to play up front in the 1970s with one of Leicester's finest ever players, Frank Worthington – and hence the reference to the player in the Shire-Ode. A gifted and acknowledged flair player, Frank Worthington played for Leicester City between 1972 and 1977, making 239 appearances and scoring 78 goals. He also made eight appearances for England – all during his spell at Leicester – and scored two goals for his country, too.

Finally, Worthington (the village) has owned some

fairly unusual nicknames in the past. Firstly, it was known as Paraffin City due to its late adoption of electricity. But the best nickname has to be Yawny Box – a now obsolete Derbyshire miner's word for a donkey. It is well-known that many Derbyshire miners found work in the coalfields of north-west Leicestershire in the 19th and 20th century … but as to the Yawny Box connection with a donkey … answers on a postcard please …

The Round House at Worthington dates from the late 18th century and was used to detain suspected criminals, prior to bringing them before the local Justices.

The Best of the Rest

The following table includes all places not featured so far in the *Quirky Leicestershire and Rutland* section.

WHITWELL	STATUS:	POPULATION:	DISTRICT:	EARLIEST RECORD:
	Village	c.300	North West Leics	19th century
MEANING/DERIVATION:	Named after Johnny Battram who owned the original cottage sited here before the village expanded with the onset of coal mining.			

BELCHER'S BAR	STATUS:	POPULATION:	DISTRICT:	EARLIEST RECORD:
	Hamlet	c.20	Hinckley & Bosworth	Late 18th century
MEANING/DERIVATION:	Probably named after a local family of rectors.			

BLASTON	STATUS:	POPULATION:	DISTRICT:	EARLIEST RECORD:
	Village	54	Harborough	*Bladestone*, 1086 (Domesday Book)
MEANING:	Farmstead of a man called Blath or Blēath.			
DERIVATION:	From the Old Scandinavian or Old English personal name, *Blath* or *Blēath*, plus the Old English word *tūn*, meaning "farmstead".			

BROUGHTON LODGES	STATUS:	POPULATION:	DISTRICT:	EARLIEST RECORD:
	Unknown	Unknown	Melton	Unknown
MEANING/DERIVATION:	*The AA Close-Up Britain Road Atlas* places Broughton Lodges on the A606 just south of Nether Broughton, a place where you will now find Bouverie Lodge – a farm that is home to American Bison and Red Deer! There is however, a Broughton Lodge Farm around 2 miles to the west on the A46.			

CARE VILLAGE	STATUS:	POPULATION:	DISTRICT:	EARLIEST RECORD:
	Residential Home	29 rooms	Harborough	N/A
MEANING/DERIVATION:	A care village for the elderly and for people with learning disabilities, but which is signed up on the B6047 and is marked on *The AA Close-Up Britain Road Atlas*.			

CARLTON CURLIEU	STATUS:	POPULATION:	DISTRICT:	EARLIEST RECORD:
	Village	30	Harborough	*Carletone*, 1086 (DB); *Carletone Curly*, 1273
MEANING:	Farmstead or estate of the freeman or peasants.			
DERIVATION:	From the Old Scandinavian word *karl*, meaning "freeman or peasant", and the Old English word *tūn* (farmstead). The *Curlieu* part is a manorial affix from the *de Curly* family, who lived here in the 13th century.			

Quirk Alert: *Battram Wood and the Grumbling Vicar*

Battram Wood is a 48ha site owned by the Royal Forestry Society. Between 1998 and 2001, the area was planted with hundreds of trees, including 350 oaks and yews forming the Millennium Circle, the focal point of the woodland, while in 2005, 630 "Trafalgar Oaks" were planted to commemorate the bicentennial of Lord Nelson's famous victory. Meanwhile, Humphrey Michel, known as the "Grumbling Vicar" of neighbouring Horninghold, was clearly so disenchanted with his own 18th century parish that he chose to be buried in Blaston instead!

SWIFT	STATUS:	POPULATION:	DISTRICT:	EARLIEST RECORD:
	River	N/A	Harborough	10th century
MEANING/DERIVATION:	Most river names are Celtic in origin, but unlike the Swift River in Canada, New Zealand and Alaska, the Leicestershire one is unlikely to be named because of a fast flow, as the river is minor and certainly doesn't flow from any significant upland country.			

THE BRAND	STATUS:	POPULATION:	DISTRICT:	EARLIEST RECORD:
	House, Rock Face	N/A	Charnwood	18th century
MEANING/DERIVATION:	Before the land enclosures of the late 18th and early 19th century, stock was driven annually to places on the edge of Charnwood Forest to be marked with the brands of the owners, and The Brand was one such place.			

THE VALLEY	STATUS:	POPULATION:	DISTRICT:	EARLIEST RECORD:
	Housing estate	3286*	Melton	20th century
MEANING/DERIVATION:	Probably means "the part of Asfordby in the valley". As for Asfordby (*Osferdebie*, 1086), it means either "farmstead of a man called Ásfrøthr", deriving from the Scandinavian personal name plus the Old Scandinavian word *bý* (farmstead, village or settlement), or "farmstead by the ash-tree ford" deriving from the Old English words *æsc* (ash) *ford* (ford) and Old Scandinavian *bý*.			

WEST END	STATUS:	POPULATION:	DISTRICT:	EARLIEST RECORD:
	Housing estate	411*	Harborough	*Carletone*, 1086 (DB); *Carletone Curly*, 1273
MEANING/DERIVATION:	Probably means "the West End of Osgathorpe". As for Osgathorpe (*Osgodtorp*, 1086), the name means "outlying farmstead or hamlet of a man called Ásgautr", again deriving from an Old Scandinavian personal name, plus the Old Scandinavian word *thorp* (secondary settlement, dependent outlying farmstead or hamlet).			

Blaston's only road.

St Mary the Virgin church, Carlton Curlieu.

Saint Mary the Blessed Virgin church at Osgathorpe.

Quirk Alert: *The Toughest Climb and the UK's Only High-Speed Test Track*

Offering some of the toughest climbing in Leicestershire, the rock face known as The Brand is actually located in the private garden of the house of the same name, and therefore permission is required before climbing! In the 17th and 18th centuries, it was also part of a quarry producing quality Swithland Slate. Meanwhile, Asfordby Valley (aka The Valley) is the HQ of the Alstom Midlands Test Centre, who control the testing of conventional and tube trains on the test line formerly known as Old Dalby, and which runs between Melton Mowbray and Edwalton.

* Populations of Asfordby and Osgathorpe, respectively

Bibliography

Books

Arthur Mee, *The King's England: Leicestershire and Rutland* (The King's England Press, 1997)

Roy Millward, *A History of Leicestershire and Rutland* (Phillimore & Co. Ltd., 1985)

A.D. Mills, *Oxford Dictionary of British Place Names* (Oxford University Press, 1991)

Information Panels at:

Aylestone Hall	Grace Dieu Priory	Oakham Castle
Battram Wood	Hallaton	Shenton Station
Beacon Hill	Hathern	Swannington Incline
Billesdon	Jewry Wall Museum	Stoke Dry: Eyebrook Reservoir
Bosworth Field	Kirby Muxloe	Stoke Dry: St Andrew's church
Burrough Hill	Leicester (multiple)	Uppingham
Foxton Locks	Medbourne	Wing
Glen Parva	Moira Furnace	Worthington

Websites:

http://beltoninrutland.co.uk

http://earlshilton.org.uk

http://en.wikipedia.org/wiki

http://leicestercathedral.org

http://neighbourhood.statistics.gov.uk

http://rutnet.co.uk

http://tonge-and-breedon-hs2-action-group.co.uk

http://www.belvoircastle.com

http://www.bouverielodge.co.uk

http://www.britishlistedbuildings.co.uk

http://www.discover-rutland.co.uk

http://www.everards.co.uk

http://www.frisbyonthewreake.net

http://www.ilivehere.co.uk

http://www.kegworthvillage.com

http://www.leics.gov.uk

http://www.leicester.gov.uk

http://www.leicestermercury.co.uk

http://www.leicestermorris.co.uk

http://www.leicestershirechurches.co.uk

http://www.leicestershireclimbs.co.uk

http://www.leicestershirevillages.com

http://www.megalithic.co.uk

http://www.moiraparish.org.uk

http://www.nationalforest.org

http://www.old-dalby.com/

http://www.roman-britain.org

http://www.rutland-times.co.uk

http://www.rutlandchurches.co.uk

http://www.staplefordpark.com

http://www.vicbikerspub.co.uk

http://www.victorianlondon.org

http://www.whitwick.org.uk